Collins

GCSE 9-1
Maths
Foundation

Revision Guide

Linda Couchman and Rebecca Evans

About this Revision & Practice book

Revise

These pages provide a recap of everything you need to know for each topic on the 9-1 AQA, Edexcel, OCR and WJEC Eduqas specifications.

You should read through all the information before taking the Quick Test at the end. This will test whether you can recall the key facts.

Quick Test
1. Factorise $5x + 10$
2. Solve $7x - 2 = 12$
3. Simplify $2y - 7 + 4y + 2$
4. Work out the value of $3p^3 - 7q$, when $p = -4$ and $q = -3$.
5. Expand the following expression: $3t(4t - 1)$

Practise

These topic-based questions appear shortly after the revision pages for each topic and will test whether you have understood the topic. If you get any of the questions wrong, make sure you read the correct answer carefully.

Review

These topic-based questions appear later in the book, allowing you to revisit the topic and test how well you have remembered the information. If you get any of the questions wrong, make sure you read the correct answer carefully.

Mix it Up

These pages feature a mix of questions for all the different topics, just like you would get in an exam. They will make sure you can recall the relevant information to answer a question without being told which topic it relates to.

Test Yourself on the Go

Visit our website at **collins.co.uk/collinsGCSErevision** and print off a set of flashcards. These pocket-sized cards feature questions and answers so that you can test yourself on all the key facts anytime and anywhere. You will also find lots more information about the advantages of spaced practice and how to plan for it.

Workbook

This section features even more topic-based questions as well as practice exam papers, providing two further practice opportunities for each topic to guarantee the best results.

ebook

To access the ebook revision guide visit
collins.co.uk/ebooks
and follow the step-by-step instructions.

Contents

N Number   **A** Algebra   **G** Geometry and Measures

S Statistics   **P** Probability   **R** Ratio, Proportion and Rates of Change

N Number   **A** Algebra   **G** Geometry and Measures

S Statistics   **P** Probability   **R** Ratio, Proportion and Rates of Change

Review Questions

Recap of KS3 Key Concepts

1. Write down two million and five as a number. [1]

2. Work out 15% of 300kg. [1]

3. Write 60 as the product of prime factors. [1]

4. Find **a)** the HCF and **b)** the LCM of 36 and 90. [2]

5. $6 + 4 \div 2 =$ _____ [1]

6. $(-2)^3 =$ _____ [1]

7. $(2^3)^2 =$ _____ [1]

8. Simplify: $5 + 2(m - 1)$ [1]

9. Simplify: $y^2 + y^2 + y^2$ [1]

10. **a)** Write the next two terms in the number sequence: 5, 8, 11, 14, __, __ [1]

    b) Is 140 a term in the sequence? Explain your answer. [2]

11. $0.3 \times 0.2 =$ _____ [1]

12. A regular polygon has an interior angle of 140°. How many sides does the polygon have? [1]

13. Work out $4.152 \div 1.2$ [1]

14. If $A = (2, 3)$ and $B = (7, 11)$, work out the coordinates of the midpoint of the line AB. [2]

15. $3 \times 3 \times 3 =$ _____ [1]

16. Lorna left her home at 11.00am and went for a 20km run. She arrived back home at 1.00pm.

    Work out Lorna's average running speed. [1]

17. The cross-section of a prism has an area of 25cm². The length of the prism is 5cm.

    Work out the volume of the prism. [1]

18. The probability of it raining is 0.6

    Work out the probability of it **not** raining. [1]

19. Write $\frac{7}{8}$ as a decimal. [1]

20. Write down 0.78 as a fraction in its simplest form. [2]

21. Find a fraction that lies between $\frac{2}{3}$ and $\frac{3}{4}$. [2]

22 Pat threw three darts. The lowest score was 10. The range was 10. The mean was 15.

Work out the score for each dart. [3]

23 Write down the number that is one less than one million. [1]

24 Share £56 in the ratio 3 : 5 [2]

25 Put the following numbers in order, smallest first: 0.4, 0.04, 0.39, 0.394 [1]

26 Calculate a value for m if:

a) $m - 5 = -1$ [1]

b) $m \div 4 = 12$ [1]

c) $2m + 13 = 16$ [1]

27 A square has a perimeter of 24cm. Work out its area. [1]

28 Work out $1616 \div 4$. [1]

29 Temi spends £7.25. She pays with a £20 note.

How much change does she receive? [1]

30 Simplify $10a - 6y + 3a - 4y$ [1]

31 Increase £60 by 35%. [1]

32 A circle has a radius of 10cm. Taking π as 3.14, work out the area of the circle. [2]

33 How many cubes of side length 2cm will fit inside a hollow cube of side length 4cm? [3]

34 Write down the square root of 225. [1]

35 $\frac{3}{4}$ of a number is 63. Write down the number. [2]

36 Work out the value of m if $2 - m = 5$. [1]

37 Give the coordinates of the point where the graph of $x + y = 5$ crosses the x-axis. [2]

38 The two shorter sides of a right-angled triangle are 5cm and 12cm.

Work out the length of the third side. [1]

39 If $a = 3$ and $b = 4$, work out the value of $2a^2 + 3b$ [2]

40 Find the median of 1, 4, 6, 13, 21, 10, 3 and 7. [1]

Total Marks _____ / 57

Number 1

You must be able to:

- Use the four operations: addition, subtraction, multiplication and division
- Use BIDMAS
- Carry out calculations using a calculator.

The Four Operations

- You must be able to identify which operations are needed to answer a question.
- **Addition** problems might use words like: *sum*, *total*, *increase* and *plus*.
- **Subtraction** problems might use words like: *minus*, *decrease*, *take away* and *difference*.
- **Multiplication** problems might use words like: *multiply*, *times* and *product*.
- **Division** problems might use words like: *divide* and *share*.

Key Point
You may have to break some questions down and use a different operation at each stage.

Over five years, the population of a town increased by 3246 people.

If there were 15 628 people originally, how many were there at the end of the five-year period?

$$15628$$
$$3246 +$$
$$18874$$
1

18874 people

A theatre can seat 600 people. On one night, 476 people watched a play.

How many seats were **not** filled?

$$\overset{5\ \ 9\ 1}{6\cancel{0}\cancel{0}}$$
$$476 -$$
$$124$$

124 seats

Borrow across the top.

Cauliflowers are delivered to a supermarket in 48-kilogram crates. On Friday, 26 crates of cauliflowers were delivered.

What was the total mass of the delivery on Friday?

×	40	8
20	800	160
6	240	48

→

$$800$$
$$160$$
$$240$$
$$48 +$$
$$1248$$
1

1248kg

Multiply the tens and units and then add the products.

In an aquarium, a large tank can hold nine exotic fish.

How many tanks would be needed for 936 exotic fish?

$$\begin{array}{r} 104 \\ 9\overline{)93^36} \end{array}$$ 104 tanks ←

9 goes into 9 once.
9 goes into 3 zero times, with 3 left over.
9 goes into 36 four times.

BIDMAS

- BIDMAS gives the order in which operations should be carried out:
  - **B**rackets (carry out the calculation in brackets first)
  - **I**ndices (roots and powers)
  - **D**ivision and **M**ultiplication
  - **A**ddition and **S**ubtraction.

Work out $6 + 4 \times 3$ ←

$6 + 12 = 18$

Multiplication must be carried out before addition.

Using a Calculator

Use your calculator to work out $(18 + 37) \times 12$

$\boxed{ON}\,\boxed{(}\,\boxed{1}\,\boxed{8}\,\boxed{+}\,\boxed{3}\,\boxed{7}\,\boxed{)}\,\boxed{\times}\,\boxed{1}\,\boxed{2}\,\boxed{=}\,660$ ←

Press the calculator keys in this order.

Use your calculator to convert $\frac{3}{8}$ to a decimal.

$\boxed{ON}\,\boxed{3}\,\boxed{\div}\,\boxed{8}\,\boxed{=}\,0.375$ ←

Press $\boxed{S \Leftrightarrow D}$ to switch between a fraction and a decimal answer.

Use your calculator to work out:

a) $\sqrt{1369}$

$\boxed{ON}\,\boxed{\sqrt{\blacksquare}}\,\boxed{1}\,\boxed{3}\,\boxed{6}\,\boxed{9}\,\boxed{=}\,37$

b) $\sqrt[3]{4096}$

$\boxed{ON}\,\boxed{SHIFT}\,\boxed{\sqrt[3]{\blacksquare}}\,\boxed{4}\,\boxed{0}\,\boxed{9}\,\boxed{6}\,\boxed{=}\,16$

c) 6^4

$\boxed{ON}\,\boxed{6}\,\boxed{x^{\blacksquare}}\,\boxed{4}\,\boxed{=}\,1296$

Key Point

Starting from the left of a calculation:

- work out division and multiplication in the order that they appear (if × appears first, complete it before the ÷)
- work out addition and subtraction in the order that they appear (if − appears first, complete it before +).

Key Point

Make sure you have practised using your calculator before the exams and know where all the main function keys are.

Quick Test

1. There are 12 greetings cards in a box. Raj needs to send 158 cards. How many boxes does he need to buy?
2. Mia says $2 + (3 + 4) + 3 \times 4 = 48$
   Molly says $2 + (3 + 4) + 3 \times 4 = 21$
   Who is correct? You must explain your answer clearly.

Key Words

addition
subtraction
multiplication
division
BIDMAS

Number 2

You must be able to:

- Order and compare positive and negative numbers
- Carry out calculations using positive and negative integers and decimals
- Understand and use standard form.

Ordering Numbers

- The value of each digit in a number depends on its position within that number. This is its place value.

Put the following numbers in order, from smallest to largest:

3400   34.03   340 000   34 030   340.3

Hundred Thousands	Ten Thousands	Thousands	Hundreds	Tens	Units		Tenths	Hundredths
		3	4	0	0			
				3	4	.	0	3
3	4	0	0	0	0			
	3	4	0	3	0			
				3	4	.	0	3

In order, smallest to largest: 34.03, 340.3, 3400, 34 030, 340 000

- A number line can help to visualise questions.

Negative Numbers   Positive Numbers

−10 −9 −8 −7 −6 −5 −4 −3 −2 −1 0 1 2 3 4 5 6 7 8 9 10

Put the following numbers in order, smallest to largest:

−10.2   −0.3 $-\frac{1}{5}$ −6.4

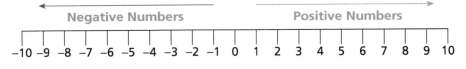

−10.2   −0.3   −0.2   −6.4

−10.2   −6.4   −0.3   −0.2

−10.2   −6.4   −0.3 $-\frac{1}{5}$

Key Point

On a number line, positive numbers (+) are to the right of zero and negative numbers (−) are to the left of zero.

Numbers on the left are smaller than numbers on the right.

A negative number is smaller than zero.

Calculating with Negative Numbers

Work out 2 − 7

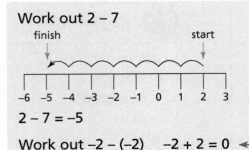

finish   start

−6 −5 −4 −3 −2 −1 0 1 2 3

2 − 7 = −5

Work out −2 − (−2)   −2 + 2 = 0

Work out −2 + (−2)

finish   start

−6 −5 −4 −3 −2 −1

−2 − 2 = −4

Key Point

−2 + (−2) and −2 − (+2) both mean −2 − 2 = −4

- When multiplying or dividing with two signs that are **different**, the answer is **negative**.
- When multiplying or dividing with two signs that are the **same**, the answer is **positive**.

$-3 \times 6 = -18$	$7 \times (-2) = -14$	$24 \div (-6) = -4$
$-5 \times (-7) = 35$	$-100 \div (-5) = 20$	

> **Key Point**
>
> $- \times - = +$ $- \times + = -$
>
> $+ \times + = +$ $+ \times - = -$

Calculating with Decimals

- When **adding** or **subtracting** decimals, keep the decimal points under each other.

Two parcels weigh 6.3kg and 11.27kg. What is their total mass?

$$\begin{array}{r} 6.30 \\ 11.27\, + \\ \hline 17.57 \\ \hline \end{array}$$

Total mass: 17.57kg

> **Key Point**
>
> The number of decimal places in the answer to a multiplication is the same as the total number of them in the original calculation.

> Remember 6.3 is the same as 6.30

> The decimal point in the answer should be in line with the other decimal points.

- When **multiplying**, remove the decimal points first.

Work out 0.6×0.2	Work out 1.46×2.3
$6 \times 2 = 12$	$146 \times 23 = 3358$
$0.6 \times 0.2 = 0.12$	$1.46 \times 2.3 = 3.358$

> Two figures after the decimal points in the question, so two figures after the decimal point in the answer.

> Three figures after the decimal points on both sides of the equals sign.

- When **dividing**, always divide by a whole number.

Work out $27.632 \div 0.2$	Work out $36.14 \div 0.002$
$276.32 \div 2 = 138.16$	$36\,140 \div 2 = 18\,070$

> In order to divide by a whole number, multiply everything by 10.

> Multiply everything by 1000.

Standard Form

- Standard form is used to represent very small or very large numbers.
- A number in standard form is written in the form $A \times 10^n$, where $1 \leqslant A < 10$ and n is an integer.
- For numbers less than 1, n is negative.

Write the following numbers in standard form:

a) 723 000 $723\,000 = 7.23 \times 10^5$

b) 0.000 0063 $0.000\,0063 = 6.3 \times 10^{-6}$

> $n = 5$ since the decimal point has to move 5 places to the left to go from 723 000 to 7.23.

> $n = -6$ since the decimal point has to move 6 places to the right to go from 0.000 0063 to 6.3.

Quick Test

1. a) -7×-3 b) $-6 - 7$
2. Write 0.001 63 in standard form.
3. Put in order, smallest to largest: 220, −220, −2201, 1022, 2200
4. Vishnaal spent £7.84.
   How much change did he receive from £20?

Key Words

place value
negative number
positive number
standard form
integer

Number 3

You must be able to:

- Use the ideas of prime numbers, factors (divisors), multiples, highest common factor, lowest common multiple and prime factors
- Show prime factor decomposition
- Use systematic listing strategies.

Types of Number

- **Multiples** are found in the 'times table' of the number, e.g.
  Multiples of 4 = {4, 8, 12, 16 ...}
- A **factor** (divisor) is a number that will divide exactly into another number, e.g.
  Factors of 12 = {1, 2, 3, 4, 6, 12}
- A **prime number** has only two factors: itself and 1.
- **Square numbers** are the results of multiplying together two numbers that are the same. They are shown using a **power** of 2, e.g.

1 × 1 = **1**	2 × 2 = **4**	3 × 3 = **9**	4 × 4 = **16**
$1^2 = 1$	$2^2 = 4$	$3^2 = 9$	$4^2 = 16$

- A **square root** is the **inverse** (opposite) of a square, e.g.
  $6^2 = 36$ $\sqrt{36} = 6$
- **Cube numbers** are the results of multiplying together three numbers that are the same. They are shown using a power of 3, e.g.

1 × 1 × 1 = **1**	2 × 2 × 2 = **8**	3 × 3 × 3 = **27**	4 × 4 × 4 = **64**
$1^3 = 1$	$2^3 = 8$	$3^3 = 27$	$4^3 = 64$

- A **cube root** is the inverse of a cube, e.g.
  $5^3 = 125$ $\sqrt[3]{125} = 5$

> **Key Point**
>
> When listing factors, look for pairs of numbers, then you will not forget any.

> **Key Point**
>
> You are expected to know the squares and square roots up to 15 × 15 = 225 and that $\sqrt[3]{1} = 1$, $\sqrt[3]{8} = 2$, $\sqrt[3]{27} = 3$, $\sqrt[3]{64} = 4$, $\sqrt[3]{125} = 5$ and $\sqrt[3]{1000} = 10$.

Prime Factors, LCM and HCF

- The **lowest common multiple (LCM)** of two numbers is the lowest integer that is a multiple of both numbers.

Find the LCM of 12 and 18.

Multiples of 12 = {12, 24, ⓛ36, 48 ...} ← Write out the multiples of 12 and 18 until you get a common value.

Multiples of 18 = {18, ⓛ36, 54 ...}

36 is the smallest number that is in both lists, so 36 is the LCM.

- The **highest common factor (HCF)** of two numbers is the largest integer that will divide exactly into both numbers.

Find the HCF of 45 and 60.

Factors of 45 = {1, 3, 5, 9, ⓛ15, 45} ← Write out the factors of 45 and 60 and look for the highest common value.

Factors of 60 = {1, 2, 3, 4, 5, 6, 10, 12, ⓛ15, 20, 30, 60}

15 is the largest number that is in both lists, so 15 is the HCF.

- Factors of a number that are also prime numbers are called prime factors.

Write 48 as a product of prime factors.

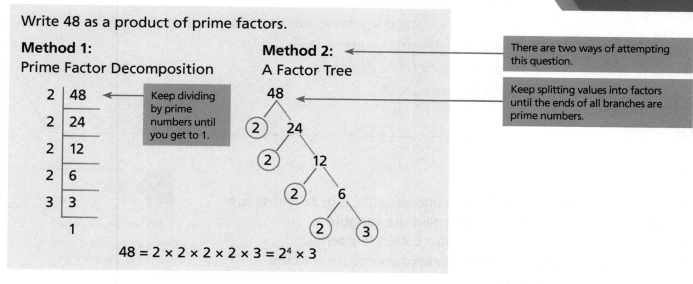

Method 1:
Prime Factor Decomposition

There are two ways of attempting this question.

Keep dividing by prime numbers until you get to 1.

Method 2:
A Factor Tree

Keep splitting values into factors until the ends of all branches are prime numbers.

$48 = 2 \times 2 \times 2 \times 2 \times 3 = 2^4 \times 3$

Choices and Outcomes

- To work out the number of ways, a listing strategy can be used.

Two coins are thrown. List all the different ways they can land.

Use abbreviations: Head (H)   Tail (T)
HH, HT, TH, TT
So there are four different outcomes.

In a restaurant there are three different starters (X, Y, Z) and six different main meals (1, 2, 3, 4, 5, 6) to choose from.

How many possible combinations are there when choosing a starter and a main meal?

Combinations are: X1, X2, X3, X4, X5, X6, Y1, Y2, Y3, Y4, Y5, Y6, Z1, Z2, Z3, Z4, Z5, Z6 (18 combinations)

There are 18 combinations altogether.

Quick Test

1. Express 36 as a product of prime factors using any method.
2. Find a) the HCF and b) the LCM of 12 and 15.
3. Red buses leave the bus garage every 12 minutes. Blue buses leave the bus garage every 20 minutes. A red bus and a blue bus both leave the garage at 9am. At what time will a red bus and a blue bus next leave the garage together?

Basic Algebra

You must be able to:

- Use and understand algebraic notation and vocabulary
- Simplify and rearrange expressions
- Expand and factorise expressions
- Solve linear equations.

Basic Algebra

- 'Like terms' are terms with the same variable, e.g. $3x$ and $4x$ are like terms because they both contain the variable x.
- To simplify an expression you must collect like terms.
- When moving a term from one side of an equation to the other, you must carry out the inverse operation.

> **Key Point**
>
> When simplifying expressions, remember to:
> - Use BIDMAS
> - Show your working.

Simplify $3x + 3y - 7x + y$

$4y - 4x$

$3x - 7x = -4x$
$3y + y = 4y$

Simplify $9p^2 + 7p - qp + pq - p^2$

$8p^2 + 7p$

$qp = pq$

$9p^2 - p^2 = 8p^2$
$-qp + pq = 0$

- Substitution means replacing variables with numbers.

If $y = 4$ and $t = 6$, work out the value of $7y - 6t$

$$7y - 6t = 7 \times 4 - 6 \times 6$$
$$= 28 - 36$$
$$= -8$$

> **Key Point**
>
> An expression does not contain an = sign.

If $q = 5$, $r = 2$ and $z = -3$, work out the value of $rq + z^2$

$$rq + z^2 = 2 \times 5 + (-3)^2$$
$$= 10 + 9$$
$$= 19$$

Use brackets as the minus sign is also squared.

> **Key Point**
>
> Always apply the rules:
> $- \times - = +$ $- \times + = -$
> $+ \times + = +$ $+ \times - = -$

- To expand (multiply out) brackets, every term in the bracket is multiplied by the term outside the bracket.

Expand $3(x + 2)$

$3x + 6$

Expand $5p(p - 2)$

$5p^2 - 10p$

$3 \times x = 3x$ and $3 \times 2 = +6$

$5p \times p = 5p^2$
$5p \times (-2) = -10p$

Expand and simplify $4y(2y - 3) - 3y(y - 2)$

$8y^2 - 12y - 3y^2 + 6y$
$= 5y^2 - 6y$

Note that $-3y \times -2 = +6y$

Factorisation

- **Factorisation** is the reverse of expanding brackets, i.e. you take out a common factor and put brackets into the expression.
- To factorise, you should look for common factors in every term.

Factorise $12x + 4$ ← 4 is the HCF of 12 and 4.

$4(3x + 1)$

Factorise $3x^2 - 6x$

$3x(x - 2)$ ← Remember $x^2 = x \times x$

Factorise $3p^3 - 2p^2 + 8p$

$p(3p^2 - 2p + 8)$

> **Key Point**
>
> To factorise completely, always take out the highest common factor, e.g. 3 is the HCF of 3 and 6.

Linear Equations

- A **linear equation** does not contain any variables with a power greater than 1.
- When you solve an equation, you are finding an unknown number, represented by a letter, e.g. x.

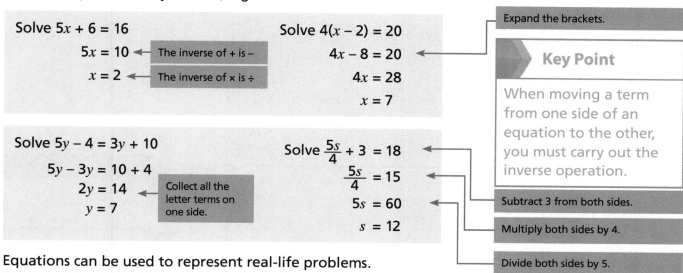

Solve $5x + 6 = 16$

$5x = 10$ ← The inverse of + is −

$x = 2$ ← The inverse of × is ÷

Solve $4(x - 2) = 20$

$4x - 8 = 20$ ← Expand the brackets.

$4x = 28$

$x = 7$

> **Key Point**
>
> When moving a term from one side of an equation to the other, you must carry out the inverse operation.

Solve $5y - 4 = 3y + 10$

$5y - 3y = 10 + 4$

$2y = 14$ ← Collect all the letter terms on one side.

$y = 7$

Solve $\frac{5s}{4} + 3 = 18$

$\frac{5s}{4} = 15$ ← Subtract 3 from both sides.

$5s = 60$ ← Multiply both sides by 4.

$s = 12$ ← Divide both sides by 5.

- Equations can be used to represent real-life problems.
- The equation should be rearranged to solve the problem.

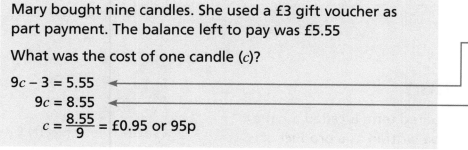

Mary bought nine candles. She used a £3 gift voucher as part payment. The balance left to pay was £5.55

What was the cost of one candle (c)?

$9c - 3 = 5.55$ ← Use the information given to set up an equation.

$9c = 8.55$ ← Solve to find the cost of one candle.

$c = \frac{8.55}{9} = £0.95$ or 95p

> **Key Words**
>
> term
> variable
> expression
> equation
> inverse operation
> factorisation
> linear equation

Quick Test

1. Factorise $5x + 10$
2. Solve $7x - 2 = 12$
3. Simplify $2y - 7 + 4y + 2$
4. Work out the value of $3p^3 - 7q$, when $p = -4$ and $q = -3$.
5. Expand the following expression: $3t(4t - 1)$

Factorisation and Formulae

You must be able to:

- Expand the product of two binomials
- Factorise a quadratic expression
- Understand and use formulae
- Rearrange and change the subject of a formula.

Binomial Expansion

- A **binomial** is an **expression** that contains two terms, e.g. $x + 2$ or $3y - 4$.
- The product of two binomials is obtained when they are multiplied together, e.g. $(2r + 7)(3r - 6)$.
- To **expand** (or multiply out) the brackets, every term in the first set of brackets must be multiplied by every term in the second set of brackets.

Expand and simplify $(x + 2)(x + 6)$

×	x	+2
x	x^2	$+2x$
+6	$+6x$	+12

$x^2 + 2x + 6x + 12$
$= x^2 + 8x + 12$ ←

Simplify by collecting like terms.

Expand and simplify $(2y + 4)(3y - 2)$

×	$2y$	+4
$3y$	$6y^2$	$+12y$
−2	$-4y$	−8

$6y^2 + 12y - 4y - 8$
$= 6y^2 + 8y - 8$

> **Key Point**
>
> Take care over + and − signs.

Quadratic Factorisation

- An expression that contains a squared term is called **quadratic**.
- Some quadratic expressions can be written as a product of two binomials.
- When written in factorised form, the new expression is equivalent to the original quadratic.

> **Key Point**
>
> Check you have factorised correctly by expanding the brackets – your expressions should be equivalent.

Factorise $x^2 + 5x + 6$

$x^2 + 5x + 6$ ←

Find a pair of numbers with a sum of +5 and a product of +6.

$(x + 2)(x + 3)$ ←

$(+2) + (+3) = +5$ and $(+2) \times (+3) = +6$

Factorise the expression $x^2 - 4x + 3$

×	x	-1
x	x^2	$-x$
-3	$-3x$	$+3$

$(x - 1)(x - 3)$

> The missing terms need to have a product of +3 and a sum of −4, i.e. −1 and −3.

> Write the expression as a product: the **first row** gives you the **first bracket** and the **first column** gives you the **second bracket**.

Changing the Subject of a Formula

- A formula is a way of describing a rule or fact.
- A formula is written as an algebraic equation.
- The subject of a formula appears once on the left-hand side.
- To change the subject, a formula must be rearranged using inverse operations.

Make p the subject of $5p - 7 = r$

$5p = r + 7$

$p = \dfrac{r + 7}{5}$

> **Key Point**
>
> When rearranging formulae remember to use inverse operations. Finish by writing the formula out with the new subject on the left-hand side.

This formula can be used to change temperature in degrees Fahrenheit to temperature in degrees Celsius:
$C = \frac{5}{9}(F - 32)$

In Iceland, the lowest recorded temperature on a certain day is −20°C.

What is this temperature in degrees Fahrenheit?

$-20 = \frac{5}{9}(F - 32)$

$-180 = 5(F - 32)$

$-36 = F - 32$

$F = -4°F$

> The formula must be rearranged to find the value of F.

> The answer is −4 degrees Fahrenheit.

Make r the subject of the formula $P = 3(r - 1)$

$\dfrac{P}{3} = r - 1$

$r = \dfrac{P}{3} + 1$

The formula for calculating the area of a circle is $A = \pi r^2$.

Make r the subject.

$\dfrac{A}{\pi} = r^2$

$r = \sqrt{\dfrac{A}{\pi}}$

> π can be treated as a numerical term.

> Only the positive root is needed as r is a length.

> **Key Words**
>
> binomial
> expression
> expand
> quadratic
> formula
> subject
> inverse operation

Quick Test

1. $T = 30w + 20$. Work out the value of w when $T = 290$.
2. Factorise $x^2 + 8x + 7$
3. Make q the subject of $6q - 5 = 2t$
4. Make y the subject of the formula $\dfrac{x + 2}{3} = 2(y - 1)$

Ratio and Proportion

You must be able to:

- Use ratio notation and reduce ratios to their simplest form
- Divide quantities into given ratios
- Apply ratio to real contexts and problems, including best buys
- Solve problems using direct and inverse proportion.

Ratio

- **Ratios** are used to compare quantities.
- You can **simplify** a ratio. This is like cancelling down a fraction.

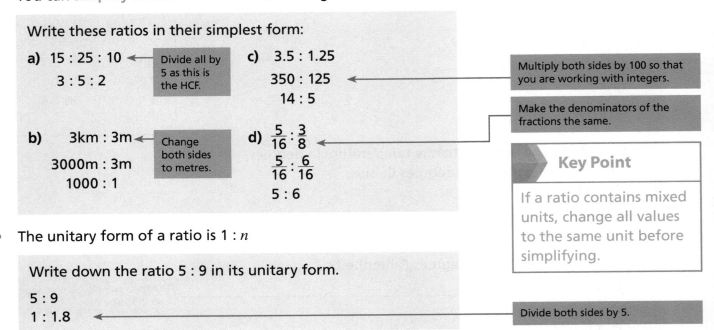

Write these ratios in their simplest form:

a) 15 : 25 : 10 ← Divide all by 5 as this is the HCF.

3 : 5 : 2

b) 3km : 3m ← Change both sides to metres.

3000m : 3m

1000 : 1

c) 3.5 : 1.25

350 : 125 ← Multiply both sides by 100 so that you are working with integers.

14 : 5

d) $\frac{5}{16} : \frac{3}{8}$ ← Make the denominators of the fractions the same.

$\frac{5}{16} : \frac{6}{16}$

5 : 6

Key Point

If a ratio contains mixed units, change all values to the same unit before simplifying.

- The unitary form of a ratio is 1 : n

Write down the ratio 5 : 9 in its unitary form.

5 : 9

1 : 1.8 ← Divide both sides by 5.

- To divide a quantity into a given ratio, you must first work out the value of one part.

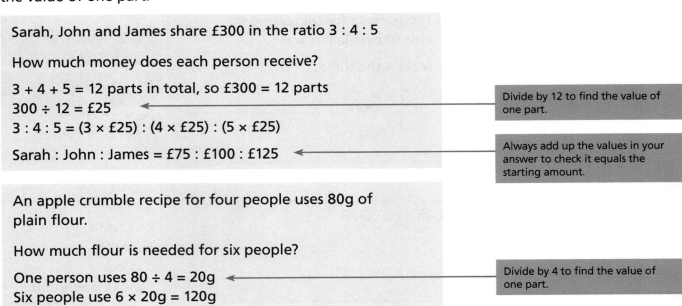

Sarah, John and James share £300 in the ratio 3 : 4 : 5

How much money does each person receive?

3 + 4 + 5 = 12 parts in total, so £300 = 12 parts

300 ÷ 12 = £25 ← Divide by 12 to find the value of one part.

3 : 4 : 5 = (3 × £25) : (4 × £25) : (5 × £25)

Sarah : John : James = £75 : £100 : £125 ← Always add up the values in your answer to check it equals the starting amount.

An apple crumble recipe for four people uses 80g of plain flour.

How much flour is needed for six people?

One person uses 80 ÷ 4 = 20g ← Divide by 4 to find the value of one part.

Six people use 6 × 20g = 120g

Best Buys

- Working out the value of one part allows you to make like-for-like comparisons.

Teabags are sold in two different sized packs:

Pack A holds 80 teabags and costs £1.80.

Pack B holds 200 teabags and costs £3.80.

Which is the best buy?

Pack A   180 ÷ 80 = 2.25p

Pack B   380 ÷ 200 = 1.9p

Packet B is the best buy (the cheaper price per teabag).

> Work out the cost of one teabag in each pack.

Direct Proportion Problems

- Quantities are in **direct proportion** if their ratio remains the same as they are increased or decreased.
- Direct proportion uses the symbol α.
- $y \, \alpha \, x$ means y is directly proportional to x or $y = kx$.
- k is called the **constant of proportionality**.
- Quantities can also be in **inverse proportion**.
- This is shown by $y \, \alpha \, \frac{1}{x}$ or $y = \frac{k}{x}$.

Key Point

If quantities are in inverse proportion, as x increases, y decreases.

The graph produced is a curve.

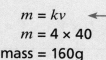

Mass is directly proportional to volume. When mass = 100g, then volume = 25cm³.

Work out the mass for a volume of 40cm³.

Stage 1

$m \, \alpha \, v$

$m = kv$

$100 = k \times 25$

$k = 4$

> Substitute in the values for m (mass) and v (volume).

> You now have a value for k.

Stage 2

$m = kv$

$m = 4 \times 40$

mass = 160g

> Substitute in the values for k and v (volume).

Quick Test

1. £180 is shared in the ratio 2 : 3
   What is the value of the larger share?
2. Simplify 3 hours : 45 minutes
3. a) Cat food comes in two different sized boxes:
      Box A has 12 sachets and costs £3.80.
      Box B has 45 sachets and costs £14.00.
      Which is the best buy? Explain your answer clearly.
   b) Tiggles the cat eats three sachets a day. How many of the best buy boxes have to be bought to feed Tiggles in June?

Key Words

ratio
simplify
direct proportion
constant of
   proportionality
inverse proportion

Variation and Compound Measures

You must be able to:

- Use compound units and solve problems involving compound measures
- Calculate compound interest
- Understand graphs that illustrate direct and inverse proportion.

Compound Measures

- A compound measure is a measure that involves two or more other measures.
- Speed is a compound measure – it involves measures of distance and time.

 LEARN

$$\text{Speed } (S) = \frac{\text{Total Distance } (D)}{\text{Time Taken } (T)} \qquad D = S \times T \qquad T = \frac{D}{S}$$

> **Key Point**
>
> Units for speed include kilometres per hour (km/h) or metres per second (m/s).

A snail crawls a distance of 30cm in 3 minutes 20 seconds.

Work out its speed in m/s.

30cm = 0.3m ◄──────── *Change 30cm into metres by dividing by 100 (100cm = 1m).*

3 minutes 20 seconds = 200 seconds ◄── *Change the total time into seconds.*

$$\text{Speed} = \frac{\text{Distance}}{\text{Time}}$$
$$= \frac{0.3}{200}$$
$$= 0.0015\text{m/s}$$

- Density and pressure are compound measures.

 LEARN

$$\text{Density } (D) = \frac{\text{Mass } (M)}{\text{Volume } (V)} \qquad M = D \times V \qquad V = \frac{M}{D}$$

> **Key Point**
>
> Always check that the units in the question are the same as the units required in the answer.

LEARN

$$\text{Pressure } (P) = \frac{\text{Force } (F)}{\text{Area } (A)} \qquad F = P \times A \qquad A = \frac{F}{P}$$

> **Key Point**
>
> Units for density include kg/m³ or g/cm³.
>
> Pressure is expressed in newtons (N) per square metre (m²). A force of 1N applied to 1m² is called 1 pascal (Pa).

Compound Interest and Repeated Percentage Change

- Compound interest is calculated based on the total amount of money invested, plus any interest previously earned.
- This formula can be used to calculate how money invested grows with time:

 LEARN

$$\text{Final Amount } (A) = \text{Original Amount} \times \left(1 + \frac{\text{Rate}}{100}\right)^{\text{time}}$$

> **Key Point**
>
> Simple interest is when the interest is paid out rather than being added to the money invested.

- To calculate depreciation (loss in value), the plus sign in the formula is changed to a minus sign.

£3000 is invested at 2% compound interest per annum.

Calculate how much money there will be after four years.
Give your answer to the nearest pound.

$A = 3000 \times \left(1 + \dfrac{2}{100}\right)^4$

Use the formula:
$A = \text{Original Amount} \times \left(1 + \dfrac{\text{Rate}}{100}\right)^{\text{time}}$

$= 3000 \times (1.02)^4$

$= 3000 \times 1.0824 = £3247$ (to the nearest £)

The value of a new car is £8000.
The car depreciates in value by 10% each year.

Work out the car's value after five years.

$A = 8000 \times \left(1 - \dfrac{10}{100}\right)^5$

Use the formula:
$A = \text{Original Amount} \times \left(1 - \dfrac{\text{Rate}}{100}\right)^{\text{time}}$

$= 8000 \times (0.9)^5$

$= 8000 \times 0.5905 = £4723.92$

Direct Proportion

- In a graph, direct proportion can be represented by a straight line that passes through the origin (0, 0).

This table gives information about the journey of a car during a half-hour time period.

Distance (miles)	0	6	12	18
Time (mins)	0	10	20	30

a) Plot the graph of distance against time.

b) Is distance directly proportional to time?
Give a reason for your answer.

Distance is directly proportional to time, because it produces a straight line graph that passes through the origin.

c) What speed was the car travelling at in mph?

Speed = $\dfrac{\text{Distance}}{\text{Time}}$ ← This is the gradient.

$= \dfrac{18 \text{ miles}}{30 \text{ minutes}}$

$= \dfrac{36 \text{ miles}}{60 \text{ minutes}} = 36\text{mph}$

Quick Test

1. An aircraft travels 134 miles in 20 minutes.
   What is the aircraft's speed in mph?
2. Work out the compound interest on £1200 invested at 1.4% per annum for three years.
3. A new plasma television is worth £429. If you want to sell it six years later, it will be worth £214.50.
   What would be the percentage loss?

Key Words

compound measure
speed
density
pressure
compound interest
depreciation

Angles and Shapes 1

You must be able to:

- Recognise relationships between angles
- Use the properties of angles to work out unknown angles
- Recognise different types of triangle
- Understand and use the properties of special types of quadrilaterals.

Angle Facts

- You should know these three types of angle:
  - **acute**: less than 90°
  - **obtuse**: between 90° and 180°
  - **reflex**: between 180° and 360°.
- Angles on a straight line add up to 180°.
- Angles around a point add to 360°.
- **Vertically opposite** angles are equal.

Angles in Parallel Lines

- Parallel lines never meet. The lines are always the same distance apart.
- **Alternate** angles are equal.
- **Corresponding** angles are equal.
- Co-interior or **allied** angles add up to 180°.

Work out the sizes of angles a, b, c and d.
Give reasons for your answers.

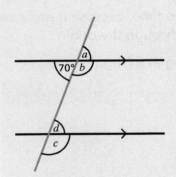

$a = 70°$ (vertically opposite angles are equal)

$b = 110°$ (angles on a straight line add up to 180°, so $b = 180° - 70°$)

$c = 110°$ (corresponding to b; corresponding angles are equal)

$d = 70°$ (corresponding to a; corresponding angles are equal)

Alternate Angles

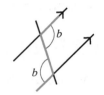

Corresponding Angles

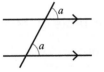

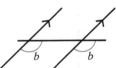

Allied Angles

$c + d = 180°$

> **Key Point**
>
> Examiners will **not** accept terms like 'Z angles' or 'F angles'. Always use correct terminology when giving reasons.

Triangles

- Angles in a triangle add up to 180°.
- There are several types of triangle:
  - **equilateral**: three equal sides and three equal angles of 60°
  - **isosceles**: two equal sides and two equal angles (opposite the equal sides)
  - **scalene**: no sides or angles are equal
  - **right-angled**: one 90° angle.

ABC is an isosceles triangle and *HE* is parallel to *GD*.
BAF is a straight line. Angle *FAE* = 81°

Calculate **a)** angle *ABC* and **b)** angle *ACB*.
Give reasons for your answers.

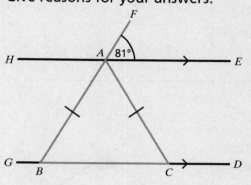

There are several different ways of solving this question.

a) Angle *HAB* = 81° (vertically opposite *FAE*), so angle *ABC* = 81° (alternate angle to *HAB*)

b) Angle *ACB* = 81° (angle *ABC* = angle *ACB*; base angles of an isosceles triangle are equal.)

Special Quadrilaterals

- The interior angles in a quadrilateral add up to 360°.
- The order of rotational symmetry is the number of times a shape looks the same when it is rotated 360° (one full turn).
- You need to know the properties of these special quadrilaterals:

	Sides	Angles	Lines of Symmetry	Rotational Symmetry	Diagonals
parallelogram	opposite sides are equal and parallel	diagonally opposite angles are equal	none	order 2	diagonals bisect each other
rhombus	all sides are equal and opposite sides are parallel	opposite angles are equal	two	order 2	diagonals bisect each other at 90°
kite	two pairs of adjacent sides are equal	one pair of opposite angles are equal	one	none	diagonals cross at 90°
trapezium	one pair of opposite sides are parallel		none (an isosceles trapezium has one)	none	

Quick Test

1. Name all the quadrilaterals that can be drawn with lines of lengths:
   a) 4cm, 7cm, 4cm, 7cm   b) 6cm, 6cm, 6cm, 6cm
2. *EFGH* is a trapezium with *EH* parallel to *FG*.
   FE and *GH* are produced (made longer) to meet at *J*.
   Angle *EHF* = 62°, angle *EFH* = 25° and angle *JGF* = 77°.
   Calculate the size of angle *EJH*.

Key Words

acute	equilateral
obtuse	isosceles
reflex	scalene
vertically opposite	right-angled
	parallelogram
alternate	rhombus
corresponding	kite
allied	trapezium

Angles and Shapes 2

You must be able to:

- Work out angles in a polygon
- Answer questions on regular polygons
- Understand scale drawings and use bearings.

Angles in a Polygon

- A **polygon** is a closed shape with at least three straight sides.
- **Regular** polygons are shapes where all the sides and angles are equal.
- **Irregular** polygons are shapes where some or all of the sides and angles are different.
- For all polygons:
  - at any **vertex** (corner): **interior** angle + **exterior** angle = 180°
  - sum of all exterior angles = 360°.
- To work out the sum of the interior angles in a polygon, you can split it into triangles from one vertex.
- For example, a pentagon can be divided into three triangles, so the sum of the interior angles is 3 × 180° = 540°.
- The sum of the interior angles for any polygon can be calculated using the formula:

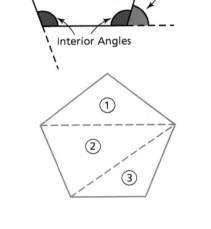

Pentagon   Exterior Angles

Interior Angles

> **Sum = (*n* − 2) × 180°**   Where *n* = number of sides

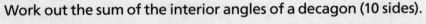
Work out the sum of the interior angles of a decagon (10 sides).

Sum = (10 − 2) × 180°
    = 8 × 180°
    = 1440°

> Use the formula:
> Sum = (*n* − 2) × 180°

Regular Polygons

- In regular polygons:

> Number of Sides (*n*) × Exterior Angle = 360°
> So, Exterior Angle = 360° ÷ *n*

Work out the size of the interior angles in a regular hexagon (six sides).

Exterior angle   = 360° ÷ 6 = 60°
Interior angle + 60°   = 180°
Interior angle   = 180° − 60°
                   = 120°

> Use the formula:
> Exterior Angle = 360° ÷ *n*

> Interior Angle + Exterior Angle = 180°

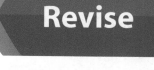

A regular polygon has an interior angle of 156°.

Work out the number of sides that the polygon has.

Exterior angle   = 180° – interior angle
                 = 180° – 156° = 24°
Number of sides = 360° ÷ 24° = 15

Scale Drawings and Bearings

- **Bearings** are always measured in a clockwise direction from north (000°) and have three figures.

This is a radar screen showing the position of four aircraft.
Scale 1mm : 4km

> 1mm on the diagram represents 4km in real life.

Describe the locations of aircraft A, B, C and D in relation to the centre (airport).

Aircraft A is on a bearing of 030° and 80km from the airport.

Aircraft B is on a bearing of 210° and 60km from the airport.

Aircraft C is on a bearing of 330° and 100km from the airport.

Aircraft D is on a bearing of 120° and 40km from the airport.

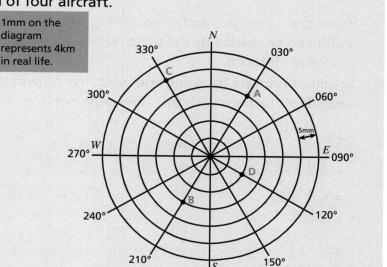

A ship sails from Mevagissey on a bearing of 130° for 22km.

a) Draw an accurate diagram to show this information and state the scale you have used.

b) What bearing would take the ship back to the harbour?

New bearing to return to harbour = 310°

> Measure with a protractor.

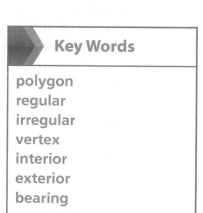

> Always place the 0 to 180 line of the protractor onto the north-south line.

1cm : 10km

> **Quick Test**

1. For a regular icosagon (20 sides), work out a) the sum of the interior angles and b) the size of one interior angle.
2. A regular polygon has an interior angle of 150°.
   How many sides does the polygon have?
3. Two yachts leave port at the same time.
   Yacht A sails on a bearing of 040° for 35km.
   Yacht B sails on a bearing of 120° for 60km.
   Using a scale of 1cm : 10km, draw the route taken by both yachts.
   Measure the bearing of yacht B from yacht A.

> **Key Words**
>
> polygon
> regular
> irregular
> vertex
> interior
> exterior
> bearing

Fractions

You must be able to:

- Add, subtract, multiply and divide fractions
- Change terminating decimals into corresponding fractions and vice versa
- Express one quantity as a fraction of another
- Use a calculator to change a fraction to a decimal.

Adding, Subtracting and Calculating with Fractions

- When the numerator and denominator of a fraction are both multiplied or divided by the same number, the result is an equivalent fraction.
- To add or subtract fractions, you must first convert them to equivalent fractions with the same denominator.

$$5\tfrac{3}{5} + 1\tfrac{2}{7}$$

$$= 6\tfrac{21}{35} + \tfrac{10}{35}$$

$$= 6\tfrac{31}{35}$$

$$4\tfrac{1}{4} - 2\tfrac{3}{5}$$

$$= \tfrac{17}{4} - \tfrac{13}{5}$$

$$= \tfrac{85}{20} - \tfrac{52}{20}$$

$$= \tfrac{33}{20} = 1\tfrac{13}{20}$$

> **Key Point**
>
> The top number in a fraction is called the **numerator**.
>
> The bottom number in a fraction is called the **denominator**.

Add whole numbers and then change fractions so that they have the same denominator.

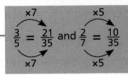

Convert mixed numbers into improper fractions and then change fractions so that they have the same denominator.

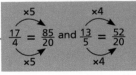

Multiplying and Dividing Fractions

- When multiplying fractions:
  - Convert mixed numbers to improper fractions
  - Cancel diagonally (or vertically) only
  - Then multiply the numerators together and the denominators together.
- When dividing fractions:
  - Invert the second fraction
  - Change the ÷ sign to a × sign
  - Then multiply.

> **Key Point**
>
> A **mixed number** contains a whole number and a fraction.
>
> An **improper fraction** has a numerator larger than the denominator.

Cancel down and then multiply. If the answer is an improper fraction, convert it back to a mixed number.

Reciprocals and Terminating and Recurring Decimals

- The reciprocal of a number (n) is 1 divided by the number, i.e. $\frac{1}{n}$
- A terminating decimal is a decimal with a finite number of digits (it ends), e.g. 0.75, 0.364
- A recurring decimal has a digit or group of digits that repeat indefinitely. It is shown with a dot over the recurring digit(s), e.g.

$0.1\dot{6} = 0.1666666...$
$0.\dot{3}\dot{7} = 0.37373737...$

- Rational numbers are numbers that **can be written exactly** as a fraction or decimal, e.g. $\frac{1}{4} = 0.25$
- π is an irrational number as it would continue forever as a decimal 3.141 592...

Key Point

To change $\frac{3}{5}$ to a decimal on a calculator, press

ON 3 ÷ 5 =

Use S ⇔ D to change the answer between a decimal and a fraction.

Change $\frac{3}{5}$ into a decimal.

$\frac{3}{5} = 3.00 \div 5$
$= 0.60$

Change the following decimals into fractions.

Give your answers in their simplest form.

a) 0.7 $\frac{7}{10}$

b) 0.35 $\frac{35}{100} = \frac{7}{20}$

c) 0.417 $\frac{417}{1000}$

One Quantity as a Fraction of Another

Express 20 minutes as a fraction of 3 hours 20 minutes.

3 hours 20 minutes = 200 minutes ← Convert to minutes.

20 minutes as a fraction of 200 minutes $= \frac{20}{200} = \frac{1}{10}$ ← Cancel down.

A school has 712 students.
$\frac{5}{8}$ of the students travel to school by bus and the rest walk.

How many students walk to school?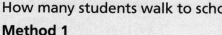

To find the number of students who take the bus, work out $\frac{1}{8}$ of 712 and then multiply by 5 to get $\frac{5}{8}$.

Method 1
$712 \div 8 = 89$
$89 \times 5 = 445$

Number who walk = $712 - 445$
$= 267$ students

Method 2
$1 - \frac{5}{8} = \frac{3}{8}$

$\frac{3}{8} \times 712 = 267$ students

Start by working out how many students walk to school as a fraction.

Key Words

numerator
denominator
equivalent
reciprocal
terminating decimal
recurring
rational number
irrational number

Quick Test

1. Which is larger: $\frac{3}{4} + \frac{1}{5}$ or $\frac{3}{4} \div \frac{1}{5}$?
   You must show your working.
2. a) Use your calculator to change $\frac{1}{9}$ to a decimal.
   b) Is the resulting decimal terminating or recurring?
3. Express 15cm as a fraction of 4m in its simplest form.

Percentages 1

You must be able to:

- Convert percentages to fractions and decimals and vice versa
- Calculate a percentage of a quantity
- Work out percentage change.

Converting Between Fractions, Decimals and Percentages

- To change **from a** percentage to a fraction or a decimal, **divide** by 100.

  Change 35% to:

  a) a fraction.

  $35\% = \frac{35}{100} = \frac{7}{20}$

  b) a decimal.

  $35\% = 0.35$

- To change from a fraction or a decimal **to a percentage**, **multiply** by 100.

  a) Convert $\frac{2}{5}$ to a percentage.

  $\frac{2}{5} \times 100 = \frac{200}{5} = 40\%$

  b) Convert 0.567 to a percentage.

  $0.567 = 56.7\%$

> **Key Point**
>
> Percentages to learn:
>
> $100\% = 1$ (the whole)
>
> $75\% = \frac{3}{4} = 0.75$
>
> $50\% = \frac{1}{2} = 0.5$
>
> $25\% = \frac{1}{4} = 0.25$
>
> $10\% = \frac{1}{10} = 0.1$

Move the decimal point two places to the **left** when **dividing** by 100.

Move the decimal point two places to the **right** when **multiplying** by 100.

A Percentage of a Quantity

Work out 15% of £80.

10% of £80 = £8

5% of £80 = £4

15% of £80 = £8 + £4 = £12

$80 \div 10$

5% is half of 10%, so half of £8.

$10\% + 5\% = 15\%$

Calculate 15% of £80.

$\frac{15}{100} \times 80 = \frac{1200}{100} = £12$

Remember, 15% means $\frac{15}{100}$.

Remember, 125% is greater than 100%, so the answer will be greater than 40kg.

What is 125% of 40kg?

$\frac{125}{100} \times 40 = \frac{5000}{100} = 50\text{kg}$

> **Key Point**
>
> $125\% = 100\% + 25\% =$ (original quantity) + (25% of original quantity)

Percentage Change

- To calculate percentage change, work out the change in value, e.g. the increase or decrease, and use the formula:

$$\text{Percentage Change} = \frac{\text{Change in Value}}{\text{Original Value}} \times 100$$

In Ashtonville (USA), there were 450 houses. After a tornado, only 300 remained standing.

What percentage of the houses in Ashtonville was destroyed by the tornado? Give your answer to 1 decimal place.

Change in values = 450 – 300 = 150
Original number of houses = 450

Percentage change = $\frac{150}{450} \times 100 = 33.3\%$ ← This is $\frac{1}{3}$.

Yesterday, Chris caught twelve fish. Today, he caught eight fewer.

What percentage decrease is this?
Give your answer to 2 decimal places.

$\frac{8}{12} \times 100 = 66.67\%$ ← This is $\frac{2}{3}$.

A car park increases its daily rate from £4.00 to £4.60.

What is this increase as a percentage?

$\frac{60}{400} \times 100 = 15\%$ ← Convert values to pence first.

Quick Test

1. Change 15% to **a)** a fraction and **b)** a decimal.
2. Without a calculator, work out 30% of 90 Turkish Lira.
3. Shima bought a necklace for £125. Three years later, she sold it online for £85. Calculate the percentage loss.
4. Put these values in order of size, smallest first:
   $\frac{1}{5}$, 15%, 1.15, $\frac{5}{20}$
5. James says that 20% of £60 is the same as 60% of £20. Is he correct?
6. Draw a rectangle measuring 6cm by 5cm.
   Divide the rectangle into 30 centimetre squares and then shade 40% of it.

Key Words

percentage

Percentages 2

You must be able to:

- Increase and decrease quantities by a percentage
- Express one quantity as a percentage of another
- Solve percentage problems using a multiplier
- Understand and use reverse percentages.

Increasing and Decreasing Quantities by a Percentage

- When **increasing** a quantity by a percentage, work out the increase and then **add** it to the original amount.
- When **decreasing** a quantity, work out the decrease and then **subtract**.
- Percentage increase and decrease problems can also be solved using a multiplier.

> **Key Point**
>
> Harder percentages to learn:
>
> $20\% = \frac{1}{5}$
>
> $33.3\% = \frac{1}{3}$
>
> $66.7\% = \frac{2}{3}$
>
> $12.5\% = \frac{1}{8}$

Last year, Dandelion Place had 14 240 visitors.

This year, the attraction will be closed for three months for refurbishment. This means there will be a 15% decrease in the total number of visitors for the year.

How many visitors are expected this year?

Method 1:

$\frac{15}{100} \times 14\,240 = 2136$

Number of visitors

$= 14\,240 - 2136$

$= 12\,104$

Method 2:

10% of 14 240 = 1424

5% of 14 240 = 712 ←

15% of 14 240 = 2136 ←

so, the number of visitors

$= 14\,240 - 2136$ ←

$= 12\,104$

10% ÷ 2 = 5%

10% + 5% = 15%

Alternatively, using a multiplier: 15% decrease means 85% of last year's visitors, so
0.85 × 14 240 = 12 104

Molly bought a new tumble dryer.
She visited three shops to compare prices:

A. Sean's Electricals
Normal price: £250, Sale price: 5% off

B. Mandeep's Deals
Tumble dryer: £200, plus tax at 17.5%

C. Chet's Cut Price Store
Normal price: £280, Sale price: $\frac{1}{7}$ off

a) Which shop offered the best deal?

b) How much did it sell the tumble dryer for?

A. Sean's Electricals:

$\frac{5}{100} \times £250 = £12.50$

Tumble dryer costs £250 − £12.50 = £237.50

B. Mandeep's Deals:

$\frac{17.5}{100} \times £200 = £35$

Tumble dryer costs £200 + £35 = £235.00

C. Chet's Cut Price Store:

$\frac{1}{7} \times £280 = £40$

Tumble dryer costs £280 − £40 = £240.00

a) Mandeep's Deals **b)** £235

> If working without a calculator, remember:
> 17.5% = 10% + 5% + 2.5%

Sanjeev's salary is £32000 per year. His salary is increased by 6%.

Work out his new salary.

100% + 6% = 106% = 1.06

1.06 × £32000 = £33920

> This is the multiplier.

Expressing One Quantity as a Percentage of Another

- When expressing one quantity as a percentage of another, write two quantities as a fraction and then multiply by 100 to convert to a percentage.

Key Point

Make sure all quantities are in the same units first.

In two separate maths tests, Vinay got 18 out of 30 and Derek got 24 out of 45.

Who got the greater percentage in their maths test?

Vinay: $\frac{18}{30} \times 100 = 60\%$

Derek: $\frac{24}{45} \times 100 = 53.33\%$

Vinay got the greater percentage.

Work out 16 minutes as a percentage of 4 hours. Give your answer to 3 decimal places. $\frac{16}{240}$

$\frac{16}{240} \times 100 = 6.667\%$

(to 3 d.p.)

> 4 hours = 4 × 60 = 240 minutes

Reverse Percentages

- **Reverse percentages** involve working backwards from the final amount to **find the original amount**.

In a Thai restaurant, there were $27\frac{1}{2}$ dumplings left on a plate after 45% had been eaten. How many dumplings were on the plate at the start of the meal?

100% − 45% = 55%

1% = 27.5 ÷ 55

100% = 100 × 27.5 ÷ 55 = 50 dumplings

> $27\frac{1}{2}$ dumplings is 55% of the original quantity.

Quick Test

1. This year Curt grew 220 carrots. This is 20% less than last year. How many carrots did Curt grow last year?
2. Increase £60 by 17.5%.
3. Express 18cm as a percentage of 12m.

Key Words

multiplier

Probability 1

You must be able to:
- Know and use words associated with probability
- Construct and use a probability scale
- Understand what mutually exclusive events are
- Calculate probabilities using experimental data.

Calculating Probabilities

- The probability of an outcome occurring can be described using words or using a numerical scale from 0 to 1.

```
        Unlikely        Likely
   |────────┬────────┬────────|
Impossible      Evens      Certain
  (0)          (0.5)        (1)
```

- Relative frequencies are probabilities based on experiments.
- Random means each possible outcome is equally likely.
- An event is biased when outcomes are **not** equally likely.
- The sample space represents all possible outcomes from an event. This can be shown as a list or a diagram.

> There are seven counters in a bag.
> Four counters are red, two are green and one is blue.
>
> One counter is taken from the bag at random.
>
> Write down the probability that the counter taken is:
>
> **a)** Red   Four of the counters are red, so P(red) = $\frac{4}{7}$ ◄
> **b)** Green   Two of the counters are green, so P(green) = $\frac{2}{7}$
> **c)** Blue.   One of the counters is blue, so P(blue) = $\frac{1}{7}$ ◄

Mutually Exclusive and Exhaustive Outcomes

- Mutually exclusive outcomes **cannot** happen at the same time.
- When two events are mutually exclusive P(A or B) = P(A) + P(B).
- Events are exhaustive if all possible outcomes have been included.
- The probabilities of a set of exhaustive outcomes add up to 1.

> Shelby looks at the weather forecast every morning.
> On Monday, the forecast says that there is a $\frac{7}{10}$ chance of rain.
>
> What is the probability that it will **not** rain?
>
> P(no rain) = $1 - \frac{7}{10} = \frac{3}{10}$

> **Key Point**
>
> Probability is the chance that an event is likely to occur.
>
> Probabilities can be based on theory or the results of an experiment.
>
> The sum of the probabilities of all possible outcomes is 1.

> **Key Point**
>
> Probabilities can be given as fractions, decimals or percentages.

There are seven counters, so seven possible outcomes. Each outcome is equally likely.

Note: $\frac{4}{7} + \frac{2}{7} + \frac{1}{7} = 1$

> **Key Point**
>
> P(A') is the probability of A **not** happening.
>
> P(A') = 1 − P(A)

A spinner has segments that are coloured red, blue, green or yellow. The probability that it will land on a particular colour is shown below:

Colour	Red	Blue	Green	Yellow
Probability	0.4	x	0.2	0.3

What is the probability that the spinner will land on blue?

$0.4 + x + 0.2 + 0.3 = 1$

$x = 1 - 0.9$

$= 0.1$

$P(\text{blue}) = 0.1$

Expectation

- When you know the probability of an outcome, you can predict how many times you would expect that outcome to occur in a certain number of trials. This is called expectation.

Kelly rolls a six-sided dice 120 times and records her results.

Score	1	2	3	4	5	6
Frequency	19	29	14	18	20	20

a) Kelly throws the dice again.

Estimate the probability that she will throw a 2.

Estimate of probability of a 2 is $\frac{29}{120}$.

b) The dice is thrown another 200 times.

How many times would you expect it to land on a 2?

$\frac{29}{120} \times 200 = 48$

c) Is there enough evidence to suggest the dice is biased? Explain your answer.

If the dice is fair, you would expect to roll 20 of each number. This did not happen, so the dice may be biased.

Probability 2

You must be able to:

- Calculate the probability of independent and dependent combined events
- Calculate probabilities using sample space and tree diagrams
- Calculate sets and combinations of sets using tables, grids, frequency trees and Venn diagrams.

Probability Diagrams

Julie thinks that in her class, you are more likely to wear glasses if you are a boy.
Based on the data below, is she correct?

	Boys	Girls	Total
Glasses	8	6	14
No Glasses	12	9	21
Total	20	15	35

P(of a boy wearing glasses) $= \frac{8}{20} = \frac{2}{5}$

P(of a girl wearing glasses) $= \frac{6}{15} = \frac{2}{5}$

Julie is incorrect as the probabilities are equal.

The same information could be shown using a frequency tree:

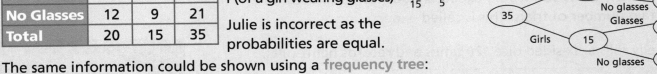

Students in a school study either French, Spanish, both or neither. There are 250 students. 75 students study both French and Spanish, 225 study French and 90 study Spanish.

Work out how many students do **not** study French or Spanish.

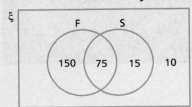

$250 - 150 - 75 - 15 = 10$

10 students do not study French or Spanish.

> The crossover represents students who study both subjects.

> **Key Point**
>
> To calculate the probabilities involving more than one event, you can use a **two-way table**, **Venn diagram** or tree diagram to represent all the possible outcomes.

Combined Events and Tree Diagrams

- When calculating probabilities for combined events, you can draw a sample space diagram.

Two fair six-sided dice are thrown and their scores are added.

a) Construct a sample space diagram to show all the possible outcomes.

b) Using your sample space diagram, work out P(8).

The sample space diagram shows there are 6 × 6 = 36 possible outcomes.

8 appears five times in the diagram out of 36 possible outcomes, therefore P(8) $= \frac{5}{36}$

		Dice 1				
+	**1**	**2**	**3**	**4**	**5**	**6**
1	2	3	4	5	6	7
2	3	4	5	6	7	8
3	4	5	6	7	8	9
4	5	6	7	8	9	10
5	6	7	8	9	10	11
6	7	8	9	10	11	12

(Dice 2 labels the rows)

- When dealing with successive events you can use a tree diagram.

Two fair coins are tossed one after the other.

Work out the probability of each possible outcome.

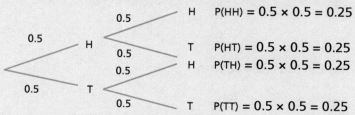

H   P(HH) = 0.5 × 0.5 = 0.25

T   P(HT) = 0.5 × 0.5 = 0.25

H   P(TH) = 0.5 × 0.5 = 0.25

T   P(TT) = 0.5 × 0.5 = 0.25

Probability of a Head and a Tail = P(HT) + P(TH)

= 0.25 + 0.25 = 0.5

Each coin can give us two possible outcomes: a Head (H) or a Tail (T).

Key Point

Always multiply along the branches of a probability tree.

Independent Events

- If A and B are independent events, one outcome does **not** depend on the other. P(A and B) = P(A) × P(B).

A fair two-sided coin is tossed and a fair six-sided dice is rolled.

What is the probability of getting a Head and rolling a 6?

$P(H) \times P(6) = \frac{1}{2} \times \frac{1}{6} = \frac{1}{12}$

The two outcomes are independent, therefore: P(A) × P(B)

Dependent Events

- If A and B are dependent events, one outcome depends on the other.

A bag contains 3 red and 5 blue counters. Two counters are taken out at random.

Work out the probability of each possible outcome.

First counter   Second counter

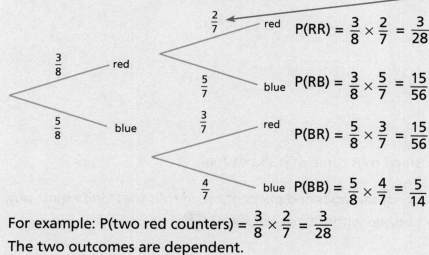

$\frac{2}{7}$ red $P(RR) = \frac{3}{8} \times \frac{2}{7} = \frac{3}{28}$

$\frac{5}{7}$ blue $P(RB) = \frac{3}{8} \times \frac{5}{7} = \frac{15}{56}$

$\frac{3}{7}$ red $P(BR) = \frac{5}{8} \times \frac{3}{7} = \frac{15}{56}$

$\frac{4}{7}$ blue $P(BB) = \frac{5}{8} \times \frac{4}{7} = \frac{5}{14}$

If red was the first counter, there are now only 2 reds left out of 7 counters.

For example: P(two red counters) = $\frac{3}{8} \times \frac{2}{7} = \frac{3}{28}$

The two outcomes are dependent.

Key Words

frequency tree
two-way table
Venn diagram
sample space diagram
tree diagram
independent
dependent

Quick Test

1. A fair three-sided spinner has one red section. Work out the probability of the spinner landing on red and a fair six-sided dice landing on 5.
2. A bag contains 3 red balls, 4 blue balls and 2 yellow balls. Two balls are taken from the bag at random. What is the probability that both balls are the same colour?

Practice Questions

Number 1, 2 & 3

1 The average distance from the Moon to the Earth is 384 000km.

    a) Write this distance in standard form.   [2]

    b) A spaceship is travelling from the Earth to the Moon.
        It has travelled 1.96×10^4km.

        How many kilometres are left to travel?   [2]

2 On one evening in December, the temperature in Birmingham was –3°C and the temperature in Aberdeen was –8°C.

    Work out the difference in temperature between Aberdeen and Birmingham.   [1]

3 Which is larger?

    $3 + 6 \times 2$ OR $(-3 - 6) - (-25)$ [2]

4 What is the largest multiple of 4 and 7 that is smaller than 105?   [1]

5 What is the lowest common multiple (LCM) of 12 and 15?   [1]

6 Which is greater, the fifth square number OR the third cube number?   [3]

7 256 can be expressed as 2^n.

    What is the value of n?   [2]

8 Is 2^3 equal to 3^2?
    Explain your answer.   [2]

9 Sausages come in packs of six. Bread rolls come in packs of four.

    What is the least number of packs of sausages and packs of bread rolls that Linda must buy, so that there is a roll for every sausage without any left over?   [2]

> **Total Marks** _____ / 18

Basic Algebra & Factorisation and Formulae

1 Expand $5(x + 6)$ 📟 [2]

2 Factorise $15x + 10$ 📟 [1]

3 Expand $6(5 - 2x)$ 📟 [2]

4 Make t the subject of $p = 4t - q$ 📟 [2]

5 Simplify $5x - 2y + 4x + 6y$ 📟 [2]

6 Simplify $5 - 3z + y - 5z + 7 + 3y$ 📟 [2]

7 Simplify $3x^2 + 3x + x^2 + 4 - x$ 📟 [1]

8 Work out the value of $3z^2 - 2q + 5$, when $z = -2$ and $q = -3$. 📟 [1]

9 Solve $4(2b - 3) = 2$ 📟 [2]

10 Solve $3(p + 2) = 2(p + 3)$ 📟 [2]

11 Solve $\frac{5}{2}x - \frac{1}{3} = \frac{2}{3}x + \frac{1}{2}$ 📟 [3]

12 Expand $6(x - 5y + 6)$ 📟 [2]

13 Expand $6p - 4(q - 3)$ 📟 [2]

14 Factorise completely $4xyz - 4xz$ 📟 [2]

15 Factorise $x^2 + 3x + 2$ 📟 [2]

16 Write $3(2x - 5) + 4(x + 3) - 4x$ in the form $a(bx + c)$, where a, b and c are integers. 📟 [3]

17 Choose a word from those below to make the statement correct. 📟

equation   expression   formula   identity

$A = \frac{1}{2}(a + b)h$ is an example of a/an _____ . [1]

> **Total Marks** _____ / 32

Practice Questions

Ratio and Proportion

1. Simplify 5g : 10kg 🖩 [1]

2. The angles in a triangle are in the ratio 2 : 3 : 4

   What is the size of the largest angle? 🖩 [2]

3. Six sticks of celery are needed to make celery soup for four people.

   How many sticks of celery would be needed to make soup for 20 people? 🖩 [2]

4. It took six people four days to build a wall.

   Working at the same rate, how long would it have taken one person to build the wall? [2]

   > **Total Marks** _____ / 7

Variation and Compound Measures

1. A bar of lead has a volume of 400cm³ and a mass of 4560g.

   Work out the density of the bar of lead in g/cm³. [2]

2. A rabbit runs 200 metres in 22 seconds.

   What is the rabbit's average speed in m/s?
   Give your answer to 2 decimal places. [2]

3. Khalid left his home at 10am and went for a 15km run.
   He arrived back home at 1pm.

   What was his average speed in km/h? [2]

4. Work out the compound interest earned on £4000 invested at 4% for four years. [3]

   > **Total Marks** _____ / 9

Angles and Shapes 1 & 2

1   Work out the size of angles j, k, l and m, giving a reason for each answer.

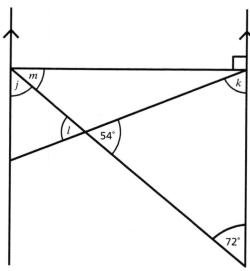

m

j

k

l   54°

72°

[4]

2   Three angles in a quadrilateral are 46°, 107° and 119°.

Calculate the size of the fourth angle.   [1]

3   Work out the exterior angle of a regular decagon.   [1]

4   A and B are two points.

If the bearing of B from A is 036°, what is the bearing of A from B?   [1]

5   A map is drawn using a scale of 1cm : 4km.

If the length of Loch Ness is 36km, what would its length be on the map?   [1]

6   A boat sails in a north-westerly direction.

What bearing is this?   [1]

Total Marks .... / 9

Practice Questions

Fractions

1 A teacher took 32 books home to mark. She marked $\frac{1}{8}$ of them.

How many books does she still have to mark? [2]

2 On a farm, $\frac{1}{3}$ of the livestock are cows, $\frac{1}{6}$ are sheep, $\frac{1}{4}$ are chickens and the remainder are horses.

Express the number of horses on the farm as a fraction. [2]

3 Write these fractions in order, smallest first:

$\frac{2}{3}$ $\frac{4}{12}$ $\frac{1}{6}$ $\frac{12}{24}$ [2]

4 **a)** Work out the area of a rectangle measuring $\frac{4}{5}$ of a metre by $\frac{2}{3}$ of a metre. [1]

     b) What is the rectangle's perimeter? Give your answer as an improper fraction. [2]

5 Write down:

     a) 0.45 as a fraction in its simplest form. [2]

     b) $\frac{7}{8}$ as a decimal. [2]

> **Total Marks** _____ / 13

Percentages 1 & 2

1 Whizzy Garage sells cars. It offers a discount of 20% off the retail price for cash purchases. Pat pays £4800 cash for a car.

Calculate the retail price of the car before the cash discount. [2]

2 In a box containing 36 bananas, nine of the bananas are bad.

What percentage of the bananas are bad? [2]

3 What is 28 minutes of 2 hours as a percentage?
Give your answer to 1 decimal place. [2]

> **Total Marks** _____ / 6

Probability 1 & 2

1 Two fair six-sided dice are thrown and the product of their scores is calculated.

a) Draw a sample space diagram to represent all the possible outcomes. [2]

b) What is the probability that the product of the scores is greater than 12? [1]

c) What is the probability that the product of the scores is a square number? [1]

2 There are 20 pens in a box: ten black, six blue and four red.
A pen is picked at random from the box.

a) What is the probability that the pen is black? [1]

b) What is the probability that the pen is **not** black? [1]

3 A three-sided spinner has sides labelled 1, 2 and 3. The spinner is biased.
Thomas spins the spinner 500 times and records the outcomes in a table.

Score	1	2	3
Frequency	98	305	97

a) Thomas spins the spinner again. Estimate the probability that it lands on a 2. [1]

b) He takes another 100 spins. Estimate how many times it will land on a 3. [2]

4 Ten coloured counters are placed in a bag.
Six counters are pink, three counters are green and one counter is blue.

a) One counter is taken from the bag at random.

Work out the probability that the counter taken is:
i) Pink   ii) Green   iii) Blue. [3]

b) A counter is taken from the bag at random and replaced.
A second counter is then taken from the bag at random.

Work out the probability that both counters are the same colour. [2]

5 Bhavna conducts a survey about the pets owned by her classmates.
There are 35 students in her class. Her results are: 25 students own cats,
15 students own dogs and 10 students own both.

a) Draw a Venn diagram to represent the results. [3]

b) How many students do **not** own a cat or a dog? [1]

Total Marks _____ / 18

Number Patterns and Sequences 1

You must be able to:

- Work out missing terms in sequences using term-to-term rules and position-to-term rules
- Recognise and use arithmetic and geometric sequences
- Work out the rule for a given pattern.

Patterns in Number

- A sequence is a series of shapes or numbers that follow a particular pattern or rule.
- A term-to-term rule links the next term in the sequence to the previous one.
- A position-to-term rule, also called the nth term, can be used to work out any term in the sequence.

> Write down the next two terms in the following sequence:
>
> 7, 11, 15, 19, __, __
>
> The term-to-term rule is +4, so the next two terms are 23 and 27.

> Write down the next two terms in the following sequence:
>
> 50, 25, 12.5, __, __
>
> The term-to-term rule is ÷2, so the next two terms are 6.25 and 3.125.

General Rules from Given Patterns

Here is a sequence of patterns made from matchsticks:

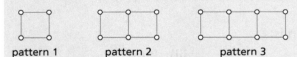

pattern 1   pattern 2   pattern 3

a) Draw the next pattern in the sequence.

b) Write down the sequence of numbers that represents the total number of matchsticks used in each pattern and state the term-to-term rule.

Pattern No.	1	2	3	4
No. of Matchsticks	4	7	10	13

The term-to-term rule is +3.

Key Point

When finding the term-to-term rule, remember to look at consecutive terms.

The nth term of a number sequence is $5n + 2$.

Write down the first five terms of the sequence.

$(5 \times 1) + 2 = 7$ ⟵

$(5 \times 2) + 2 = 12$ ⟵

$7, 12, 17, 22, 27$ ⟵

> To work out the first term, substitute $n = 1$ into the expression.

> To work out the second term, substitute $n = 2$ into the expression.

> Continue until $n = 5$ to produce the first five terms of the sequence.

Number Sequences

- In an **arithmetic sequence**, there is a common difference between consecutive terms, e.g.

  $5, 8, 11, 14, 17 \dots$ ⟵

  > The terms have a common difference of $+3$.

- In a **geometric sequence**, each term is found by multiplying the previous term by a constant, e.g.

  $20, 10, 5, 2.5, 1.25 \dots$ ⟵

  > The constant (or ratio) is 0.5

The nth term of an arithmetic sequence is $4n - 1$.

a) Write down the term-to-term rule.

The sequence of numbers is $3, 7, 11, 15, 19 \dots$ ⟵
The term-to-term rule is $+4$.

> Work out the first five terms.

b) Marnie thinks that 50 is a number in this sequence. Is Marnie correct? Give a reason for your answer.

$4n - 1 = 50$, $n = 12.75$ ⟵
n is not a whole number, so 50 is **not** in this sequence.
Marnie is wrong.

> Use the nth term to find the value of n for an output of 50.

Here is a geometric sequence: $4, 6, 9, \_\_, 20.25$

What is the missing term?

$\dfrac{6}{4} = \dfrac{9}{6} = 1.5$ ⟵

$9 \times 1.5 = 13.5$ ⟵
The missing term is 13.5

> Divide at least two given terms by the previous term to work out the ratio.

> Multiply by the ratio to find the missing term.

Quick Test

1. Here are the first five terms of a sequence: $16, 12, 8, 4, 0 \dots$
   Write down the next two terms.
2. The nth term of a sequence is $5n - 7$.
   Work out the 1st term and the 10th term of this sequence.
3. In the sequence below the next pattern is formed by adding another layer of tiles around the previous pattern:

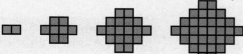

Work out how many tiles will be needed for the 6th pattern.

Key Words

sequence
term-to-term rule
position-to-term rule
nth term
arithmetic sequence
geometric sequence

Number Patterns and Sequences 2

You must be able to:

- Work out and use expressions to calculate the *n*th term of a linear sequence
- Recognise and use sequences of triangular numbers, squares, cubes and other special sequences.

Finding the *n*th Term of a Linear Sequence

- A number sequence that increases or decreases by the same amount each time is called a linear sequence.
- To work out the expression for the *n*th term in a linear sequence, look for a pattern in the numbers.
- Using a function machine to represent a sequence of numbers can help.

The first five terms of a sequence are: 9, 12, 15, 18, 21 …

What is the expression for the *n*th term of this sequence?

Input (*n*)	× 3 (3*n*)	Output
1	3	9
2	6	12
3	9	15
4	12	18
5	15	21
n	3*n*	3*n* + 6

The 'input' is the position of the term and the 'output' is the value of the term.

The term-to-term rule is +3, so the expression for the *n*th term starts with 3*n*.

The difference between 3*n* and the output in each case is 6, so the expression for the *n*th term is **3*n* + 6.**

- The alternative method is to work out the zero term.

The first five terms of a sequence are: 20, 16, 12, 8, 4 …

What is the expression for the *n*th term of this sequence?

Input	Output
0	zero term
1	20
2	16
3	12
4	8
5	4
n	*n*th term

The expression for the *n*th term is −4*n* + 24 or 24 − 4*n*.

Key Point

The zero term is the term that would come before the first term in a given sequence of numbers.

The zero term is (20 + 4 =) 24

The difference between terms is −4.

The *n*th term = 'the difference' × *n* + the zero term

Special Sequences

- It is important to be able to recognise special sequences of numbers, e.g. the square numbers, the cube numbers, the triangular numbers and the Fibonacci sequence.

Here is a sequence of numbers: 1, 4, 9, 16, 25 ...

Write down:

a) The next two terms.

36, 49 ⟵————————————————— The sequence is the square numbers.

b) The nth term of the sequence.

The nth term is n^2.

Here is a sequence of numbers: 1, 8, 27, 64 ...

Write down:

a) The next two terms.

125, 216 ⟵————————————————— The sequence is the cube numbers.

b) The nth term of the sequence.

The nth term is n^3.

Here is a sequence of numbers: 1, 3, 6, 10, 15 ...

Write down:

a) The next two terms.

21, 28 ⟵————————————————— The sequence is the triangular numbers.

b) The nth term of the sequence.

The nth term is $\frac{n}{2}(n + 1)$.

Write down the next two terms in the following sequence:
1, 1, 2, 3, 5, 8, 13, 21 ...

34, 55 ⟵————————————————— This is the Fibonacci sequence. The next term is found by adding the previous two terms together.

> **Quick Test**
>
> 1. Write down the next two terms in the following sequence:
>   6, 9, 12, 15, __, __
> 2. a) Write down the nth term for the following sequence:
>   7, 10, 13, 16, 19 ...
>   b) Work out the 50th term in this sequence.
> 3. Write down the nth term for the following sequence:
>   0, 3, 8, 15, 24 ...

> **Key Words**
>
> linear sequence
> zero term
> Fibonacci sequence

Transformations

You must be able to:

- Identify, describe and construct transformations of shapes, including reflections, rotations, translations and enlargements.

Reflection

- When a shape is reflected:
  - Each point on the image is the same distance from the mirror line as the corresponding point on the object
  - The object and the image are congruent (same size and shape)
  - To define a reflection on a coordinate grid, the equation of the mirror line should be stated.

Rotation

- Rotation is described by stating the:
  - Direction rotated (clockwise or anticlockwise)
  - Angle of rotation (which is usually a multiple of 90° in the exam)
  - Centre of rotation (point about which the shape is rotated).

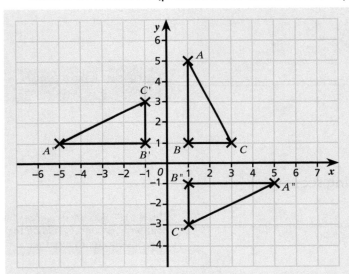

> **Key Point**
>
> There is no need to state clockwise or anticlockwise for a rotation of 180°.

a) Describe the transformation that maps triangle ABC onto triangle $A'B'C'$.

The transformation that maps ABC to $A'B'C'$ is a rotation 90° anticlockwise (or 270° clockwise) about the origin (0, 0).

b) Describe the transformation that maps triangle $A'B'C'$ onto triangle $A''B''C''$.

The transformation that maps $A'B'C'$ to $A''B''C''$ is a rotation of 180° about the origin (0, 0).

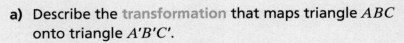

Translation

- When a shape is translated:
  - The shape does not rotate – it moves left or right and up or down – and stays the same size
  - The translation is represented by a column vector $\binom{x}{y}$.

Describe the transformation that takes shape A to shape B.

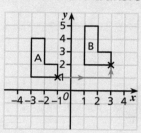

Four right, one up.

A translation through $\binom{4}{1}$

Enlargement

- When a shape is enlarged:
  - The shape of the object is not changed, only its size
  - The enlarged shape is similar to the original shape
  - The scale factor determines whether the object gets bigger (scale factor > 1) or smaller (scale factor < 1)
  - When describing the enlargement, state the scale factor and the centre of enlargement.

a) Enlarge triangle A by scale factor 2, centre of enlargement (1, 2). Label the transformed triangle, B.

b) Enlarge triangle A by scale factor $\frac{1}{2}$, centre of enlargement (1, 2). Label the transformed triangle, C.

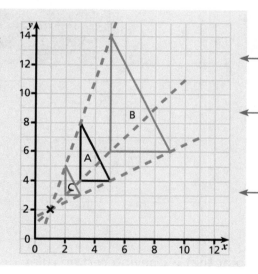

All construction lines must remain.

The side **lengths** of triangle B are **twice** the length of the corresponding sides of triangle A. However, the **area** of triangle B is **four times** bigger.

The side **lengths** of triangle C are **half** the length of the corresponding sides of triangle A. However, the **area** of triangle C is **four times** smaller.

Quick Test

1. Describe the single transformation that takes:
   a) Triangle A to triangle B
   b) Triangle A to triangle C
   c) Triangle A to triangle D.

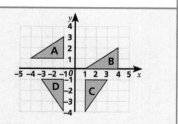

Constructions

You must be able to:

- Use a ruler and a pair of compasses to produce different constructions, including bisectors
- Describe a locus and solve problems involving loci.

Constructions

- The **perpendicular bisector** of line AB.

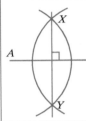

> Open compasses to more than half AB. Put compass point on A. Draw arc. Put compass point on B. Draw arc. XY is the perpendicular bisector.

- A **perpendicular from a given point** to the line AB.

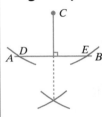

> Put compass point on C. Draw arc. Keep radius the same. Put compass point on E. Draw arc. Put compass point on D. Draw arc. Join C to the point where the arcs cross.

Key Point

The perpendicular distance from a point to a line is the shortest distance to the line.

- An **angle bisector.**

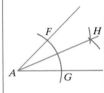

> Put compass point on A. Draw arc FG. Put compass point on F. Draw arc. Put compass point on G. Draw arc. Join HA.

- An **equilateral triangle** and an **angle of 60°.**

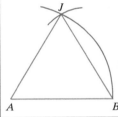

> Open compasses to length AB. Put point on A. Draw arc. Put compass point on B. Draw arc. Join AJ and BJ. Angle $A = 60°$

- A **perpendicular** to line AB **at a given point**.

> Put compass point on M. Draw arcs at K and L. Construct the perpendicular bisector of K and L.

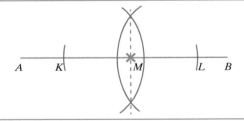

Defining a Locus

- A **locus** is the path taken by a point that is obeying certain rules.
- The plural of locus is **loci**.

- The locus of points that are a **fixed distance from a given point**, A, is a circle.

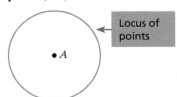

Locus of points

- The locus of points that are a **fixed distance from a line** AB.

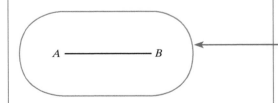

Locus of points

Key Point

In the exam, the fixed distance is likely to be given, e.g. 4cm.

- The locus of points that are the **same distance from two lines** AB and AC. This is the angle bisector.

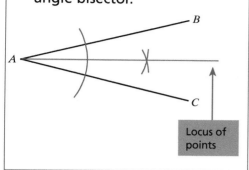

Locus of points

- The locus of points that are **equidistant from two points** A and B. This is the perpendicular bisector.

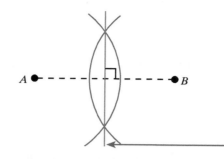

Locus of points

Loci Problems

A guard dog is tied to a post by a 4-metre long rope.

Accurately draw the locus of the points the dog can reach using a scale of 1cm : 1m.

The solution would be a shaded circle of radius 4cm. The dog could reach the circumference of the circle and any point inside it.

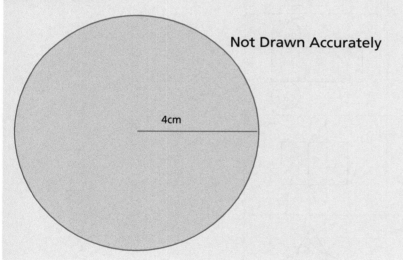

Not Drawn Accurately

4cm

Quick Test

1. Describe how you would accurately construct an angle of 30°.
2. A rectangular vegetable plot $ABCD$ measures 6m by 3m. A goat is tethered at corner A by a 4m rope. Accurately draw the plot and construct the locus of the points that the goat can reach. Scale 1cm : 1m. Shade the region of the vegetable plot that can be eaten by the goat.

Key Words

perpendicular
bisector
locus / loci
equidistant

Nets, Plans and Elevations

You must be able to:

- Identify a 3D shape from its net
- Draw nets of 3D shapes
- Use isometric grids
- Interpret and draw plans and elevations of 3D shapes.

Nets

- A **net** is a 2D shape that can be folded to form a 3D solid.

Name	Shape	Net
Cube		
Cuboid		
Cylinder		
Triangular Prism		
Square-Based Pyramid		

> **Key Point**
>
> There are many different nets for a cube.

Plans and Elevations

- An **isometric grid** can be used to draw 3D shapes.
- The **plan view** of a 3D shape shows what it looks like from above, i.e. a bird's eye view.
- The side **elevation** is the view of a 3D shape from the side.
- The front elevation is the view of a 3D shape from the front.

> **Key Point**
>
> An isometric grid can be made up of equilateral triangles or dots.

Here is a 3D shape made of centimetre cubes:

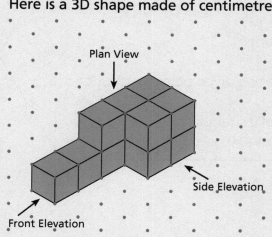

Plan View

Side Elevation

Front Elevation

Draw:

a) The plan view

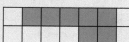

Count the number of cubes for each length carefully.

b) The front elevation

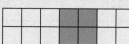

c) The side elevation.

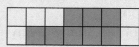

Here are the three views of a 3D shape:

Plan View

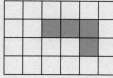

Front Elevation

Side Elevation

Draw the 3D shape on isometric paper.

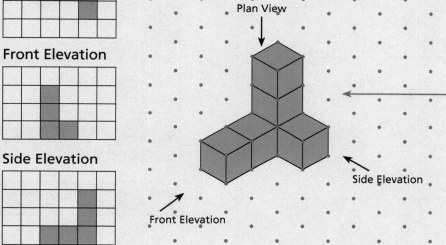

Plan View

Side Elevation

Front Elevation

Check that your final drawing matches the given views.

Quick Test

1. A can of soup has a height of 10cm. The length of the label required to go once around the can is 22cm.

Draw an accurate plan view and front elevation of the can of soup.

Key Words

net
isometric grid
plan view
elevation

Linear Graphs

You must be able to:

- Work with coordinates in all four quadrants
- Plot graphs of linear functions
- Work out the equation of a line through two given points or through one point with a given gradient
- Work out the gradient and y-intercept of a straight line $y = mx + c$
- Use number machines to work out inputs and outputs.

Algebra

Drawing Linear Graphs from Points

- **Linear graphs** are straight-line graphs.
- The equation of a straight-line graph is usually given in the form $y = mx + c$, where m is the **gradient** of the line and c is the **intercept** of the y-axis.
- $y = mx + c$ is a function of x, where the **input** is the x-coordinate and the **output** is the y-coordinate.

Write down the gradient and y-intercept of the line of equation $y = 5x + 1$.

The gradient is 5.
The y-intercept is $(0,1)$.

> **Key Point**
>
> To draw a straight line, only two coordinates are needed.

Draw the graph of the equation $y = 2x + 5$.
Use values of x from -3 to 3.

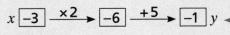

You can set up a flow chart to work out the y-coordinates.

x	-3	0	3
y	-1	5	11

Draw a table of values. Include a third value as a check.

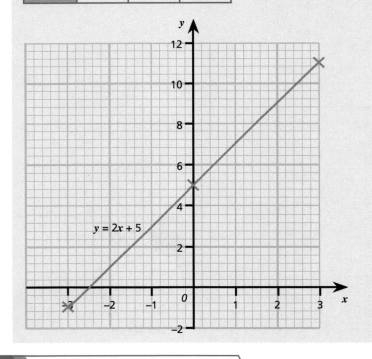

The Cover-Up Method

- The cover-up method can be used to draw graphs of equations given in the form $ax + by = c$.

Draw the graph of the equation $2x + 3y = 6$.

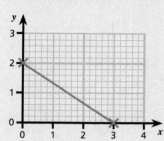

$3y = 6$

$y = 2$ The y-intercept is (0, 2).

$2x = 6$

$x = 3$ The x-intercept is (3, 0).

> Cover up the x term and solve to find y.

> Cover up the y term and solve to find x.

The Equation of a Straight Line

- To find the equation of a straight line in the form $y = mx + c$, work out the gradient and y-intercept.

Work out the equation of the line that joins the points (1, 20) and (4, 5).

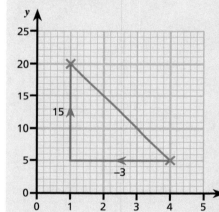

Gradient $= \dfrac{15}{-3}$

$= -5$

$y = mx + c$

$y = -5x + c$

$20 = -5 \times 1 + c$

$c = 25$

The equation of the line is $y = -5x + 25$

> To work out the value of c, substitute in the gradient and point (1, 20) or (4, 5).

> Substitute your values for m and c into the equation.

Functions

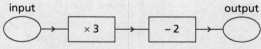

a) Work out the output when the input is 8.
   Output $= 8 \times 3 - 2 = 22$
b) Work out the input when the output is 16.
   Input $= (16 + 2) \div 3 = 6$

Quick Test

1. Draw the graph with equation $y = 4x + 1$ from $x = 0$ to $x = 6$.
2. Write down the gradient and y-intercept of the line with equation $y = 5 - 2x$.
3. Work out the equation of the line that joins the points (5, 7) and (3, 10).

Graphs of Quadratic Functions

You must be able to:

- Recognise, sketch and interpret graphs of quadratic functions
- Identify and interpret roots, intercepts and turning points of quadratic functions
- Work out roots using algebraic methods
- Work out turning points.

Plotting Quadratic Graphs

- A quadratic equation is an equation that contains an unknown term with a power of 2, e.g. x^2.
- You can use a table of values to draw quadratic graphs.

Draw the graph of the function $y = 2x^2 + 1$.

$x \boxed{-2} \xrightarrow{x^2} \boxed{4} \xrightarrow{\times 2} \boxed{8} \xrightarrow{+1} \boxed{9} y$

x	−2	−1	0	1	2	3	4
y	9	3	1	3	9	19	33

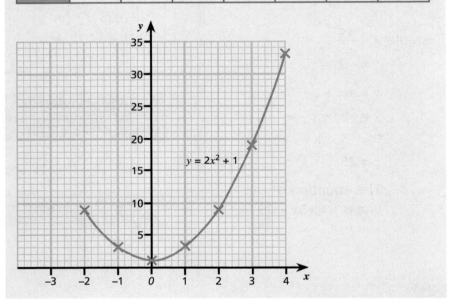

$y = 2x^2 + 1$

> **Key Point**
>
> Remember to use BIDMAS when working out the y-coordinates.

The Significant Points of a Quadratic Curve

- A sketch is used to show the shape and significant points on a graph, but it is not an accurate drawing.
- To sketch a quadratic, work out the roots, the intercept and the turning point.
- The roots are found by solving the quadratic when $y = 0$.
- Because quadratic curves are symmetrical, the turning point is halfway between the two roots.

> **Key Point**
>
> All quadratic graphs have a line of symmetry, which passes through the turning point.
>
> The roots of a quadratic equation are the points where the graph crosses the x-axis. Not all quadratic curves will have roots.

Sketch the graph of equation $y = x^2 + 5x + 4$.

Roots:

$x^2 + 5x + 4 = 0$

$(x + 4)(x + 1) = 0$

$x = -4$ and $x = -1$

Work out the values for x when $y = 0$.

y-intercept:

$y = 4$

y-intercept is $(0, 4)$.

Substitute $x = 0$ into the equation.

Turning Point:

$x = -4$ and $x = -1$, therefore $x = -2.5$

The value of x for the turning point is in the middle of the two roots.

$y = (-2.5)^2 + (5 \times -2.5) + 4$

$\quad = -2.25$

Turning point is $(-2.5, -2.25)$.

Substitute the value of x into the equation.

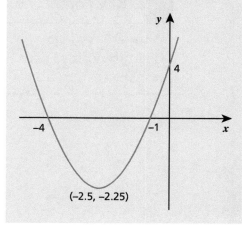

Graph showing parabola with labels y, x, 4, -4, -1, and turning point $(-2.5, -2.25)$.

> **Quick Test**

1. Sketch the graph of the equation $y = x^2 - 3x + 2$.
2. Draw the graph with the equation $y = x^2 - 6$.
3. Draw the graph of $y = 3x^2 - 2x + 1$, for values of x between -2 and 2.
4. Write down the coordinates of the roots and turning point of the quadratic curve shown.

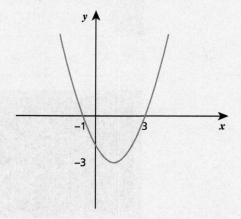

Graph showing parabola with labels y, x, -1, 3, -3.

> **Key Words**

quadratic equation
quadratic graph
roots
intercept
turning point

Powers, Roots and Indices

You must be able to:

- Recognise and recall powers of 2, 3, 4 and 5
- Recognise and recall the square numbers up to 15×15
- Calculate with powers and roots, including negative indices.

Roots and Powers (Indices)

- Powers or indices are a shorthand method of showing that a number is multiplied by itself a number of times, e.g.
$5 \times 5 = 5^2$
$5 \times 5 \times 5 = 5^3$
$5 \times 5 \times 5 \times 5 = 5^4$, etc.
- A root is the inverse function of a power.
- You must learn all the square numbers up to 15×15, i.e.
1, 4, 9, 16, 25, 36, 49, 64, 81, 100, 121, 144, 169, 196, 225.
- You must also learn the cubes of 1, 2, 3, 4, 5 and 10, i.e.
1, 8, 27, 64, 125 and 1000.
- You must be able to recognise powers of 2, 3, 4 and 5, e.g.
$16 = 2^4$ and $243 = 3^5$, and work out real roots.

> **Key Point**
>
> A square root can be both positive or negative.

Write down the value of 10^6.	$2^x = 64$
$10^6 = 10 \times 10 \times 10 \times 10 \times 10 \times 10$ $= 1\,000\,000$	Write down the value of x. $2^6 = 64$, so $x = 6$

Work out the value of 3^4.	Write down the value of $\sqrt[3]{8}$.
$3 \times 3 \times 3 \times 3 = 81$	$2^3 = 8$, so $\sqrt[3]{8} = 2$

Multiplying and Dividing Powers

- When completing calculations involving powers, apply the following rules:

$$x^m \times x^n = x^{m+n}$$
$$x^m \div x^n = x^{m-n}$$
$$(x^m)^n = x^{mn}$$

> **Key Point**
>
> $x^0 = 1$

$(a^m)^n = a^{mn}$
Power of a Power

Write each of the following as a single power of 2.

a) $2^3 \times 2^4$

$= 2^{3+4} = 2^7$

b) $2^9 \div 2^4$

$= 2^{9-4} = 2^5$

c) $(2^3)^4$

$= 2^{3 \times 4} = 2^{12}$

d) $2^3 \times 2^2 \times 2^4$

$= 2^{3+2+4} = 2^9$

e) Write the following as a single power of 5.

i) $\dfrac{5^6 \times 5^2}{5^4}$

$= \dfrac{5^8}{5^4} = 5^4$

ii) $\dfrac{5 \times 5^7}{(5^3)^2}$

$= \dfrac{5^8}{5^6} = 5^2$

When no power is shown, the power is 1, i.e. $5 = 5^1$.

Negative Powers

- A negative power occurs when the power on the denominator (bottom number) of a fraction is higher than the power on the numerator (top number).

 LEARN

$$\frac{1}{x^n} = x^{-n}$$

Write down $\dfrac{6^3}{6^5}$ in its simplest form.

$\dfrac{6^3}{6^5} = \dfrac{\cancel{6} \times \cancel{6} \times \cancel{6}}{\cancel{6} \times \cancel{6} \times \cancel{6} \times 6 \times 6}$

$= \dfrac{1}{6 \times 6} = 6^{-2}$

Write each of the following as a single power of 7.

a) $7^3 \div 7^9$

$= 7^{3-9}$

$= 7^{-6}$

b) $(7^{-2})^{-3}$

$= 7^{(-2 \times -3)}$

$= 7^6$

Remember, $- \times - = +$

Simplify $(3x^2y)^{-2}$

$= 3^{-2} \times (x^2)^{-2} \times y^{-2}$

$= \dfrac{1}{9}x^{-4}y^{-2}$

$= \dfrac{1}{9x^4y^2}$

Quick Test

1. Simplify $2x^3 \times 3x^2$
2. Write $2^3 \times 2^5$ as a single power of 2.
3. What is the value of 3^{-3}?
4. Simplify $(x^{-2}y^5)^{-2}$

 Key Words

index / indices

root

Area and Volume 1

You must be able to:

- Calculate the perimeter and area of rectangles and triangles
- Calculate the perimeter and area of composite shapes
- Calculate the volume and surface area of a cuboid.

Rectangles

- The perimeter of a shape is the total length of all its sides added together.
- The area is the space enclosed within the perimeter.

LEARN

Area of a Rectangle (A) = Length (l) × Width (w)

$$A = lw$$

Perimeter of a Rectangle (P) = 2 × Length (l) + 2 × Width (w)

$$P = 2l + 2w$$

Calculate the perimeter and area of the rectangle.

5cm

8cm

Area

$A = 5 \times 8$

$= 40\text{cm}^2$

Perimeter

$P = 2 \times 5 + 2 \times 8$

$= 10 + 16 = 26\text{cm}$

Triangles

LEARN

Area of a Triangle (A) = $\frac{1}{2}$ × Base (b) × Height (h)

$$A = \frac{1}{2}bh$$

Work out the perimeter and area of the triangle.

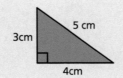

5 cm

3cm

4cm

Area

$A = \frac{1}{2}bh = \frac{1}{2} \times 4 \times 3$

$= 6\text{cm}^2$

Perimeter

$P = 3 + 4 + 5$

$= 12\text{cm}$

> **Key Point**
>
> When calculating the area of a triangle, always use the perpendicular height.

Composite Shapes

- Composite shapes are made up of other shapes.
- To find the perimeter and area of composite shapes, break them down into their component shapes.

Calculate the perimeter and area of the shape below.

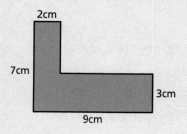

Key Point

When calculating area, remember to give your answer in units², e.g. cm².

Area

$A = 7 \times 2 + 7 \times 3$

$= 14 + 21$

$= 35\text{cm}^2$

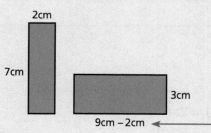

Work out the unknown length.

Perimeter

$P = 2 + 7 + 9 + 3 + 7 + 4$

$= 32\text{cm}$

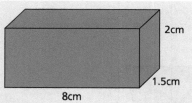

Cuboids

LEARN

Volume of a Cuboid (V) = Length (l) × Width (w) × Height (h)

$V = lwh$

Surface Area of a Cuboid (SA) = $2lw + 2lh + 2hw$

Key Point

When calculating volume, remember to give your answer in units³, e.g. cm³.

Work out the volume and surface area of the cuboid.

$V = 8 \times 1.5 \times 2$

$= 24\text{cm}^3$

$SA = 2 \times 8 \times 1.5 + 2 \times 8 \times 2 + 2 \times 2 \times 1.5$

$= 24 + 32 + 6$

$= 62\text{cm}^2$

Quick Test

1. A rectangle has a length of 4m and a width of 3m. Calculate the area and perimeter.
2. A triangle has a base of length 5cm and a perpendicular height of 4cm. Calculate the area.
3. A cuboid has a length of 3cm, a width of 3cm and a height of 2cm. Work out the volume and surface area of the cuboid.

Key Words

perimeter
area
composite shapes

Area and Volume 2

You must be able to:

- Recall and use the formulae for the circumference and area of a circle
- Recall and use the formula for the area of a trapezium
- Recall and use the formulae for the volume and surface area of a prism
- Recall and use the formulae for the volume and surface area of a cylinder.

Circles

LEARN

Circumference of a Circle (C) = $2\pi r$ or $C = \pi d$

Area of a Circle (A) = πr^2

Work out the circumference and area of a circle with radius 9cm. Give your answers to 1 decimal place.

Circumference

$C = 2 \times \pi \times 9$

$= 18 \times \pi$

$= 56.5$cm (to 1 d.p.)

Area

$A = \pi \times 9^2$

$= \pi \times 81$

$= 254.5$cm^2 (to 1 d.p.)

Key Point

The symbol π represents the number **pi**.

π can be approximated by 3.14 or $\frac{22}{7}$.

Trapeziums

LEARN

The area of a trapezium is:

$$A = \tfrac{1}{2}(a + b)h$$

where a and b are the parallel sides and h is the perpendicular height

Key Point

Perpendicular means 'at right angles'.

Parallel means 'in the same direction and always the same distance apart'.

- This formula can be proved:

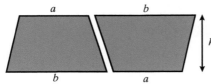

- – Two identical trapeziums fit together to make a parallelogram with base $a + b$ and height h
- – The area of the parallelogram is $(a + b)h$
- – Therefore, the area of each trapezium is $\tfrac{1}{2}(a + b)h$.

Key Point

The area of a parallelogram is: $A = bh$

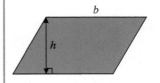

Work out the area of the trapezium.

$A = \tfrac{1}{2} \times (5 + 10) \times 4$

$= 30$cm^2

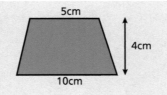

Prisms

- A right prism is a 3D shape that has the same cross-section running all the way through it.

 LEARN Volume of a Prism = Area of Cross-Section × Length

- The surface area is the sum of the areas of all the faces.

Work out the volume and surface area of the triangular prism.

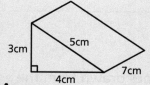

Volume
Area of the cross-section
$= \frac{1}{2} \times 3 \times 4 = 6 \text{cm}^2$
Volume = 6 × 7
$= 42 \text{cm}^3$

Surface Area
Five faces:
Two triangular faces = 6 + 6 = 12
Base = 4 × 7 = 28
Side = 3 × 7 = 21
Slanted side = 5 × 7 = 35
Total surface area =
12 + 28 + 21 + 35 = 96cm²

Cylinders

 LEARN
Volume of a Cylinder = $\pi r^2 h$

Surface Area of a Cylinder = $2\pi rh + 2\pi r^2$

Work out the volume and the surface area of the cylinder. Give your answers in terms of π.

Volume
$V = \pi \times 4^2 \times 7$
$= 112\pi \text{cm}^3$

Surface Area
$SA = 2 \times \pi \times 4 \times 7 + 2 \times \pi \times 4^2$
$= 56\pi + 32\pi$
$= 88\pi \text{cm}^2$

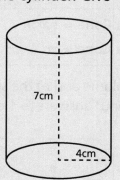

> **Key Point**
>
> A cylinder is just like any other right prism. To find the volume, you multiply the area of the cross-section (circular face) by the length of the cylinder.

Quick Test

1. Calculate the volume and surface area of a cylinder with radius 4cm and height 6cm.
2. Work out the area of the trapezium.

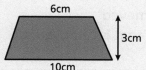

3. Calculate the circumference and area of a circle, diameter 7cm.

> **Key Words**
>
> trapezium
> parallel
> perpendicular
> cross-section
> face

Area and Volume 3

You must be able to:

- Find the volume of a pyramid
- Find the volume and surface area of a cone
- Find the volume of a frustum
- Find the volume and surface area of a sphere
- Find the area and volume of composite shapes.

Pyramids

- A **pyramid** is a 3D shape in which lines drawn from the **vertices** of the base meet at a point.

 LEARN
Volume of a Pyramid = $\frac{1}{3}$ × Area of the Base × Height

> **Key Point**
>
> A pyramid is usually defined by the base, e.g. a square-based pyramid or a triangular-based pyramid.

Work out the volume of the square-based pyramid.

$V = \frac{1}{3} \times 9 \times 9 \times 7$

$= 189\text{cm}^3$

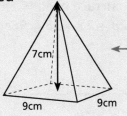

> You must use the perpendicular height to calculate volume.

Cones

- A **cone** is a 3D shape with a circular base that tapers to a single vertex.

 LEARN
Volume of a Cone = $\frac{1}{3}\pi r^2 h$

Surface Area of a Cone = $\pi r l + \pi r^2$

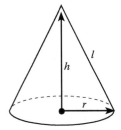

Work out **a)** the volume and **b)** the surface area of the cone. Give your answers to 1 decimal place.

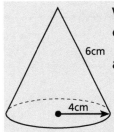

a) $h = \sqrt{6^2 - 4^2}$

$h = \sqrt{20}$

$V = \frac{1}{3} \times \pi \times 4^2 \times \sqrt{20} = 74.9\text{cm}^3$

> First find the height using Pythagoras' Theorem (see p.84–85).

b) $SA = (\pi \times 4 \times 6) + (\pi \times 4^2) = 125.7\text{cm}^2$

- A **frustum** is the 3D shape that remains when a cone is cut parallel to its base and the top cone removed.
- The original cone and the smaller cone that is removed are always **similar**.

 LEARN
Volume of a Frustum
= Volume of Whole Cone – Volume of Top Cone

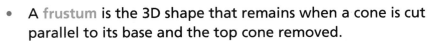

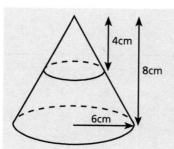

Calculate the volume of the frustum. Leave your answer in terms of π.

Radius of small cone = 3cm

The two cones are similar with scale factor 2.

$V = \frac{1}{3}(\pi \times 6^2 \times 8) - \frac{1}{3}(\pi \times 3^2 \times 4)$
$= 84\pi\,\text{cm}^3$

Spheres

- A **sphere** is a 3D shape that is round, like a ball. At every point, its surface is equidistant from its centre.

Volume of a Sphere = $\frac{4}{3}\pi r^3$

Surface Area of a Sphere = $4\pi r^2$

- A **hemisphere** is half of a sphere; a dome with a circular base.

Work out **a)** the volume and **b)** the surface area of the sphere. Leave your answers in terms of π.

a) $V = \frac{4}{3} \times \pi \times 6^3 = 288\pi\,\text{cm}^3$

b) $SA = 4 \times \pi \times 6^2 = 144\pi\,\text{cm}^2$

Composite Shapes and Composite Solids

This shape is made from a quarter-circle and a square.

Work out **a)** the perimeter and **b)** the area. Leave your answers in terms of π.

4 cm

Perimeter = $\frac{1}{4} \times 2 \times \pi \times 4 + (4 \times 4) = (2\pi + 16)$ cm

Area = $\frac{1}{4} \times \pi \times 4^2 + (4 \times 4) = (4\pi + 16)$ cm²

Key Point

To find the volume of a composite solid, you must break the solid down.

Work out the volume of the shape.
Give your answers to 2 decimal places.

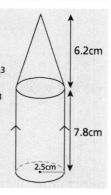

6.2cm

7.8cm

2.5cm

Volume of the Cylinder = $2.5^2 \times \pi \times 7.8 = 153.15\,\text{cm}^3$

Volume of the Cone = $\frac{1}{3} \times \pi \times 2.5^2 \times 6.2 = 40.58\,\text{cm}^3$

Total Volume = $153.15 + 40.58 = 193.73\,\text{cm}^3$

Key Words

pyramid
vertex / vertices
cone
frustum
similar
sphere
hemisphere

Quick Test

1. Work out the volume of a sphere with diameter 10cm.
2. Calculate the surface area of a cone with radius 3cm and perpendicular height 6cm.
3. Work out the volume of a square-based pyramid with side length 5cm and perpendicular height 8cm.
4. Calculate the surface area of a hemisphere with radius 6cm.

Review Questions

Number 1, 2 & 3

1 An adult theatre ticket costs £38.60 and a child ticket costs £12.76

Work out the total cost for eight adult tickets and four child tickets. [2]

2 If $1.263 \times 2.47 = 3.11961$, work out:

   a) 126.3×2.47 [1]

   b) 1.263×0.247 [1]

3 What is the value of $(-3)^3$? [1]

4 In a restaurant, there are three different starters and eight different main meals.

How many possible combinations are there when choosing a starter and a main meal? [1]

5 9, 13, 15, 27, 35, 100

From the list of numbers above, find:

   a) a factor of 72 [1]

   b) a multiple of 7 [1]

   c) a square number [1]

   d) a cube number [1]

   e) a prime number. [1]

6 Find a number (other than 1) that is a square number and also a cube number. [1]

7 Peter says $(2^3)^2 = (2^2)^3$

Is Peter correct?
Write down a calculation to support your answer. [2]

8 Express 105 as the product of prime factors. [2]

Total Marks _____ / 16

Basic Algebra & Factorisation and Formulae

1 There are k children in a room.
The number of children who wear glasses is g.

Write an expression in terms of k and g for the number of children who **do not** wear glasses. [1]

2 Simplify $7x - 2y + 5x - 3y$ [2]

3 Work out the value of the following expression when $a = -3$. [2]

$$\frac{4a^2 - a^3}{a^4}$$

4 Solve $2x + 6 = 5x - 10$ [3]

5 Factorise $5ab - 3b^2c$ [1]

6 Solve $4(x - 3) = 10$ [3]

7 Solve $\frac{x}{3} + 3 = 1$ [1]

8 The shape below is a rectangle.

6x + 5

3x + 2

Mitan thinks the correct expression for the perimeter of the rectangle is $9x + 7$.

a) Mitan is wrong. Write down the correct expression for the perimeter. [1]

b) The perimeter of the rectangle is 56cm. Work out the value of x. [2]

9 The formula for the volume of a cylinder is $V = \pi r^2 h$.

a) Make r the subject of the formula. [2]

b) Work out the value of r when $V = 50$ and $h = 10$. [2]

Total Marks _____ / 20

Review Questions

Ratio and Proportion

1 The square of the speed (v) at which a ball is thrown is directly proportional to the height (h) reached, so $v^2 = kh$.

A ball thrown at a speed of 10 metres per second reaches a height of 5 metres.

Calculate the constant of proportionality (k). [2]

2 £60 is divided in the ratio 5 : 7

What is the difference in value between the two shares? [3]

3 Simplify 6 hours : 4 minutes [2]

> **Total Marks** _____ / 7

Variation and Compound Measures

1 **a)** Calculate the distance travelled by a mouse moving at 1.5 metres per second for 1.5 seconds. [2]

b) The maximum speed that an antelope can run at is 55 miles per hour.
The maximum speed that a zebra can run at is 64 kilometres per hour.
Assume 8km = 5 miles

Which animal can run the fastest?
You **must** show your working. [2]

2 The density of aluminium is 2700kg/m³.

Work out the mass of a piece of aluminium that has a volume of 4.5m³. [2]

3 A woman with a weight (force) of 588 newtons is wearing stiletto heels. The point of each heel has an area of 0.0001m².

What is the pressure that each heel exerts on the ground? [2]

> **Total Marks** _____ / 8

Angles and Shapes 1 & 2

1 The three interior angles of a triangle are $y°$, $2y°$ and $3y°$.

Work out the size of the largest angle. [2]

2 A quadrilateral has angles of 80°, 123°, 165° and 40°.

Why is it impossible to draw this quadrilateral? [1]

3 Name all the quadrilaterals that can be drawn with four lines of length 5cm, 8cm, 5cm and 8cm. [2]

4 An aircraft flies from airport A on a bearing of 054° to airport B.

Work out the bearing that the aircraft must fly on in order to return to airport A. [1]

5 What is the size of one interior angle in an equilateral triangle? [1]

6 Calculate:

a) The sum of the interior angles in a regular octagon [2]

b) The size of one interior angle in a regular octagon. [1]

7 A map has a scale of 1cm : 3km. A lake on the map is 6.5cm long.

What is the actual length of the lake in kilometres? [1]

8 The angles in a triangle are $y + 5$, $3y - 16$ and $2y + 5$ degrees.

a) Write down an equation for the sum of the angles in the triangle.
Give your answer in its simplest form. [1]

b) Solve your equation to find the value of y. [1]

c) Work out the size of each angle in the triangle. [3]

9 Elaine calculates that the interior angle of a regular polygon is 158°.
Pauline says that Elaine has made a mistake.

Who is correct?
Give a reason for your answer and show all your working. [3]

Total Marks _____ / 19

Review Questions

Fractions

1. Work out $6 \div \frac{3}{4}$ 📱 [1]

2. What is half of a half of a quarter? 📱 [1]

3. A box contained 344 dog biscuits.
Fluff ate one-eighth of them.

   How many biscuits were left? 📱 [2]

4. Lee spends £95 a week.

   If this is five-sixths of Lee's weekly wage, what does he earn in total each week? 📱 [2]

5. Change $\frac{5}{8}$ to a decimal. 📱 [1]

Total Marks _____ / 7

Percentages 1 & 2

1. A coat costs £56. It is reduced by 35% in a sale.

   What is the sale price of the coat? [2]

2. Richard says that 30% of £40 is the same as 40% of £30.

   Is he correct?
   Write down a calculation to support your answer. [2]

3. A house is purchased for £215 000 and sold for £300 000.

   What is the percentage profit?
   Give your answer to 1 decimal place. [2]

4. Write down 15cm as a percentage of 5m. [1]

Total Marks _____ / 7

Probability 1 & 2

1 The sides of a spinner are coloured red, blue, green and yellow.
The probability that the spinner will land on each colour is shown in the table below:

Colour	Red	Blue	Green	Yellow
Probability	0.3	0.3		0.1

    a) Complete the table to work out the probability of landing on green. [1]

    b) Estimate the number of times the spinner will land on the colour red if it is spun 50 times. [2]

    c) Georgia and Annie are playing a game using the spinner.
Georgia suggests that she wins if the spinner lands on red or blue and Annie wins if the spinner lands on green or yellow.

        Georgia thinks this is fair. Is she correct? Give a reason for your answer. [2]

2 A restaurant serves three courses: starters, mains and desserts. All customers have a main course.
The Venn diagram shows information about whether customers ordered starters and desserts.

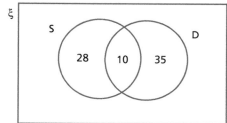

S = Starter
D = Dessert

The total number of customers served at lunchtime was 82.

Work out the number of customers who ordered neither a starter nor a dessert. [3]

3 Two events, A and B, are mutually exclusive: P(A) = 0.3 and P(B) = 0.6

    a) Draw a Venn diagram to represent this information. [2]

    b) Write down P(A and B) [1]

    c) Work out P(A or B) [2]

4 Helen has ten yogurts. Four are vanilla flavoured and six are banana flavoured.
She takes a yogurt at random for breakfast on Monday.

Work out the probability that she takes a banana yogurt.   [2]

Total Marks _____ / 15

Number Patterns and Sequences 1 & 2

1 For each of the following sequences write down **i)** the next two terms in the sequence
and **ii)** the term-to-term rule:

   a) 5, 8, 11, 14, 17, __, __   [2]

   b) 16, 12, 8, 4, 0, __, __   [2]

   c) 189, 63, 21, 7, $\frac{7}{3}$, __, __   [2]

2 Here is a sequence:

   20, 16, 12, 8, 4 ...

   Work out the expression for the nth term of the sequence.   [2]

3 Work out the first five terms in the sequence with the nth term $3n - 5$.   [2]

4 The first five terms of an arithmetic sequence are 14, 17, 20, 23, 26 ...

   a) Write an expression for the nth term of this sequence.   [2]

   b) Calculate the 100th term in this sequence.   [1]

5 **a)** A sequence of numbers is given as 5, 8, 12, 17 ...

   Write down the next two terms in the sequence.   [2]

   b) A second sequence of numbers is given as 2, 3, 2, 3, 2, 3 ...

   Write down the 100th term.   [1]

6 Here is a sequence of patterns made from matchsticks:

   a) Draw the next two patterns in the sequence.   [2]

   b) Write down the rule for the number of matchsticks required for pattern number n. [2]

   c) Use the rule to work out how many matchsticks are required for pattern 100. [1]

   Total Marks _____ / 21

Transformations, Constructions & Nets, Plans and Elevations

1   a) Plot the following points: $A(2, 0)$ $B(5, 0)$ $C(5, 2)$ $D(3, 2)$ $E(3, 5)$ $F(2, 5)$
        Join the points together and label the shape M.   [1]

    b) Rotate shape M by 180° about the origin to form shape N.   [1]

    c) Reflect shape N in the x-axis to form shape O.   [1]

    d) Describe fully the single transformation that maps shape O to shape M.   [2]

2   Rectangle R has a width of 3cm and a length of 5cm.
    It is enlarged by scale factor 3 to give rectangle T.

    a) What is the area of rectangle T?   [2]

    b) How many times bigger is the area of rectangle T than the area of rectangle R?   [2]

3   Describe how to construct an angle of 45°.   [2]

4   Describe the locus of points in the following:

    a) A person sitting on the London Eye as it rotates around.   [1]

    b) The seat of a moving swing.   [1]

    c) The end of the minute hand on a clock moving for one hour.   [1]

    d) The end of a moving see-saw.   [1]

5   The diagram represents a solid made from ten identical cubes.

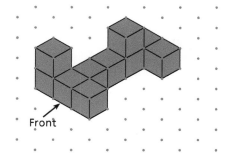

    On a squared grid, draw the:

    a) Front elevation   b) Plan view.   [2]

Practice Questions

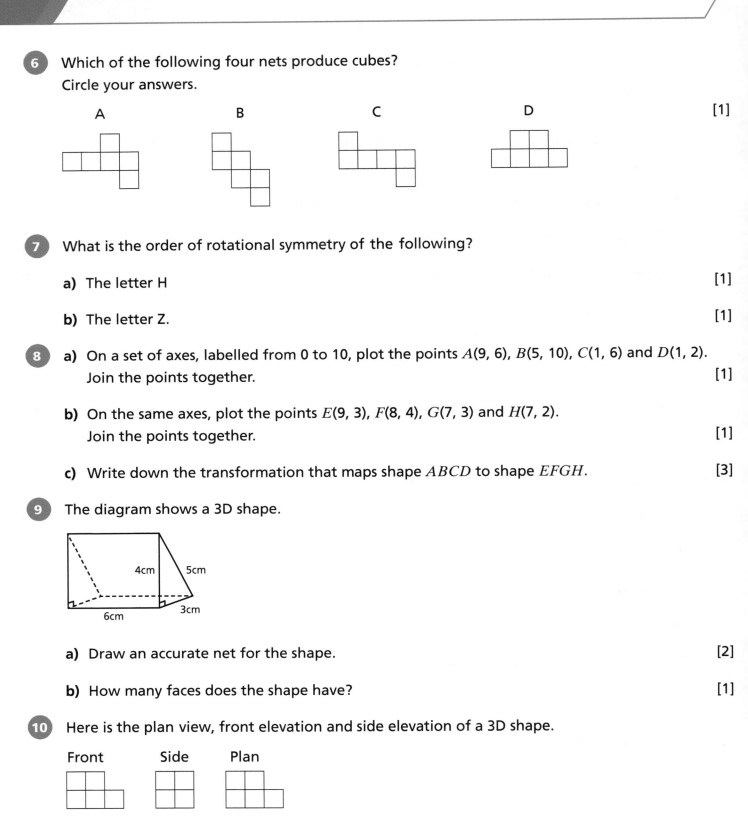

6 Which of the following four nets produce cubes?
Circle your answers. [1]

A   B   C   D

7 What is the order of rotational symmetry of the following?

a) The letter H [1]

b) The letter Z. [1]

8 a) On a set of axes, labelled from 0 to 10, plot the points A(9, 6), B(5, 10), C(1, 6) and D(1, 2). Join the points together. [1]

b) On the same axes, plot the points E(9, 3), F(8, 4), G(7, 3) and H(7, 2). Join the points together. [1]

c) Write down the transformation that maps shape $ABCD$ to shape $EFGH$. [3]

9 The diagram shows a 3D shape.

4cm   5cm   6cm   3cm

a) Draw an accurate net for the shape. [2]

b) How many faces does the shape have? [1]

10 Here is the plan view, front elevation and side elevation of a 3D shape.

Front   Side   Plan

Sketch the 3D shape. [3]

Total Marks _____ / 31

Linear Graphs & Graphs of Quadratic Functions

1 A straight-line graph has the equation $y = 3x + 7$.

    a) To plot the graph, you need to work out values of x and y for the equation.

        Draw a flow diagram that can be used to work out values for x and y, where x is the input and y is the output. **[2]**

    b) Use your flow diagram to complete the table below. **[2]**

x	−3	−2	−1	0	1	2	3
$y = 3x + 7$	−2				10		

    c) Draw the graph of $y = 3x + 7$ for values of x from −3 to 3. **[2]**

2 **a)** Sketch the graph of $y = x^2 + 3x + 2$.
        Clearly label the points where the graph crosses the axes. **[3]**

    b) Write down the x-coordinate of the turning point of the graph. **[1]**

3 Draw the graph of $y = 4x − 2$ for values of x from −4 to 4. **[2]**

4 Draw the graph of the function with gradient 5 and y-intercept $(0, 3)$ for values of x between −2 and 2. **[2]**

5 Write down the gradient and y-intercept of the graph with equation $y = 5 − 2x$. **[1]**

6 Draw the graph with equation $y = 3x^2 − 2x + 1$ for values of x from −3 to 3. **[2]**

7 Work out the equation of the line that joins the points $(−3, 5)$ and $(3, −1)$. **[3]**

8 Work out the equation of the line shown. **[3]**

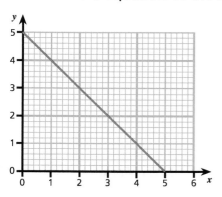

Total Marks _____ / 23

Practice Questions

Powers, Roots and Indices

1 Write down the following as a single power of 5:

    a) $5^2 \times 5^3$ [1]

    b) $5^7 \div 5^3$ [1]

    c) $\dfrac{5^4 \times 5^2}{5^3}$ [2]

2 Simplify $(x^2)^4$ [2]

3 Write down the following as a single power of 7:

    a) $7^2 \times 7^5 \times 7^{-3}$ [2]

    b) $\dfrac{7^4}{7^{-4}}$ [2]

    c) $\left(7^3\right)^{-2}$ [2]

4 Dan thinks that $2^2 \times 5^2 = 10^4$

    Rebecca thinks $2^2 \times 5^2 = 100$

    Who is correct?
    Write down a calculation to support your answer.   [2]

5 Simplify $\left(9x^2\right)^{-2}$ [2]

6 Expand and simplify $x^{-3}\left(x^2 + x^3\right)$ [2]

7 Simplify $\left(3r^2p\right)^3$ [2]

8 Write down the value of:

    a) $2^3 \times 2^2$ [2]

    b) $3^3 \div 2$ [2]

    c) 4^{-3} [1]

    d) 5^0 [1]

Total Marks _____ / 26

Area and Volume 1, 2 & 3

1. Work out:

   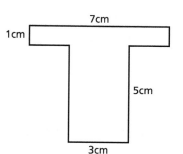

   a) The perimeter of the shape [2]

   b) The area of the shape. [2]

2. Here is a cuboid. The volume of the cuboid is 300cm³.

   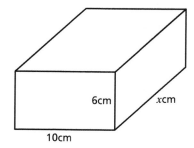

   Work out the value of x. [2]

3. Two identical circles sit inside a square of side length 6cm.

   Work out the area of the shaded region. [4]

4. A vase is made from two cylinders. The larger cylinder has a radius of 15cm.
   The total volume of the vase is 6000πcm³.
   The ratio of volumes of the smaller cylinder to the larger cylinder is 1 : 3.

   a) Calculate the height of the larger cylinder. [3]

   b) The height and radius of the smaller cylinder are equal.

      Work out the radius of the smaller cylinder. [3]

5. A cat's toy is made out of plastic. The top of the toy is a solid cone with radius 3cm and
   height 7cm. The bottom of the toy is a solid hemisphere. The base of the hemisphere and
   the base of the cone are the same size.

   Calculate the volume of plastic needed to make the toy. Give your answer in terms of π. [3]

   Total Marks _____ / 19

Uses of Graphs

You must be able to:

- Use the form $y = mx + c$ to identify parallel lines
- Interpret the gradient of a straight-line graph as a rate of change
- Recognise and interpret graphs that illustrate direct and inverse proportion.

Parallel Lines

- **Parallel** lines travel in the same direction and have the same gradient.

Write down the gradient of the line that is parallel to the line with the equation $y = 6x + 2$.

The line has a gradient of +6, so the line that is parallel to it also has a gradient of +6.

> **Key Point**
>
> The gradient of a straight line in the form $y = mx + c$ is m.

Write down the gradient of the line that is parallel to the line with the equation $y = 7 - 2x$.

The line has a gradient of –2, so the line that is parallel to it also has a gradient of –2.

Work out the equation of the line that goes through the point (2, 9) and is parallel to the line with equation $y = 7x + 10$.

$y = mx + c$

$y = 7x + c$ ← Substitute in $m = 7$.

$9 = (7 \times 2) + c$ ← Goes through the point (2, 9), so $x = 2$ when $y = 9$.

$c = -5$

The equation of the parallel line is $y = 7x - 5$.

Gradient of a Line

- The **rate of change** is the rate at which one quantity changes in relation to another.
- The gradient of a straight-line graph represents a rate of change – it describes how the variable on the y-axis changes when the variable on the x-axis is increased by 1.

LEARN

$$\text{Gradient} = \frac{\text{Change in } y}{\text{Change in } x}$$

Write down the gradient of the line that joins points (1, 3) and (5, 9).

Gradient = $\frac{6}{4}$

= 1.5

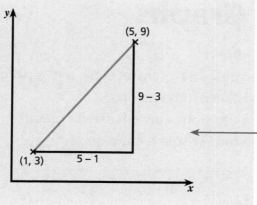

Draw a right-angled triangle and find the lengths of both sides.

The graph shows the volume of liquid in a container over time.

What is the rate of change?

Gradient = $\frac{4}{5}$

= $\frac{4}{5}$ = 0.8cm³/s

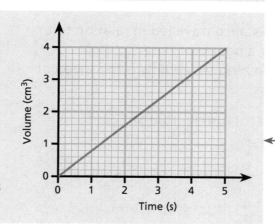

The gradient is the rate of change.

Real-Life Uses of Graphs

The graph below is the conversion graph between miles and kilometres.

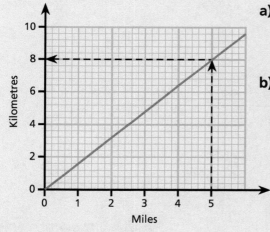

a) How many kilometres are there in 5 miles?

5 miles = 8km

Read from graph.

b) What is the gradient of the line?

Gradient = $\frac{8}{5}$

= 1.6

1 mile = 1.6km

Quick Test

1. Work out the equation of the line that is parallel to the line $y = -2x + 6$ and goes through the point (4, 7).
2. Write down the gradient of the line that joins points (4, 7) and (6, 11).

Key Words

parallel
rate of change

Other Graphs

You must be able to:

- Recognise, draw and interpret cubic and reciprocal graphs
- Interpret distance–time graphs
- Work out speed from a distance–time graph
- Draw and interpret speed–time graphs.

Distance–Time Graphs

- A distance–time graph shows distance travelled in relation to a fixed point (starting point) over a period of time.
- The gradient of a straight line joining two points is the speed of travel between those two points.

The graph below shows Val's car journey from St Bees to Cockermouth and back.

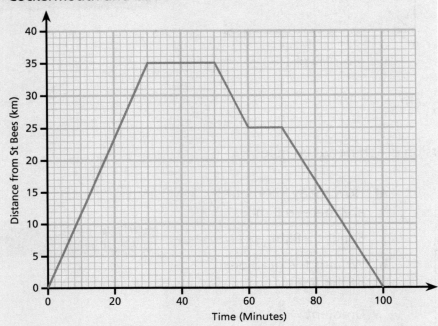

a) Val sets off at 12 noon and travels directly to Cockermouth. At what time does she arrive?

Val travels for 30 minutes so arrives at 12.30pm.

b) For how long does Val stop in Cockermouth?

20 minutes ←——— This is represented by the horizontal line on the graph – where the distance does not change.

c) Val begins her journey home but stops to fill up with petrol.

Calculate the average speed of Val's journey from the petrol station to home in kilometres per hour.

Speed = $\dfrac{\text{Distance}}{\text{Time}}$ = $\dfrac{25}{0.5}$ ←——— Convert minutes into hours.

    = 50km/h

Speed–Time Graphs

- A speed–time graph shows the speed of travel in relation to a fixed point (starting point) over a period of time.
- The gradient of a straight line joining two points is the acceleration of travel between those two points.

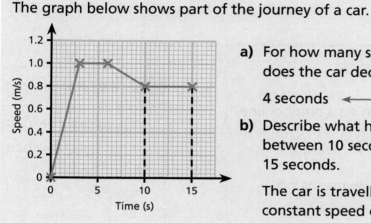

The graph below shows part of the journey of a car.

a) For how many seconds does the car decelerate?

4 seconds

b) Describe what happens between 10 seconds and 15 seconds.

The car is travelling at a constant speed of 0.8 m/s

Other Graphs

- A cubic function is one that contains an x^3 term.
- $y = \frac{1}{x}$ is called a reciprocal function.

Cubic Function

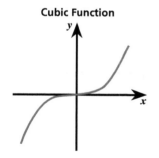

Reciprocal Function

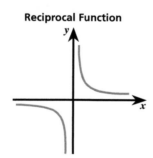

Quick Test

1. Plot the graph $y = x^3 - 5$ for x values -2 to 2.
2. Below is a graph for the journey of a car.

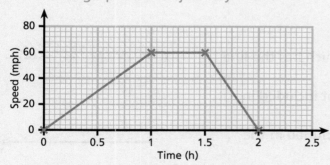

a) What was the maximum speed of the car?
b) For how many minutes was the car decelerating?

Inequalities

You must be able to:

- Solve linear inequalities in one or two variables
- Represent solutions to inequalities on number lines or graphs.

Linear Inequalities

- The solution to an inequality can be shown on a number line.

  ◄———○ means $x <$ ○———► means $x >$

  ◄———● means $x \leqslant$ ●———► means $x \geqslant$

Solve these inequalities and show the solutions on a number line:

a) $x + 3 > 4$

$x > 4 - 3$

$x > 1$

b) $2(x + 4) \leqslant 18$

$x + 4 \leqslant 9$

$x \leqslant 5$

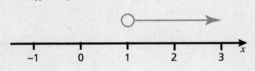

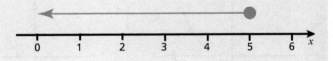

Work out all the possible integer values of n for these inequalities:

a) $-4 < n < 4$

$n = -3, -2, -1, 0, 1, 2, 3$

b) $-3 < 10n \leqslant 53$

$-0.3 < n \leqslant 5.3$ ◄——— Divide each part of the inequality by 10.

$n = 0, 1, 2, 3, 4, 5$ ◄——— n must be a whole number.

Graphical Inequalities

- The graph of the equation $y = 6$ is a line.
- The graph of the inequality $y > 6$ is a **region**, which has the line $y = 6$ as a boundary.
- For inequalities $>$ and $<$ the boundary line is **not included** in the solution and is shown as a **dashed line**.
- For inequalities $\geqslant$ and $\leqslant$ the boundary line is **included** in the solution and is shown as a **solid line**.

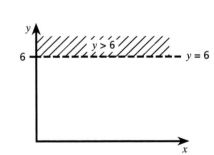

On a graph, show the region that satisfies $x \geqslant 0$, $x + y < 3$ and $y > 3x - 1$.

$x + y = 3$

$\quad y = 3 - x$

Work out values of y for $x + y = 3$ and $y = 3x - 1$. You need three values.

x	0	1	2
y	3	2	1

$y = 3x - 1$

x	0	1	2
y	−1	2	5

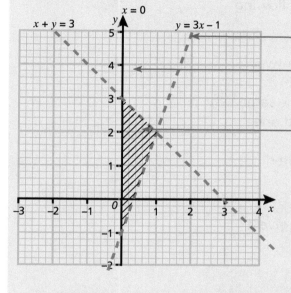

Draw the dashed lines $x + y = 3$ and $y = 3x - 1$.

The line $x = 0$ is the y-axis.

This is the region that satisfies all three inequalities.

- The region that satisfies $x \geqslant 0$ is to the right of the y-axis. All the points in this region have a value of x greater than 0.
- The region that satisfies $x + y < 3$ is below the line $x + y = 3$. When the values of x and y are added together, the result is always less than 3.
- The region that satisfies $y > 3x - 1$ is above the line $y = 3x - 1$.
- The overlap of the three regions is the region that satisfies all three inequalities.

Quick Test

1. Solve the inequality $2x - 5 < 9$ and show the solution on a number line.
2. Write down all the possible integer values for $-5 \leqslant y < -1$.
3. Which inequality sign is missing between the numbers?
   a) $-3.2 \underline{\quad} -3.3$
   b) $3.2 \underline{\quad} 3.3$

Key Words

inequality
region

Congruence and Geometrical Problems

You must be able to:

- Identify congruent and similar shapes
- State the criteria that congruent triangles satisfy
- Solve problems involving similar figures
- Understand geometrical problems.

Congruent Triangles

- If two shapes are the same size and shape, they are congruent.
- Two triangles are congruent if they satisfy one of the following four criteria:
  - SSS – three sides are the same
  - SAS – two sides and the included angle (the angle between the two sides) are the same
  - ASA – two angles and one corresponding side are the same
  - RHS – there is a right angle, and the hypotenuse and one other corresponding side are the same.
- Sometimes angles or lengths of sides have to be calculated before congruency can be proved.

State whether these two triangles are congruent and give a reason for your answer.

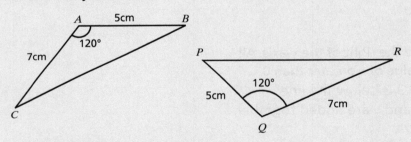

Angle CAB = Angle PQR (given)
$AC = QR$ (given)
$AB = PQ$ (given)
Triangles ABC and PQR are congruent because they satisfy the criteria SAS.

> **Key Point**
>
> Congruent shapes can be reflected, rotated or translated and remain congruent.

Similar Figures

- Similar figures are identical in shape but can differ in size.
- In similar triangles:
  - corresponding angles are identical
  - lengths of corresponding sides are in the same ratio $y : z$
  - the area ratio = $y^2 : z^2$
  - the volume ratio = $y^3 : z^3$.

Triangles AED and ABC are similar.

Calculate **a)** AC and **b)** DC.

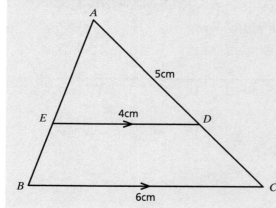

a) $\dfrac{4}{6} = \dfrac{5}{AC}$

The corresponding sides of both triangles are in the same ratio.

$4 \times AC = 6 \times 5$

Cross multiply.

$AC = \dfrac{6 \times 5}{4}$

$= 7.5\text{cm}$

b) $DC = AC - AD$

$= 7.5 - 5$

$= 2.5\text{cm}$

Geometrical Problems

- Congruency and similarity are used in many geometric proofs.

Prove that the base angles of an isosceles triangle are equal.

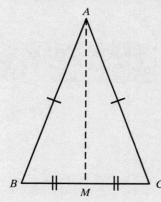

Given $\triangle ABC$ with $AB = AC$
Let M be the midpoint of BC
Join AM
$AB = AC$ (given)
$BM = MC$ (from construction)
$AM = AM$ (common side)
$\triangle ABM$ and $\triangle ACM$ are congruent (SSS)
So, angle ABC = angle ACB

Quick Test

1.

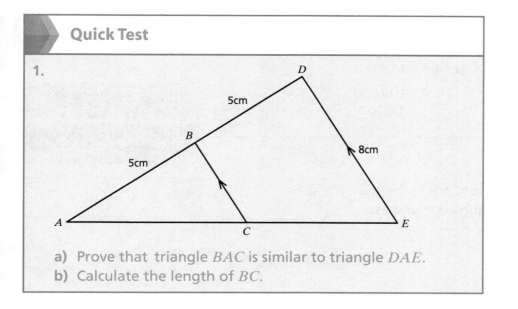

a) Prove that triangle BAC is similar to triangle DAE.
b) Calculate the length of BC.

Geometry and Measures

Right-Angled Triangles 1

You must be able to:

- Recall and use the formula for Pythagoras' Theorem
- Calculate the length of an unknown side in a right-angled triangle
- Apply Pythagoras' Theorem to real-life problems
- Use Pythagoras' Theorem in isosceles triangles.

Pythagoras' Theorem

- The longest side (c) of a right-angled triangle is called the hypotenuse.
- Pythagoras' Theorem states that $a^2 + b^2 = c^2$.

$$a^2 + b^2 = c^2$$

> **Key Point**
>
> a^2 means $a \times a$ **not** $2 \times a$

Calculating Unknown Sides

Calculate the length of side c.

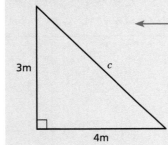

$$3^2 + 4^2 = c^2$$
$$9 + 16 = c^2$$
$$25 = c^2$$
$$c = \sqrt{25}$$
$$= 5m$$

> c is the hypotenuse (the longest side).

Calculate the length of side b.

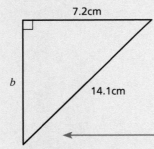

$$14.1^2 - 7.2^2 = b^2$$
$$198.81 - 51.84 = b^2$$
$$146.97 = b^2$$
$$b = \sqrt{146.97}$$
$$= 12.1cm$$

> Rearrange the formula:
> $a^2 + b^2 = c^2 \rightarrow c^2 - a^2 = b^2$

> Give the answer to 3 significant figures unless you are told otherwise.

> b is one of the shorter sides, so the answer must be less than 14.1cm.

- The following length combinations are Pythagorean triples. They regularly appear in right-angled triangles:
  - (3, 4, 5)
  - (6, 8, 10)
  - (5, 12, 13)
  - (7, 24, 25).

> **Key Point**
>
> Memorise the Pythagorean triples to help identify unknown sides quickly.

Real-Life Problems

A boat sails 15km due north and then 10km due east.

How far is the boat from its starting point?
Give your answer to 3 decimal places.

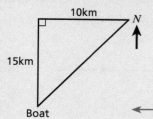

$$15^2 + 10^2 = c^2$$
$$225 + 100 = c^2$$
$$325 = c^2$$
$$c = \sqrt{325} = 18.028\text{km}$$

A sketch makes it clear that you are looking for the hypotenuse (c) of a right-angled triangle.

A four-metre ladder leans against a tree.
It reaches three metres up the side of the tree.

Calculate how far the base of the ladder is from the bottom of the tree.

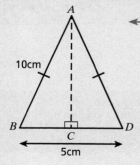

$$4^2 - 3^2 = a^2$$
$$16 - 9 = a^2$$
$$7 = a^2$$
$$a = \sqrt{7}$$
$$= 2.65\text{m}$$

You are looking for one of the shorter sides of a right-angled triangle.

Isosceles Triangles

Calculate the height of the isosceles triangle ABD.

$$10^2 - 2.5^2 = AC^2$$
$$100 - 6.25 = AC^2$$
$$93.75 = AC^2$$
$$AC = \sqrt{93.75}$$
$$= 9.68\text{cm}$$

The height of the triangle is AC (one of the short sides of a right-angled triangle).

C is the midpoint of BD, so $BC = 5 \div 2 = 2.5$cm.

Quick Test

1. A rectangle measures 12cm by 5cm.
   Work out the length of its diagonal.
2. A triangle has sides 8cm, 15cm and 17cm.
   Show that it is a right-angled triangle.
3. A caterpillar was eating a cabbage. The wind blew the caterpillar 24cm due north. The wind suddenly changed direction and then blew the caterpillar 56cm due west.
   How far was the caterpillar from the cabbage?

Key Words

hypotenuse
Pythagoras' Theorem
Pythagorean triple

Right-Angled Triangles 2

You must be able to:

- Recall and use the trigonometric ratios
- Calculate unknown lengths and angles using trigonometry
- Recall the exact trigonometric values for certain angles without using a calculator.

The Trigonometric Ratios

- Unknown sides or angles in right-angled triangles can be calculated using the trigonometric ratios: sine, cosine and tangent.
- The symbol θ (theta) is used to represent an unknown angle.

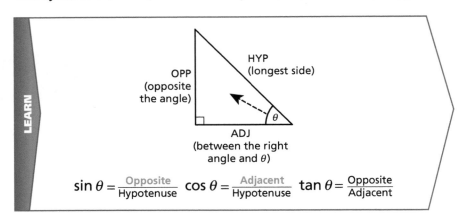

$$\sin \theta = \frac{\text{Opposite}}{\text{Hypotenuse}} \quad \cos \theta = \frac{\text{Adjacent}}{\text{Hypotenuse}} \quad \tan \theta = \frac{\text{Opposite}}{\text{Adjacent}}$$

> **Key Point**
>
> Sine, cosine and tangent ratios can only be used in right-angled triangles.

- The above formulae can be remembered using:
  Some **O**ld **H**orses **C**arry **A** **H**eavy **T**on **O**f **A**pples
     SOH   **CAH**   **TOA**

For example:

$$\sin \theta \, (\text{Some}) = \frac{\text{Opposite (Old)}}{\text{Hypotenuse (Horses)}}$$

Calculating Unknown Sides

Work out the length of x. Give your answer to 1 decimal place.

You have the hypotenuse (H) and you are looking for the side opposite (O) the given angle, so use sine (SOH).

$\sin 40° = \dfrac{x}{7}$

Rearrange, using inverse operations, to work out the value of x.

$x = 7 \times \sin 40°$

$x = 7 \times 0.6428$

$x = 4.499$

$x = 4.5\text{cm}$ (to 1 decimal place)

The diagram shows a lookout tower.
Ann is standing 30m from the base of the tower.

If the angle of elevation to the top of the tower is 50°, calculate the height of the tower. Give your answer to 1 decimal place.

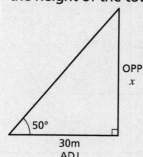

$$\tan 50° = \frac{x}{30}$$
$$x = 30 \times \tan 50°$$
$$x = 30 \times 1.1918$$
$$= 35.8\text{m (to 1 decimal place)}$$

> You have the adjacent (A) side and you are looking for the side opposite (O) the given angle, so use tangent (TOA).

Key Point

Angles of elevation are angles above the horizontal, e.g. the angle from the ground to the top of a tower.

Calculating Unknown Angles

Work out the size of angle θ.
Give your answer to the nearest degree.

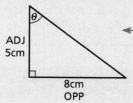

$$\tan \theta = \frac{8}{5} = 1.6$$
$$\tan^{-1} 1.6 = 57.99°$$
$$\theta = 58°$$

> You have the adjacent (A) side and the opposite side (O), so use tangent (TOA).

> On your calculator press
> SHIFT | tan | 1 | . | 6

EFG is a right-angled triangle. Angle $EFG = 90°$.
$FG = 5$cm and $EG = 8$cm.

Calculate angle EGF. Give your answer to 1 decimal place.

$$\cos \theta = \frac{5}{8} = 0.625$$
$$\cos^{-1} 0.625 = 51.3°$$

> EG is the hypotenuse (H) as it is opposite the right angle and FG is the side adjacent (A) to the unknown angle, so use cosine (CAH).

Trigonometric Values to Learn

	sin	cos	tan
0°	0	1	0
30°	$\frac{1}{2}$	$\frac{\sqrt{3}}{2}$	$\frac{1}{\sqrt{3}}$
45°	$\frac{1}{\sqrt{2}}$	$\frac{1}{\sqrt{2}}$	1
60°	$\frac{\sqrt{3}}{2}$	$\frac{1}{2}$	$\sqrt{3}$
90°	1	0	

Key Point

Make sure your calculator is in degree mode when using the trigonometric ratios.

Key Words

trigonometric ratios
sine
cosine
tangent
theta
opposite
adjacent

Quick Test

1. An 8m ladder leans against a vertical wall. The base of the ladder is 3.5m from the wall. Calculate the angle between the top of the ladder and the wall. Give your answer to 1 decimal place.
2. A ship sails 14km on a bearing of 035°. How far north has the ship travelled? Give your answer to the nearest kilometre.

Statistics 1

You must be able to:

- Understand and identify different types of data
- Construct tally charts and frequency tables
- Construct pie charts, bar charts and line graphs to represent data.

Data and Data Collection

- Data can be qualitative (non-numerical) or quantitative (numerical).
- Numerical data can be discrete or continuous.
- A tally chart is a quick way of collecting data.
- When you use a tally chart to collect data, it is already grouped.
- To produce a frequency table, add a column to your tally chart, containing the total for each group.

> Louisa records the colour of the cars that pass by her house during a one-hour time period. She constructs a tally chart and frequency table to show the data.
>
> The last car she sees is green. Add this to the tally chart and complete the frequency column.

Colour	Tally	Frequency
Red	ЖЖ ЖЖ ЖЖ ЖЖ ЖЖ	25
Blue	ЖЖ ЖЖ ЖЖ ЖЖ I	21
Silver	ЖЖ ЖЖ IIII	14
White	ЖЖ ЖЖ ЖЖ IIII	19
Other	ЖЖ ЖЖ I	11

> **Key Point**
>
> Discrete data takes certain values in a given range. Continuous data can take any value in a given range.

Car colour is qualitative data. The number of cars is quantitative data.

Each line in the tally represents one car. Grouping them in sets of five makes them easy to count.

The frequency is the total number of cars for each group.

Statistical Diagrams

- The type of diagram you use will be dictated by the data and what aspect of the data you want to look at.
- Bar charts and vertical line graphs can be used to compare frequencies.

> Draw a bar chart and vertical line graph to represent the data on car colours (above).

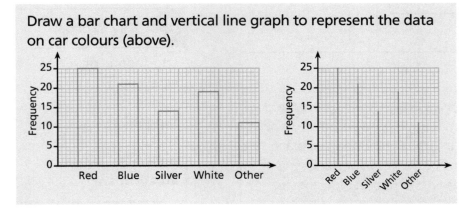

- **Pie charts** show proportion (but not exact frequencies).

Construct a pie chart to represent the data on car colours.

Colour	Frequency	Angle on Pie Chart
Red	25	25 × 4 = 100°
Blue	21	21 × 4 = 84°
Silver	14	14 × 4 = 56°
White	19	19 × 4 = 76°
Other	11	11 × 4 = 44°
Total	**90**	**360°**

The total frequency is 90 cars. A full circle is 360°.

One car = $\frac{360}{90}$ = 4°

- A **line graph** is used to show changes in trends over time.

The graph shows ice cream sales for Shelby's Ices for a one-year period.

Which two months had the highest sales? Suggest a reason for this.

July and August had the highest sales.

Sales of ice cream are higher in these months because it is the summer, so temperatures are higher and more people are on holiday.

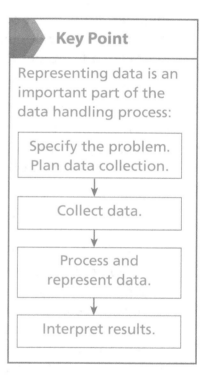

Key Point

Representing data is an important part of the data handling process:

Specify the problem. Plan data collection.

↓

Collect data.

↓

Process and represent data.

↓

Interpret results.

Quick Test

1. Jasmine surveyed the pupils in her class to find out their shoe size. Her results are shown below:

Shoe Size	Frequency
4	8
5	15
6	6
7	1

a) Draw a bar chart to represent her results.
b) Draw a pie chart to represent her results.
c) Which diagram do you think is most suitable for this data and why?

Key Words

qualitative
quantitative
discrete
continuous
tally chart
frequency table
bar chart
pie chart
line graph

Statistics 2

Statistics

You must be able to:

- Understand how a sample can be used to represent a population and its limitations
- Use and interpret scatter graphs
- Calculate the mean, median, mode and range of a set of data.

Sampling

- A population is a collection of individuals or items.
- For a large population, collecting information from all members is not practical and so information is obtained from a proportion of the population, referred to as a sample.
- There are advantages and limitations associated with sampling:

Advantages	Limitations
Quicker and cheaper than investigating whole population	Bias can occur
Can be impractical to investigate whole population	Different samples could give different results

Key Point

Limitations can be minimised by ensuring the sample is large enough to be representative and an appropriate method is used to select the sample.

- Primary data is collected by yourself or on your behalf.
- Secondary data is collected from a different source, e.g. the Internet.

Statistical Measures

- To compare data sets you should compare:
  - a measure of average: mean, median or mode
  - a measure of spread, i.e. the range – the difference between the largest and smallest value in the data set.
- A stem and leaf diagram orders data from smallest to largest and can be used to find the median and range of discrete data.

The Ages of Competitors in a Swimming Race

| 1 | 8 | 8 | 8 | 9 |
| 2 | 0 | 0 | 1 | 6 |

Key: 1 | 8 = 18 years

The data shows the ages of the competitors in a swimming race:

18, 26, 19, 21, 18, 18, 48, 20, 20

a) Identify the outlier.

The outlier is 48.

An outlier is a value within a data set that is significantly smaller or larger than the other values.

b) Remove the outlier from the data and calculate:

i) The mean age

$$\frac{18 + 26 + 19 + 21 + 18 + 18 + 20 + 20}{8} = \frac{160}{8} = 20$$

Mean = $\frac{\text{Sum of all Values}}{\text{Number of Values}}$

ii) The median age

18, 18, 18, ⑲, ⑳, 20, 21, 26

The median is 19.5

Write the data in order, from smallest to largest. The median is the middle value.

iii) The mode age.

The mode age is 18

The mode is the most common value.

The table shows the time taken by students, in minutes, to complete a mathematical puzzle.

Time Taken to Complete Puzzle (min)	Frequency (f)	Midpoint (x)	fx
$0 < t \leqslant 2$	8	1	8
$2 < t \leqslant 4$	12	3	36
$4 < t \leqslant 6$	10	5	50
$6 < t \leqslant 8$	5	7	35
	$\Sigma f = 35$		$\Sigma fx = 129$

a) Write down the modal class.

   The modal class is $2 < t \leqslant 4$ ←————

   The modal class has the highest frequency.

b) Work out which group contains the median. ←————

   The median is the middle value.

   $\dfrac{35 + 1}{2}$ = 18th value ←————

   There are 35 students.

   The median (18th value) is in the group $2 < t \leqslant 4$

c) Estimate the mean time taken.

   $\text{Mean} = \dfrac{\Sigma fx}{\Sigma f}$

   $\text{Mean} = \dfrac{129}{35} = 3.69$ minutes (to 2 d.p.) ←————

Scatter Graphs

- Scatter graphs or scatter diagrams are used to investigate the relationship between two variables.
- If a linear relationship exists, a line of best fit can be drawn. This can be used to make predictions.
- A prediction taken from the line of best fit within the data range is reliable.
- A prediction taken from the line of best fit outside the data range is less reliable.
- Positive correlation – as one variable increases, the other variable increases.
- Negative correlation – as one variable increases, the other variable decreases.

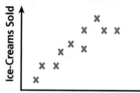

Positive Correlation

As temperature increases, ice-cream sales increase.

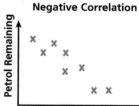

Negative Correlation

As distance travelled increases, petrol remaining decreases.

Quick Test

1. The table below shows the age of children who attend a reading group at the library. Calculate a) the mean b) the median c) the mode and d) the range of the data.

Age	6	7	8	9
Frequency	5	10	6	12

Number Patterns and Sequences 1 & 2

1 The first term that the following two sequences have in common is 17.

8, 11, 14, 17, 20 …

1, 5, 9, 13, 17 …

Work out the next term that the two sequences have in common.
You must show your working. [2]

2 Regular pentagons of side length 1cm are joined together to make a pattern.

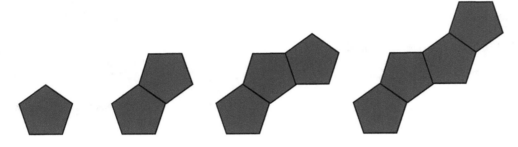

a) Use the patterns to complete the table below.

Pattern Number	Perimeter (cm)
1	
2	
3	
4	
60	
n	

[2]

b) What is the maximum number of pentagons that could be used to give a perimeter less than 1500cm? [2]

3 Write down the first three terms in the sequence with the nth term $n^2 - 6$. [2]

4 Write down the next two terms in the sequence below:

4, 6, 10, 18, 34 … [2]

Total Marks .... / 10

Transformations, Constructions & Nets, Plans and Elevations

1 Three points $X(5,1)$, $Y(3, 5)$, and $Z(1, 2)$ are reflected in the y-axis. 🖩

    a) Give the new coordinates of the three points. [3]

    b) The original points X, Y, and Z are rotated 90° about (0, 0) in a clockwise direction.

       Give the coordinates of the three points in their new positions. [3]

2 A rectangle (C) measures 3cm by 5cm. Each length of rectangle C is enlarged by scale factor 3 to form a new rectangle (D).

    What is the ratio of the area of rectangle C to rectangle D? 🖩 [3]

3 A cuboid (C) measures 3cm by 4cm by 5cm. Each length of cuboid C is enlarged by scale factor 3 to form a new cuboid (D).

    What is the ratio of the volume of cuboid C to cuboid D? [3]

4 On a 6 × 6 grid, plot the points $A(3, 2)$, $B(1, 3)$, $C(0, 6)$ and $D(2, 5)$.

    Reflect each point in the line that joins (3, 0) to (3, 6) and write down the coordinates of points A', B', C' and D' in the image produced. [4]

5 Describe the locus of points for the following: 🖩

    a) The path of a rocket for the first three seconds after take-off. [1]

    b) A point just below the handle on an opening door. [1]

    c) The central point of a bicycle wheel as the bicycle travels along a level road. [1]

    d) The end of a pendulum on a grandfather clock. [1]

6 Describe the plan view of a cube measuring 4cm by 4cm by 4cm. 🖩 [1]

7 **a)** Construct a triangle, DEF, where DE = 8cm, EF = 7cm and DF = 3cm. [2]

    b) By accurate measurement, find the size of angle FDE. [1]

    c) Construct the bisector of angle FED. [2]

Review Questions

8 The photograph shows a World War II Lancaster Bomber.

Sketch:

a) the side elevation of the Lancaster Bomber [2]

b) the front elevation of the Lancaster Bomber [2]

c) the plan view of the Lancaster Bomber. [2]

9 Below is a 3D shape made up of eight cubes.

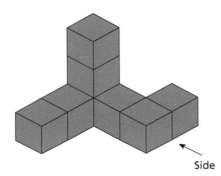

Side

a) Draw the plan view. [2]

b) Draw the side elevation. [2]

10 **a)** Here is the top half of a word. The dashed line is the line of symmetry.

Write down the word. [1]

b) Give an example of another three or four-letter word, through which a horizontal line of symmetry can be drawn. [1]

Total Marks _____ / 38

Linear Graphs & Graphs of Quadratic Functions

1   Work out the equation of the line that joins the points $\left(\frac{2}{3}, 8\right)$ and $\left(\frac{5}{6}, 5\right)$.   [3]

2   Work out the equation of the line drawn below.   [3]

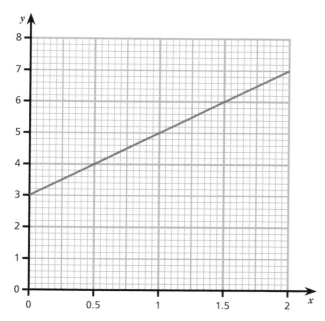

3   Sketch the graph of the function $y = x^2 + 4x + 3$, clearly stating the roots and the coordinates of the turning point.   [3]

4   The equation of a line is $4y = 3x + 1$.

     Work out the gradient and y-intercept of the line.   [2]

5   A curve has the equation $y = x^2 + ax + b$.
     The curve crosses the x-axis at the points (–7, 0) and (1, 0).

     a)   Work out the values of a and b.   [3]

     b)   Work out the x-coordinate of the turning point.   [1]

6   a)   Sketch the graph $y = \frac{1}{x}$.   [1]

     b)   On the same axes sketch the graph $y = -\frac{1}{x}$.   [1]

7   Sketch the graph of $y = x^3$.   [1]

Total Marks _____ / 18

Review Questions

Powers, Roots and Indices

1 Simplify $(2ab^{-5})^{-3} \times (3a^{-2}b^3)^2$ [3]

2 Amber states that $(x^{-2})^3 = \frac{1}{x^6}$

Is Amber's statement true or false?
Write down a calculation to support your answer. [2]

3 Write down the following as a single power of 3:

a) $3^2 \times 3^4$ [1]

b) $3^9 \div 3^6$ [1]

c) $(3^2)^3$ [1]

4 Write down the following as a single power of 5:

a) $5^4 \times 5^5 \times 5^{-2}$ [2]

b) $\frac{5^5}{5^{-4}}$ [2]

c) $(5^3)^{-6}$ [2]

5 Kirsten thinks that $3^2 + 3^3 = 3^5$
Darcey thinks $3^2 + 3^3 = 36$

Who is correct?
Write down a calculation to support your answer. [2]

6 Simplify $(16x^3)^{-2}$ [2]

7 Expand and simplify $x^5(x^{-3} + x^3)$ [2]

Total Marks _____ / 20

Area and Volume 1, 2 & 3

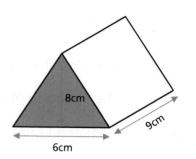

1 **a)** Work out the volume of the triangular prism. [2]

   b) A cube has the same volume as the triangular prism.

   Work out the total length of all the edges of the cube. [3]

2 The numerical values of the area and circumference of a circle are equal.

Work out the radius of this circle. [2]

3 The volume of the trapezoid is 900cm³.
All measurements are in centimetres.

Work out the value of x. [4]

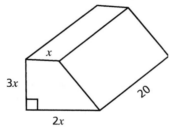

4 The surface area of a sphere is 75cm². Work out the length of the radius. [3]

5 Here is a triangle.
The area of the triangle is 7.5cm².

Work out the value of x. [3]

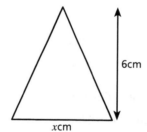

6 John is planning to paint the front of his house. He needs to estimate how much paint he should buy. He does this by calculating the area of the front of the house, including all windows and doors.

The diagram shows John's house.

If each tin of paint will cover 11m², work out an estimate of the number of tins that John needs to buy. [4]

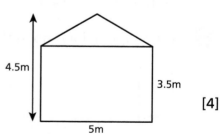

Total Marks .... / 21

Uses of Graphs & Other Graphs

1 A line is parallel to the line of equation $y = 3x - 2$ and goes through the point (1, 5).

Work out the equation of the line. [3]

2 Gemma, Naval and Esmai entered a five-mile cycling race. The graph below shows the race.

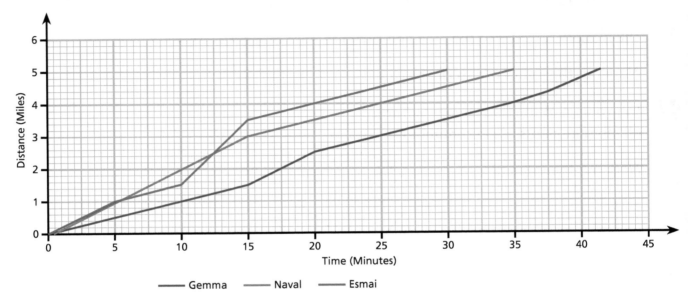

a) Who won the race? [1]

b) What speed was Naval travelling at for the last 20 minutes before he finished?
   Give your answer in miles per hour. [2]

c) Between what times was Gemma travelling her fastest?
   Give a reason for your answer. [2]

d) How many minutes after the race started did the winner move into the lead? [1]

e) Describe the race. [3]

3 The graph below shows the journey of a train. Describe the journey. [3]

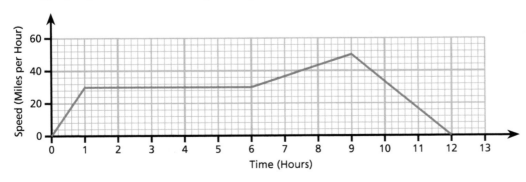

Total Marks _____ / 15

Inequalities

1 Write down all the integer values for m that satisfy $-1 \leqslant m < 4$. [1]

2 Solve $2x - 6 > 2$ [2]

3 Write down all the possible integer values for y if $12 \leqslant 3y \leqslant 36$. [2]

4

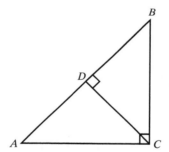

Write down the inequality represented by the number line. [2]

> **Total Marks** .... / 7

Congruence and Geometrical Problems

1 Prove that triangle ABC and triangle BCD are similar. [3]

2 Lisa has a 10cm by 8cm photograph of her pet dog. She wants a smaller copy to fit into her handbag and a larger copy for her office.

a) What will the length of the smaller copy be, if the width is 4cm? [1]

b) What will the width of the larger copy be, if the length is 25cm? [2]

> **Total Marks** .... / 6

Practice Questions

Right-Angled Triangles 1 & 2

1 A man walks 6.7km due north. He then turns due west and walks 7.6km.

How far is he now from his starting point? [3]

2 A 4m ladder leans against a vertical wire fence. The foot of the ladder is 2m from the base of the fence. Fang, the lion, can jump 3m vertically.

Will Fang be able to jump over the fence?
You must give reasons for your answer. [4]

3 ABC is an isosceles triangle. $AB = BC = 13$cm. D is the midpoint of AC and $AC = 10$cm.

Calculate the length of BD. [3]

4 A bumblebee leaves its nest and flies 10 metres due south and then 6 metres due west.

What is the shortest distance the bumblebee has to fly to return to its nest?
Give your answer to 3 significant figures. [3]

5 A triangle has side lengths of 1.5cm, 2.5cm and 2cm. Is it a right-angled triangle?
Give a reason for your answer. [3]

6 How long is the diagonal of a square of side length 3cm? [2]

7 A is the point (4, 0) and B is the point (7, 5).

Calculate the angle between line AB and the x-axis to the nearest degree. [2]

8 Molly cycles 5km in a north-easterly direction from Apton (A) to Bray (B). She then cycles 8km in a north-westerly direction from Bray to Chart (C).

a) How far is Chart from Apton? Give your answer to 2 significant figures. [2]

b) Calculate angle CAB. Give your answer to the nearest degree. [2]

9

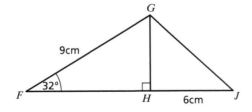

Calculate:

a) The length of GH.
Give your answer to 2 decimal places. [2]

b) The size of angle HGJ.
Give your answer to 1 decimal place. [2]

Total Marks _____ / 28

Statistics 1 & 2

1 The table shows the number of pieces of fruit eaten by a group of students in one week.

Number of Pieces of Fruit	Frequency
10	6
11	
12	
13	10
14	10

a) Use the bar chart to complete the frequency table. [2]

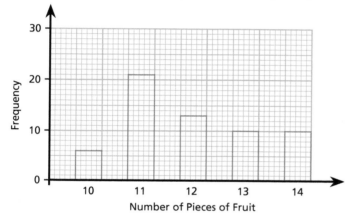

b) How many students were in the group? [1]

c) Write down the modal number of pieces of fruit eaten. [1]

d) Calculate the mean number of pieces of fruit eaten. [3]

2 The table below shows hours of sunshine and amount of rainfall for nine towns across England in one month.

Sunshine (h)	600	420	520	630	470	380	560	430	450
Rainfall (mm)	11	18	13	9	16	25	14	20	19

a) Draw a scatter diagram to represent this information. [2]

b) Describe the relationship between hours of sunshine and rainfall. [1]

Total Marks _____ / 10

Measures, Accuracy and Finance

You must be able to:

- Understand and solve problems relating to household finance
- Check calculations using approximation
- Round numbers and measures to an appropriate degree of accuracy
- Convert between metric units and use conversion factors to convert between imperial and metric units.

Solving Real-Life Problems

- Being able to understand and solve problems relating to finance is an essential life skill.

> Nadine bought a designer handbag from an online shop for £230 and sold it two years later for £184.
>
> Calculate the percentage loss.
>
> Percentage profit or loss = $\dfrac{\text{profit or loss}}{\text{original amount}} \times 100$
>
> $= \dfrac{£46}{£230} \times 100 = 20\%$

Loss = £230 – £184 = £46

> VAT is charged at the standard rate of 20%.
>
> What is the final cost after VAT has been added to a bill of £45?
>
> $\dfrac{20}{100} \times £45 = £9$
>
> Total bill = £45 + £9 = £54

This could also be calculated using a multiplier: 1.2 × £45 = £54

> Yvonne earns £36 000 per year. The first £8200 is tax free, but income tax of 20% must be paid on the rest.
>
> How much income tax does Yvonne have to pay each year?
>
> £36 000 – £8200 = £27 800
>
> Income tax = $\dfrac{20}{100} \times £27\,800 = £5560$

Work out the amount that is taxable.

Limits of Accuracy

- You will often be asked to give answers to a certain number of decimal places or significant figures. To do this, you must 'round off' the number.
- **Decimal places** refers to the number of digits after the decimal point, e.g.
  27.3652 = 27.4 (to 1 d.p.)
  27.3652 = 27.37 (to 2 d.p.)

Because the digit two places after the decimal point is 5 or more, the 3 (in the first decimal place) rounds up to 4.

The 5 rounds up the 6 to a 7.

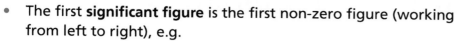

- The first **significant figure** is the first non-zero figure (working from left to right), e.g.
  - 541 = 540 (to 2 significant figures)
  - 0.0347 = 0.035 (to 2 significant figures).
- Inequality notation is used to specify simple error intervals due to rounding, e.g. $144.5 \leqslant x < 145.5$

Approximation of Calculations

- You can use approximations to estimate and check the answers to calculations.

Estimate the answer to $(2136 + 39.7) \div (9.6 \times 11.1)$

$(2000 + 40) \div (10 \times 10)$
= $2040 \div 100 = 20.4$

Key Point

Leading zeros in decimals are **not** counted when rounding to significant figures.

Approximate each number to 1 significant figure.

Converting Between Units

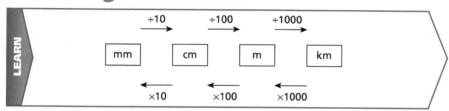

How many metres are there in 4 kilometres?

$4km = 4 \times 1000 = 4000m$

A rod is 620 millimetres long. What is its length in centimetres?

$620mm = 620 \div 10 = 62cm$

Key Point

$1000mg = 1g$
$1000g = 1kg$
$1000kg = 1$ tonne

$1000ml = 1$ litre
$1000cm^3 = 1$ litre

- Imperial / metric conversions will be given in exam questions, but you must know how to use them.

How many kilometres are there in 20 miles?
Assume 8km = 5 miles

20 miles = 32km

Multiply by 4.

How many pounds are there in 20 kilograms?
Assume 1kg = 2.2 pounds

20kg = 44 pounds

Multiply by 20.

Quick Test

1. Estimate the value of $(0.897)^2 \times 392.4$
2. A lorry travels 150 miles between two towns.
   If 5 miles is 8km, work out the distance travelled in
   a) kilometres and b) metres.

Key Words

decimal places
significant figures
approximation

Quadratic and Simultaneous Equations

You must be able to:

- Solve quadratic equations by factorising
- Solve two simultaneous equations
- Find approximate solutions to quadratic and simultaneous equations by using a graph.

Factorisation

- When solving a quadratic equation by factorisation (see p.15–17), make sure it equals zero first.

Solve the equation $x^2 + 4x + 3 = 0$ by factorisation.

×	x	$+1$
x	x^2	$+x$
$+3$	$+3x$	$+3$

$(x + 1)(x + 3) = 0$

$x + 1 = 0 \qquad x + 3 = 0$

$x = -1 \qquad x = -3$

Set up and complete a table. The missing terms need to have a product of +3 and a sum of +4.

First row = first bracket; first column = second bracket

The Method of Intersection

- Plotting a graph of a quadratic equation can give zero, one or two solutions for x when $y = 0$.
- The solutions are given by the curve's points of intersection with the x-axis.

Find approximate solutions to the equation $x^2 - 5x + 1 = 0$ by plotting a graph.

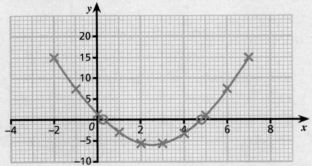

There are two solutions: $x = 0.2$ or $x = 4.8$

These solutions are approximate.

Key Point

If two brackets have a product of zero, one of the brackets must equal 0.

Key Point

The points of intersection with the x-axis are called roots.

Key Point

Solutions to simultaneous equations always come in pairs.

Simultaneous Equations

- Simultaneous equations can be solved by elimination.

Solve the following simultaneous equations:

$3x - y = 18$ \qquad Equation 1

$x + y = 10$ \qquad Equation 2

$4x = 28 \qquad 7 + y = 10$

$x = 7 \qquad y = 3$

Add equation 1 and equation 2 to eliminate the y terms.

Substitute your value for x into one of the equations.

Annabel buys three pears and two apples for £1.20.
David buys four pears and three apples for £1.65.

Work out the cost of one apple and one pear.

$$3p + 2a = 120 \quad \text{Equation 1}$$
$$4p + 3a = 165 \quad \text{Equation 2}$$

Equation 1 × 4: $12p + 8a = 480$
Equation 2 × 3: $12p + 9a = 495$

$$a = 15$$
$$3p + (2 \times 15) = 120$$
$$p = 30$$

An apple costs 15p and a pear costs 30p.

Form two equations with the information given.

Multiply so that the p terms match. Remember to multiply all terms.

Subtract equation 1 from equation 2.

Substitute your value for a into one of the equations and solve.

Solve the following equations simultaneously:

$y = 2x + 1$ Equation 1
$3y + x = 10$ Equation 2

$$3(2x + 1) + x = 10$$
$$6x + 3 + x = 10$$
$$7x + 3 = 10$$
$$7x = 7$$
$$x = 1$$
$$y = (2 \times 1) + 1$$
$$y = 3$$

Substitute $y = 2x + 1$ into equation 2.

Substitute your value for x into equation 1 to find y.

Solve the simultaneous equations:
$y = 3x^2$
$y + 5x = 3$

You can plot graphs and find the points of intersection. However the solutions are only approximate.

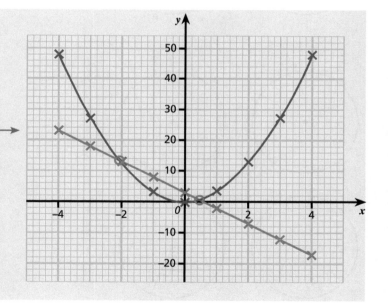

The points of intersection are (–2.1, 13.5) and (0.5, 1).

So, the two approximate solutions are
$x = -2.1$ and $y = 13.5$ or $x = 0.5$ and $y = 1$.

Quick Test

1. Solve the equation $x^2 = 2x + 5$ by the method of intersection.
2. Solve the simultaneous equations:
   $2x + y = 5$
   $x + y = 3$

Key Words

factorisation
intersection
simultaneous equation

Circles

You must be able to:

- Identify the parts of a circle and understand their basic properties
- Calculate angles in a circle.

Parts of a Circle

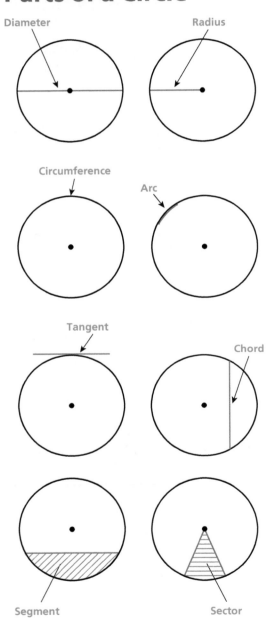

- The circumference is found with the formula:

LEARN

Circumference = π × Diameter (*d*) OR 2 × π × Radius (*r*)

= π*d* OR 2π*r*

Angles in a Circle

- When two radii are used to form a triangle, the triangle will be isosceles.
- When two radii form a triangle and the angle at the centre of the circle is 60°, the triangle will be equilateral.

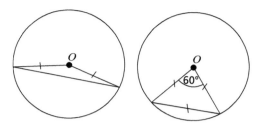

O is the centre of the circle.
AO and BO are radii.

If angle $AOB = 80°$, calculate angle ABO.

$AO = BO$, so AOB is an isosceles triangle.

Angle $ABO = \dfrac{(180° - 80°)}{2} = 50°$

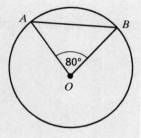

O is the centre of the circle.
AO and BO are radii.

If angle $OAB = 54°$, calculate angle AOB.

$AO = BO$, so AOB is an isosceles triangle.
Angle $OAB = OBA$
Angle $AOB = 180° - (54° + 54°) = 72°$

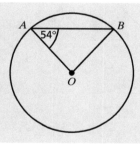

O is the centre of the circle.

If angle $EOF = 93°$, and angle $EOG = 132°$, calculate angle FOG.

Angle $FOG = 360° - (132° + 93°) = 135°$

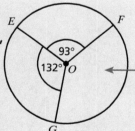

 Angles at a point have a sum of 360°.

Quick Test

1. O is the centre of a circle. OX and OY are radii. If angle $OYX = 40°$, calculate angle XOY.
2. Draw a circle with a radius of 4cm.

Vectors

You must be able to:

- Add and subtract vectors
- Multiply a vector by a scalar
- Carry out translations according to column vectors.

Properties of Vectors

- A **vector** is a quantity that has both **magnitude** (size) and direction.
- Vectors are equal only when they have equal magnitudes and are in the same direction.

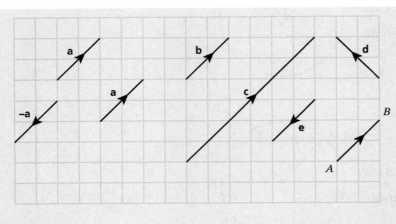

b = **a** (same direction, same length)

d ≠ **a** (different direction, same length)

e = –**a** (opposite direction, same length)

c = 3**a** (same direction, 3 × length of **a**)

$$\mathbf{a} = \overrightarrow{AB} = \underline{a} = \begin{pmatrix} 2 \\ 2 \end{pmatrix}$$

These are all ways of writing the same vector.

$$-\mathbf{a} = \begin{pmatrix} -2 \\ -2 \end{pmatrix}$$

a and **c** are parallel vectors.
a and **b** are equal vectors.

- Any number of vectors can be added together.

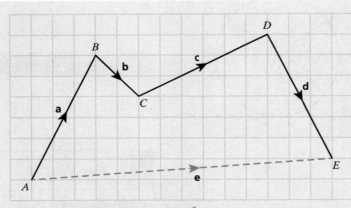

$$\mathbf{a} + \mathbf{b} + \mathbf{c} + \mathbf{d} = \begin{pmatrix} 3 \\ 6 \end{pmatrix} + \begin{pmatrix} 2 \\ -2 \end{pmatrix} + \begin{pmatrix} 6 \\ 3 \end{pmatrix} + \begin{pmatrix} 3 \\ -6 \end{pmatrix} = \begin{pmatrix} 14 \\ 1 \end{pmatrix}$$

$$\overrightarrow{AB} + \overrightarrow{BC} + \overrightarrow{CD} + \overrightarrow{DE} = \overrightarrow{AE} \text{ or } \mathbf{e}$$

This is the resultant vector.

- When a vector is multiplied by a **scalar** (a numerical value), the resultant vector will always be parallel to the original vector.
- When a vector is multiplied by a positive number (not 1), the direction of the vector does not change, only its magnitude.

- When a vector is multiplied by a negative number, the vector points in the opposite direction.

Calculating with Column Vectors

$$e = \begin{pmatrix} 4 \\ -2 \end{pmatrix} \quad f = \begin{pmatrix} -3 \\ 5 \end{pmatrix}$$

a) Work out **e + f** as a column vector.

$$e + f = \begin{pmatrix} 4 \\ -2 \end{pmatrix} + \begin{pmatrix} -3 \\ 5 \end{pmatrix} = \begin{pmatrix} 1 \\ 3 \end{pmatrix}$$

b) Work out **2e – 3f** as a column vector.

$$2e - 3f = 2\begin{pmatrix} 4 \\ -2 \end{pmatrix} - 3\begin{pmatrix} -3 \\ 5 \end{pmatrix} = \begin{pmatrix} 8 \\ -4 \end{pmatrix} - \begin{pmatrix} -9 \\ 15 \end{pmatrix} = \begin{pmatrix} 17 \\ -19 \end{pmatrix}$$

Translations

- When a shape is translated, it does not change size or rotate. It moves left or right and up or down.
- The translation is represented by a column vector $\begin{pmatrix} x \\ y \end{pmatrix}$
- x represents the distance moved **horizontally**: **positive** means to the **right**, **negative** means to the **left**.
- y represents the distance moved **vertically**: **positive** means **up**, **negative** means **down**.

Translate the shaded shape by vector $\begin{pmatrix} -4 \\ -3 \end{pmatrix}$

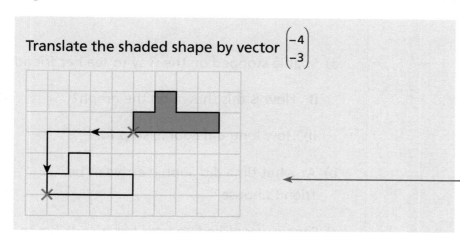

Four squares to the left and three squares down.

Quick Test

1. A point is translated from (1, 4) to (3, –2).
   Describe the translation as a column vector.

Key Words

vector
magnitude
scalar

Uses of Graphs & Other Graphs

1 The graph below shows the journey of a car.

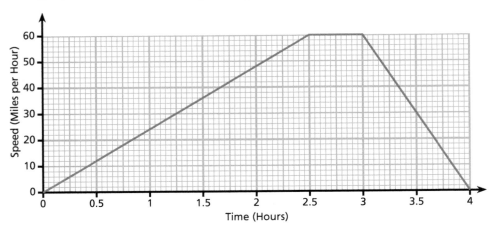

a) What is the greatest speed at which the car travels during the journey? [1]

b) Why does the graph have a gradient of zero between 2.5 and 3 hours? [1]

2 The graph shows Sophie's journey to her friend's house. Her friend lives 18km away. Sophie began her journey at 1pm.

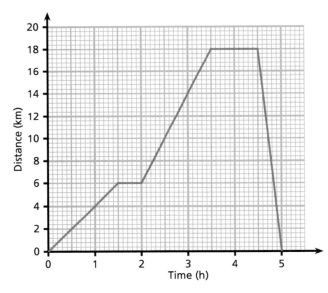

a) Sophie stopped on the way to see her friend.

  i) How is this shown on the graph? [1]

  ii) How long did Sophie stop for? [1]

b) At what time did Sophie arrive at her friend's house? [1]

c) Sophie was picked up from her friend's house by her mum.

  i) Calculate the average speed, in km/h, of her journey home. [2]

  ii) At what time did Sophie arrive home? [1]

3 Work out the equation of the line that is parallel to the line $y = 2x - 5$ and goes through the point (3, 6). [3]

Total Marks _____ / 11

Inequalities

1. Write down all the possible integer values of n if $3 \leqslant n \leqslant 7$. [1]

2. Solve $3x + 4 > 25$ [2]

3. Work out all the possible integer values of y if $15 \leqslant 5y \leqslant 35$. [2]

4. A TV salesperson is set a target to sell more than six televisions a week.
   The manufacturer can let the salesperson have a maximum of 20 televisions each week.

   Use an inequality to represent the number of televisions that could be sold
   each week if the salesperson meets or exceeds their target. [2]

5. Maisie is thinking of a number (m). $11 < m < 17$
   m is also a prime number.

   What number is Maisie thinking of? [1]

   Total Marks _____ / 8

Congruence and Geometrical Problems

1. A triangle has angles of 56°, 64° and 60°. The triangle is enlarged by scale factor 2.

   What are the angles of the enlarged triangle? [3]

2. A tree of height 5m casts a shadow that is 8.5m in length.

   Work out the height of a tree casting a shadow that is 34m in length. [2]

3. What is the difference between congruency and similarity? [2]

4. Fill in the missing criteria to complete the sentence:

   Two triangles are congruent if they satisfy one of four criteria: SSS, RHS, SAS and _____ . [1]

   Total Marks _____ / 8

Review Questions

Right-Angled Triangles 1 & 2

1 A rectangle has a length of 10cm and a width of 5cm.

Calculate the length of its diagonal. Give your answer to 3 significant figures. [2]

2 A square has a diagonal length of 12cm.

Calculate the side length of the square. Give your answer to 2 decimal places. [3]

3 PQR is a triangle. P is at (1, 0), Q is at (1, 5) and R is at (6, 0).

  a) What type of triangle is PQR? [1]

  b) Calculate the length of PR. [1]

  c) Calculate the length of PQ. [1]

  d) Calculate the length of QR. Give your answer to 2 decimal places. [3]

  e) Work out the area of triangle PQR. [2]

4 Sean and Alexander are arguing about a triangle that has side lengths of 9cm, 40cm and 41cm. Sean says it is a right-angled triangle and Alexander says it is not.

Who is correct? Write down a calculation to support your answer. [3]

5 Moira is standing 80m from the base of Blackpool Tower. The angle of elevation to the top of the tower is 63.15°.

Calculate the height of the tower to the nearest metre. [3]

6 The coordinates of a triangle XYZ are X(1, 4), Y(1, 1) and Z(6, 1).

Calculate angle XZY. Give your answer to 3 decimal places. [2]

7 Chevaun says that sin 30° + sin 60° > cos 30° + cos 60°.

Is she correct? Show working to support your answer. [3]

8 A helicopter leaves an air base in London and flies 175km in a north-easterly direction to an air base in Norwich.

  a) How far north of the London air base is the Norwich air base?
    Give your answer to the nearest kilometre. [3]

  b) How long did it take the helicopter to make the journey if it travelled 100km in 30 minutes? [2]

Total Marks _____ / 29

Statistics 1 & 2

1 The table shows information about the genre of the books sold by a bookshop one Friday.

Book Genre	Frequency
Non-Fiction	20
Crime	15
Children's	50
Science Fiction	5

a) How many books were sold in total? [1]

b) Draw a pie chart to represent this information. [3]

2 Corinna wants to sample 100 people in Malmesbury to find out how often people visit the library. She stands by the entrance to the library and asks the first 100 people she meets.

a) Suggest a reason why this is not a representative sample. [1]

b) Describe a better method that Corinna could use to collect her data. [2]

3 The scatter graph below shows the body temperature and pulse rate of ten animals.

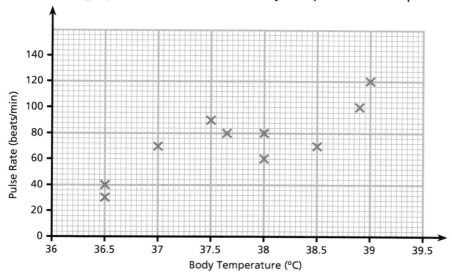

a) Draw a line of best fit and use it to estimate the pulse rate in an animal with a body temperature of 39.5°C. [2]

b) Comment on the reliability of this estimate. [1]

Total Marks _____ / 10

Practice Questions

Measures, Accuracy and Finance

1 Estimate an answer to the following calculation: 📖

$$\frac{512 \times 7.89}{38.9}$$ [2]

2 Four kilograms of carrots and five kilograms of potatoes cost £3.76.

If five kilograms of potatoes cost £1.80, work out the cost of one kilogram of carrots. [2]

3 Sabrina's take-home pay is worked out using this formula:

Take-Home Pay = Hours Worked × Hourly Rate − Deductions

Sabrina's hourly rate is £35.
Her deductions were £218.
Her take-home pay was £657.

Work out the number of hours she worked that week. [3]

4 Calculate $\dfrac{\sqrt{(6.2^2 - 3.6)}}{2.6 \times 0.15}$

Give your answer to:

a) 2 decimal places [3]

b) 3 significant figures. [1]

5 Write down the most appropriate metric unit for measuring:

a) The distance between Portsmouth and Eastbourne. [1]

b) The quantity of flour needed for a small cake. [1]

c) The capacity of a can of lemonade. [1]

6 A marathon is about 25 miles long. If 5 miles = 8km, how many kilometres is this? [1]

7 Round 8765 to:

a) The nearest thousand [1]

b) The nearest hundred [1]

c) The nearest ten. [1]

Total Marks _____ / 18

Quadratic and Simultaneous Equations

1 Solve the equation $3x^2 = 27$ [2]

2 **a)** On the same set of axes, draw the graphs $y = 2x^2$ and $y = 3x + 2$ [2]

   b) Use your graph to solve the equation $2x^2 = 3x + 2$ [2]

3 Solve the simultaneous equations:

$2x + y = 1$

$y = x - 2$ [4]

4 **a)** Factorise $x^2 + 2x - 8$ [1]

   b) Use your answer to part **a)** to help solve the equation $x^2 + 2x - 8 = 0$ [2]

5 Rebecca goes to the greengrocer's shop and buys three apples and two pears. She pays £2.20.

Mandeep goes to the same greengrocer's shop and buys six apples and two pears. She pays £3.40.

Work out the cost of one pear and the cost of one apple.
You **must** show all your working. [4]

6 Solve the simultaneous equations:

$x + y = 5$

$2x - y = 7$ [4]

7 Solve the simultaneous equations:

$4y + 3x = 17$

$3y + 2x = 12$ [4]

8 The graph has the equation $y = x^2 + 2x - 2$

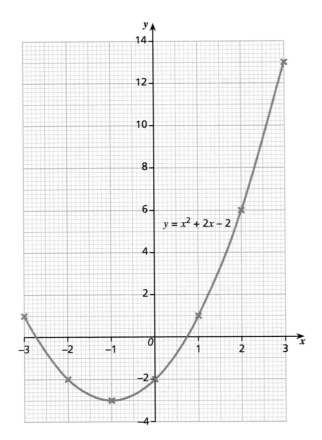

$y = x^2 + 2x - 2$

a) Using the graph, estimate solutions to the equation $x^2 + 2x - 2 = 0$ [2]

b) On the same axes, draw the graph of equation $y = x - 1$ [1]

c) Use your graphs to solve the equation $x^2 + 2x - 2 = x - 1$ [2]

9 Solve the simultaneous equations:

$4x + y = 17$

$2x + y = 9$ [4]

10 Solve the following equation by factorising:

$x^2 + 3x = 4$ [3]

11 Work out the value of a for:

$x^2 + 7x + 6 = (x + a)(x + 1)$ [1]

Total Marks _____ / 38

Circles

1. For each of the following questions, work out the lettered angles. The centre of each circle is marked with an O. 🔲 [2]

a)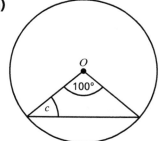

b)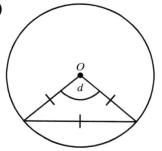

Vectors

1. On squared paper, draw a set of axes that go from –7 to +7 in each direction.

a) Plot the points $A(1, 2)$, $B(5, 2)$ and $C(5, 0)$ and join them together. Label the shape E.

What shape have you drawn? [2]

b) Translate shape E by the vector $\begin{pmatrix} 0 \\ -4 \end{pmatrix}$. Label the shape F.

What are the coordinates of shape F? [3]

c) Translate shape E by the vector $\begin{pmatrix} -7 \\ 3 \end{pmatrix}$. Label the shape G.

What are the coordinates of shape G? [3]

2. $a = \begin{pmatrix} 4 \\ -1 \end{pmatrix}$ $b = \begin{pmatrix} 2 \\ 4 \end{pmatrix}$

Work out $2a - b$ as a column vector. [2]

Review Questions

Measures, Accuracy and Finance

1 Calculate the value of $\dfrac{25.75 \times 31.3}{7.62 - 1.48}$

Give your answer to **a)** 2 decimal places and **b)** 3 significant figures. [3]

2 The Cotton family, comprising of Mum, Dad and 16-year-old daughter, are going away to Turkey.

The brochure states that for every three days booked, you receive one day free.
The price per adult per day is £42. There is a 15% reduction for a child up to the age of 17.
The package is all inclusive.

a) What would the total cost of the holiday be if the family books 12 days? [3]

b) There is an additional early booking discount of 5%.

   If the Cotton family book early, how much do they save? [2]

c) The flight to Turkey takes 4 hours 20 minutes. The departure time from Gatwick was scheduled for 11.10am but, due to bad weather, the flight was delayed by 1 hour 34 minutes.

   If Turkish time is two hours ahead of UK time, at what time did the flight arrive in Turkey? [2]

d) The distance from Gatwick to Dalyan (in Turkey) is 3672km.

   If 5 miles = 8km, what is the distance from Gatwick to Dalyan in miles? [2]

3 Complete the sentences:

a) The mass of an egg is about _____ grams. [1]

b) The floor to ceiling height of a room is about _____ metres. [1]

c) The volume of an average size mug is about _____ millilitres. [1]

Total Marks _____ / 15

Quadratic and Simultaneous Equations

1 The area of the triangle is 1.5cm². [4]

Work out the value of x.

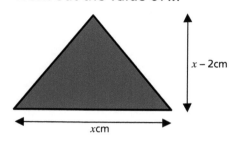

$x - 2$cm

$x$cm

2 The graph below shows the line with equation $y = x^2 - 5x + 6$

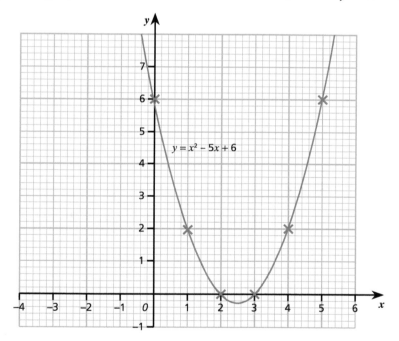

$y = x^2 - 5x + 6$

a) On the same axes, draw the line of the equation $y = 2$. [1]

b) Use the graphs to solve the equation $x^2 - 5x + 6 = 2$ [2]

3 Solve $x^2 + 8x - 9 = 0$ [3]

4 Stephen buys and downloads three apps and four singles at a total cost of £6.10.
Martin buys and downloads five apps and two singles at a total cost of £5.50.

Work out the cost of one app and one single. [4]

5 The sum of two numbers is 20 and the difference is 4.

Set up a pair of simultaneous equations and solve to find the two numbers. [4]

6 The graph has the equation $y = 3x^2$

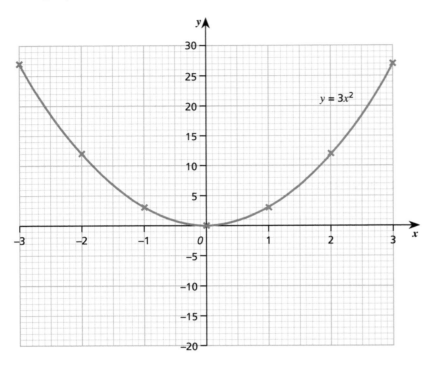

$y = 3x^2$

a) On the same axes draw the graph of $y = 4x + 2$ [1]

b) Use your graphs to find estimates to the solutions of the equation $3x^2 = 4x + 2$ [2]

7 Solve the following simultaneous equations:

$2x + y = 1$

$y = x + 2$ [3]

8 Solve the simultaneous equations:

$3x + 2y = 19$

$2x - 2y = 6$ [4]

9 Work out the value of a for:

$x^2 + 5x + 6 = 0$

$(x + 3)(x + a) = 0$ [1]

Total Marks _____ / 29

Circles & Vectors

1 Complete the sentences:

a) A curved line that is part of the circumference of a circle is an _____. [1]

b) A straight line from the centre of the circle to the circumference is a _____. [1]

c) The distance around the edge of the circle is the _____. [1]

d) A line through the centre of the circle, with both ends touching the

circumference, is the _____. [1]

e) A line that touches the circumference at both ends, but does not pass through the

centre, is a _____. [1]

f) A line outside the circle, which touches the circumference of the circle at only

one point, is a _____. [1]

g) _____ is the number 3.142 (to 3 decimal places). [1]

h) The formula used to calculate the area of a circle is _____. [1]

i) The formula used to calculate the circumference of a circle is _____. [1]

2 Choose a vector from those below to make the statement correct.

4**a** + 6**b**   8**a** + 3**b**   8**a** + 6**b**   4**a** – 3**b**

The vector _____ is parallel to 4**a** + 3**b**. [1]

3 Translate shape A by the vector $\begin{pmatrix} -8 \\ 1 \end{pmatrix}$ [1]

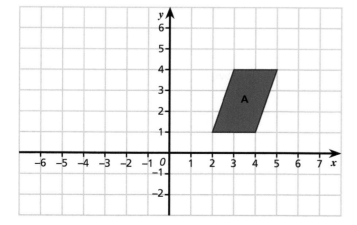

Total Marks _____ / 11

Mixed Exam-Style Questions

1 The diagram is a regular pentagon of side length P. C and G are lines in the pentagon.

Shade the area on the diagram that is represented by the expression $\frac{1}{2}CG + \frac{1}{2}PG$. 🖩

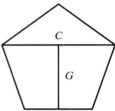

[1]

2 Factorise completely $3x^3 + 6x^2$ 🖩

Answer _____ [2]

3 Solve $3(x + 3) - 5 = 2(x - 2)$ 🖩

Answer _____ [3]

4 Work out the value of $\frac{5}{7}\left(x - \frac{2}{5}\right) + 9y$ when $x = \frac{1}{5}$ and $y = \frac{2}{7}$ 🖩

Answer _____ [2]

5 Simplify $3x^2 + 6x - 2x^2 + 4x - 2y - 6x^2$ 🖩

Answer _____ [2]

6 Simplify $3p^2y - py + p^2y + 7py$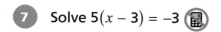

Answer _____ [1]

7 Solve $5(x - 3) = -3$

Answer _____ [2]

8 Factorise $x^2 - x - 2$

Answer _____ [1]

9 Use the formula $P = 3r - q^2$ to work out the value of q when $P = 30$ and $r = 20$.
Give your answer to 2 decimal places.

Answer _____ [2]

10 a) Factorise $x^2 - 16$

Answer _____ [2]

b) Use your answer to part a) to solve $x^2 - 16 = 0$

Answer _____ [2]

11 The formula used to calculate the area of a circle is $A = \pi r^2$.

A circle has an area of 25cm².

Ethan thinks the radius of the circle is $\dfrac{5}{\sqrt{\pi}}$

Guy thinks the radius is $\dfrac{\sqrt{\pi}}{5}$

Who is correct? Write down a calculation to support your answer.

[2]

12 Put the following numbers in order.

6.77   6.767   6.677   6.8

_____ [1]

13 **a)** Write 45 as a product of prime factors.

Answer _____ [2]

b) Write 105 as a product of prime factors.

Answer _____ [1]

c) Use your answers to parts **a)** and **b)** to work out the highest common factor of 45 and 105.

Answer _____ [2]

14 Work out $5\frac{1}{6} - 2\frac{1}{3}$

Answer _____ [3]

15 $P = xy$

x is increased by 10%.

y is increased by 10%.

Work out the percentage increase in P.

Answer _____ [2]

16 Mandeep is looking for a new 12-month phone contract.

Dave's Dongles	**Ian's Internet**
£12 a month	£10 a month
+	+
5p a minute	6p a minute
10% discount on first 6 months	15% discount on first 4 months

On average Mandeep uses 120 minutes per month.

Which phone contract is cheaper for Mandeep?
You must show your working.

Answer _____ [5]

17 97 × 1452 = 140 844

a) Use this information to write down the value of 9.7 × 145.2

Answer _____ [1]

b) Use this information to write down the value of 0.97 × 1.452

Answer _____ [1]

18 $y = \dfrac{ab}{a + b}$

$a = 3 \times 10^4$

$b = 5 \times 10^3$

Work out the value of y. Give your answer in standard form.

Answer _____ [2]

19   Write down the formula for calculating speed.

Answer _____ [1]

20   A regular polygon has 20 sides.

Calculate the size of each interior angle.

Answer _____ [2]

21   Work out the expression for the nth term of the following sequence of numbers:

8, 11, 14, 17, 20 …

Answer _____ [2]

22   A cat rescue centre recorded the age of the cats it re-homed over the course of a year.

Age	Frequency
1	10
2	21
3	16
4	12
5	6

a) Write down the modal age.

Answer _____ [1]

b) Calculate the mean age. Give your answer to 2 decimal places.

Answer _____ [3]

c) On the graph paper below draw a bar chart to represent the data.

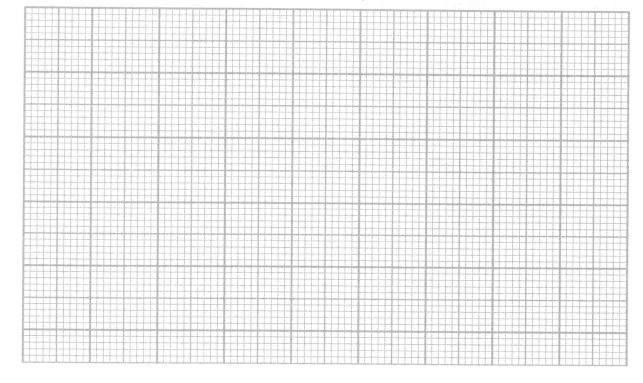

[2]

23 The force (*F*) between two objects is directly proportional to the distance (*x*) between them.

$F = 4$ when $x = 2$

a) Work out an expression for *F* in terms of *x*.

Answer _____ [2]

b) Work out the value of F when $x = 5$.

Answer _____ [1]

c) Work out the value of x when $F = 20$.

Answer _____ [2]

24 Write down the equation for the y-axis.

Answer _____ [1]

25 As part of a health and safety review, a company surveys its employees to find out how many wear glasses or contact lenses.

	Male	Female
Glasses	9	6
Contact Lenses	8	16
Neither	20	15

a) Write down the ratio of the number of females who wear glasses to the number of females who wear contact lenses. Give your answer in its simplest form.

Answer _____ [1]

b) What percentage of all employees are male and do not wear glasses or contact lenses?

Answer _____ [2]

26 Sketch the graph of $y = x^2 + 5x + 4$ [1]

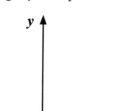

27 Solve the simultaneous equations:

$y = 2x - 1$

$y = 3x - 4$

Answer _____ [3]

28 In the diagram O is the centre of the circle.

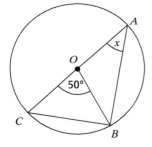

a) Work out the size of angle x.
   Give reasons for your answer.

Answer _____ [2]

b) Show that angle $ABC = 90°$ [2]

29 Simplify $(5t^3)^2$

Answer _____ [2]

30 The diagram shows a sector of a circle, centre O.
The radius of the circle is 6cm.
The angle of the sector at the centre of the circle is 115°.

Work out the perimeter of the sector.

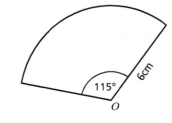

Answer _____ [4]

31 A bag contains six blue beads and five red beads.
Samuel takes a bead at random from the bag. He records its colour and replaces it.
He does this one more time.

Work out the probability that he takes one bead of each colour from the bag.

Answer _____ [3]

32 A sketch of the graph of the equation $y = x^2 + 3x + 2$ is shown below.

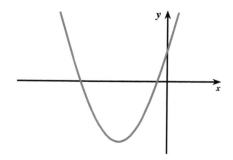

a) Write down the values for x at the points where the graph crosses the x-axis.

Answer _____ [2]

b) Work out the coordinates of the turning point.

Answer _____ [3]

Total Marks _____ / 84

Answers

Pages 6–7 Review Questions

1. 2 000 005 **[1]**
2. 45kg **[1]**
3. $2^2 \times 3 \times 5$ **[1]**
4. a) 18 **[1]**
   b) 180 **[1]**
5. 8 **[1]**
6. −8 **[1]**
7. 64 **[1]**
8. $3 + 2m$ **[1]**
9. $3y^2$ **[1]**
10. a) 17, 20 **[1]**
    b) Yes **[1]**; nth term = $3n + 2$ and
    $(3 \times 46) + 2 = 140$ **[1]** OR
    $\frac{(140 - 5)}{3} = 45$
    (term-to-term rule is +3) **[1]**
11. 0.06 **[1]**
12. 9 sides **[1]**
13. 3.46 **[1]**
14. (4.5, 7) **[2]**
15. 27 **[1]**
16. 10km/h **[1]**
17. 125cm³ **[1]**
18. 0.4 **[1]**
19. 0.875 **[1]**
20. $\frac{78}{100}$ **[1]**; $\frac{39}{50}$ **[1]**
21. $\frac{2}{3} = \frac{8}{12} = \frac{16}{24}$ and $\frac{3}{4} = \frac{9}{12} = \frac{18}{24}$ **[1]**; $\frac{17}{24}$ **[1]**
22. 10, 15, 20 **[3]**
23. 999 999 **[1]**
24. £21 : £35 **[2]**
25. 0.04, 0.39, 0.394, 0.4 **[1]**
26. a) $m = 4$ **[1]**
    b) $m = 48$ **[1]**
    c) $m = 1.5$ **[1]**
27. 36cm² **[1]**
28. 404 **[1]**
29. £12.75 **[1]**
30. $13a - 10y$ **[1]**
31. £81 **[1]**
32. $A = \pi \times r \times r$ **[1]**; $A = 314$cm² **[1]**
33. Vol (1) = $2 \times 2 \times 2 = 8$cm³ **[1]**;
    Vol (2) = $4 \times 4 \times 4 = 64$cm³ **[1]**;
    $\frac{64}{8} = 8$ cubes **[1]**
34. 15 **[1]**
35. $\frac{63}{3} \times 4$ **[1]**; = 84 **[1]**
36. $m = -3$ **[1]**
37. (5, 0) **[2]**
38. 13cm **[1]**
39. $(2 \times 3^2) + (3 \times 4) = 18 + 12$ **[1]**;
    = 30 **[1]**
40. 6.5 **[1]**

Pages 8–35 Revise Questions

Page 9 Quick Test
1. 14 boxes
2. Molly. The multiplication must be carried out before the addition.

Page 11 Quick Test
1. a) 21
   b) −13
2. 1.63×10^{-3}

3. −2201, −220, 220, 1022, 2200
4. £12.16

Page 13 Quick Test
1. $2^2 \times 3^2$
2. a) 3
   b) 60
3. 10am

Page 15 Quick Test
1. $5(x + 2)$
2. $x = 2$
3. $6y - 5$
4. −171
5. $12t^2 - 3t$

Page 17 Quick Test
1. $w = 9$
2. $(x + 7)(x + 1)$
3. $q = \frac{2t + 5}{6}$
4. $y = \frac{x + 8}{6}$

Page 19 Quick Test
1. £108
2. 4 : 1
3. a) Box A, 1 sachet costs 31.7p; Box B, 1 sachet costs 31.1p; Box B is the best buy
   b) 2

Page 21 Quick Test
1. 402mph
2. £51.11
3. 50%

Page 23 Quick Test
1. a) Rectangle, Parallelogram, Kite
   b) Square, Rhombus
2. Angle $EJH = 16°$

> When FE and GH are made longer, they produce a triangle, FGJ. Angles EHF and HFG are alternate angles on parallel lines.

Page 25 Quick Test
1. a) 3240°
   b) 162°
2. 12
3.

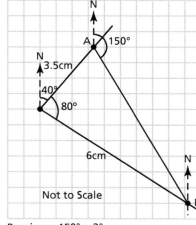

Not to Scale

Bearing = 150° ± 2°

Page 27 Quick Test
1. $\frac{3}{4} \div \frac{1}{5}$ $\left(\frac{3}{4} + \frac{1}{5} = \frac{15}{20} + \frac{4}{20} = \frac{19}{20}\right.$ and $\left. \frac{3}{4} \div \frac{1}{5} = \frac{15}{4} = 3\frac{3}{4}\right)$
2. a) $0.\dot{1}$
   b) recurring
3. $\frac{3}{80}$

Page 29 Quick Test
1. a) $\frac{3}{20}$
   b) 0.15
2. 27 Turkish Lira
3. 32%
4. 15%, $\frac{1}{5}$, $\frac{5}{20}$, 1.15
5. James is correct.
6. Any 12 squares shaded.

Page 31 Quick Test
1. 275 carrots
2. £10.50 + £60 = £70.50
3. 1.5%

Page 33 Quick Test
1. a) 0.1
   b) 45
   c) Yes, the probabilities are not equal.

Page 35 Quick Test
1. $\frac{1}{18}$
2. $\frac{5}{18}$

Pages 36–41 Practice Questions

Page 36
1. a) 3.84×10^5 **[2]** (1 mark for correct digits but decimal point in wrong position)
   b) 384 000 − 19 600 **[1]**; = 364 400 or 3.644×10^5 **[1]**
2. 5°C **[1]**
3. $3 + (6 \times 2) = 15$, $(-3 - 6) - (-25) = 16$ **[1]**; $(-3 - 6) - (-25)$ is larger **[1]**
4. 84 **[1]**
5. 60 **[1]**
6. Fifth square number = 25 **[1]**; third cube number = 27 **[1]**; The third cube number is greater **[1]**
7. $256 = 2^8$ **[1]**; $n = 8$ **[1]**
8. No **[1]**; $2^3 = 8$, $3^2 = 9$ **[1]**
9. 2 packs of sausages **[1]**; 3 packs of bread rolls **[1]**

Page 37
1. $5x + 30$ **[2]** (1 mark for each correct term)
2. $5(3x + 2)$ **[1]**
3. $30 - 12x$ **[2]** (1 mark for each correct term)
4. $4t = p + q$ **[1]**; $t = \frac{p + q}{4}$ **[1]**
5. $9x + 4y$ **[2]** (1 mark for each correct term)
6. $4y - 8z + 12$ **[2]**
7. $4x^2 + 2x + 4$ **[1]**
8. 23 **[1]**
9. $8b = 14$ or $2b = \frac{7}{2}$ **[1]**; $b = \frac{7}{4}$ OR $1\frac{3}{4}$ **[1]**
10. $3p + 6 = 2p + 6$ **[1]**; $p = 0$ **[1]**

11. $\frac{5}{2}x - \frac{2}{3}x = \frac{1}{2} + \frac{1}{3}$ **[1]**; $\frac{15}{6}x - \frac{4}{6}x = \frac{3}{6} + \frac{2}{6}$ **[1]**; $x = \frac{5}{11}$ **[1]**

> Look for a common denominator.

12. $6x - 30y + 36$ **[2]** (1 mark for 2 correct terms)
13. $6p - 4q + 12$ **[2]** (1 mark for $-4q$; 1 mark for $+12$)

> $- \times - = +$

14. $4xz(y - 1)$ **[2]** OR $4z(yx - x)$ OR $4x(yz - z)$ **[1]**
15. $(x + 1)(x + 2)$ **[2]** (1 mark for each correct bracket)
16. $6x - 15 + 4x + 12 - 4x$ **[1]**; $6x - 3$ **[1]**; $3(2x - 1)$ **[1]**
17. formula **[1]**

Page 38
1. 1 : 2000 **[1]**
2. $180° \div 9 = 20°$ **[1]**; largest angle = 80° **[1]**
3. 4 people = 6 celery sticks, 1 person = $6 \div 4$ = 1.5 sticks (OR 3.5 × 6) **[1]**; 20 people = 20 × 1.5 = 30 sticks **[1]**
4. 6 × 4 **[1]**; = 24 days **[1]**

1. Density = mass ÷ volume **[1]**; Density = 4560 ÷ 400 = 11.4g/cm³ **[1]**
2. Speed = distance ÷ time **[1]**; Speed = 200 ÷ 22 = 9.09m/s **[1]**
3. Speed = distance ÷ time **[1]**; Speed = 15 ÷ 3 = 5km/h **[1]**
4. Final amount = Original amount × $\left(1 + \frac{\text{Rate}}{100}\right)^{\text{Time}}$ **[1]**; Final Amount = $4000 \times \left(1 + \frac{4}{100}\right)^4$ = 4000×1.04^4 = £4679.43 **[1]**; Compound Interest = £4679.43 − £4000 = £679.43 **[1]**

Page 39
1.

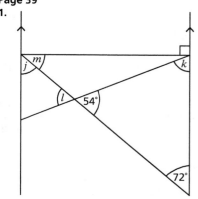

(Marks will not be awarded if reason is incorrect.) j = 72° (alternate angle) **[1]**; k = 54° (sum of the interior angles of a triangle = 180°) **[1]**; l = 54° (vertically opposite angles are equal) **[1]**; m = 18° (90° − 72°) **[1]**
2. 360° − 46° − 107° − 119° = 88° **[1]**
3. Exterior angle = $\frac{360°}{n} = \frac{360°}{10}$ = 36° **[1]**
4. Bearing = 180° + 36° = 216° **[1]**
5. 36km ÷ 4 = 9, 9cm **[1]**
6. 315° **[1]**

Page 40
1. 32 ÷ 8 = 4 **[1]**; 32 − 4 = 28 books **[1]**
2. $\frac{1}{3} + \frac{1}{6} + \frac{1}{4} = \frac{4}{12} + \frac{2}{12} + \frac{3}{12} = \frac{9}{12}$ **[1]**; Fraction that are horses is $1 - \frac{9}{12} = \frac{3}{12} = \frac{1}{4}$ **[1]**
3. $\frac{1}{6}, \frac{4}{12}, \frac{12}{24}, \frac{2}{3}$ **[2]**
4. a) $\frac{4}{5} \times \frac{2}{3} = \frac{8}{15}$ m² **[1]**
   b) $\frac{4}{5} + \frac{4}{5} + \frac{2}{3} + \frac{2}{3} = \frac{44}{15}$ m **[2]** (1 mark if answer is given as $2\frac{14}{15}$)
5. a) $\frac{45}{100}$ **[1]**; $\frac{9}{20}$ **[1]**
   b) $\frac{7.000}{8}$ **[1]**; = 0.875 **[1]**

1. £4800 × $\frac{100}{80}$ **[1]**; = £6000 **[1]**
2. $\frac{9}{36}$ × 100 **[1]**; = 25% **[1]**
3. $\frac{28}{120}$ × 100 **[1]**; = 23.3% **[1]**

Page 41
1. a) Fully correct table **[2]** (1 mark for a list of 36 outcomes)

	1	2	3	4	5	6
1	1	2	3	4	5	6
2	2	4	6	8	10	12
3	3	6	9	12	15	18
4	4	8	12	16	20	24
5	5	10	15	20	25	30
6	6	12	18	24	30	36

   b) $\frac{13}{36}$ **[1]**
   c) $\frac{8}{36} = \frac{2}{9}$ **[1]**
2. a) $\frac{1}{2}$ **[1]**
   b) $\frac{1}{2}$ **[1]**
3. a) $\frac{305}{500} = \frac{61}{100}$ **[1]**
   b) $\frac{97}{500}$ × 100 = 19.4 **[1]**; 19 or 20 **[1]**
4. a) i) $\frac{6}{10}$ OR $\frac{3}{5}$ **[1]**
      ii) $\frac{3}{10}$ **[1]**
      iii) $\frac{1}{10}$ **[1]**
   b) $\left(\frac{6}{10} \times \frac{6}{10}\right) + \left(\frac{3}{10} \times \frac{3}{10}\right) + \left(\frac{1}{10} \times \frac{1}{10}\right)$ **[1]**; $\frac{23}{50}$ **[1]**
5. a)

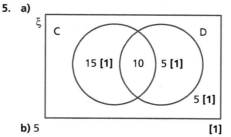

15 **[1]** 10 5 **[1]** 5 **[1]**
   b) 5 **[1]**

Pages 42–63 Revise Questions

Page 43 Quick Test
1. −4, −8
2. −2, 43
3. 72

Page 45 Quick Test
1. 18, 21
2. a) $3n + 4$
   b) 154
3. $n^2 - 1$

Page 47 Quick Test
1. a) A translation by the vector $\begin{pmatrix} 5 \\ -1 \end{pmatrix}$
   b) A reflection in the line $y = x$
   c) A rotation of 90° anticlockwise about (0, 0)

Page 49 Quick Test
1. Construct an angle of 60° and bisect it. i.e. Draw a line and mark on it two points, A and B.

   Open compasses to length AB.

   Put compass point on A and draw an arc. Put compass point on B and draw an arc.

   Draw a line to join A to the new point, C.

   Adjust compasses so less than length AB.

   Put compass point on A and draw arcs crossing AB and AC at points D and E.

   Put compass point on D and draw an arc. Put compass point on E and draw an arc. Draw a line from A to the new point, F.
2.

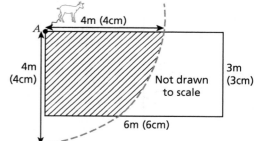

Page 51 Quick Test
1.

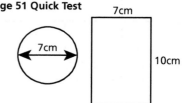

Page 53 Quick Test
1.

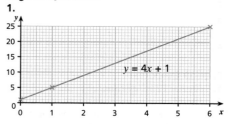

2. Gradient = −2 and y-intercept = 5
3. $y = -1.5x + 14.5$ OR $2y + 3x - 29 = 0$

Answers

Page 55 Quick Test
1.

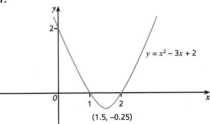

$y = x^2 - 3x + 2$

(1.5, −0.25)

2.

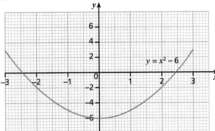

$y = x^2 - 6$

3.

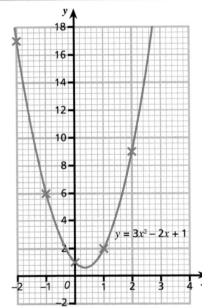

$y = 3x^2 - 2x + 1$

4. Roots = (−1, 0) and (3, 0), turning point = (1, −3)

Page 57 Quick Test
1. $6x^5$
2. 2^8
3. $\frac{1}{27}$
4. $\frac{x^4}{y^{10}}$

Page 59 Quick Test
1. Area = 12m², perimeter = 14m
2. 10cm²
3. Volume = 18cm³, surface area = 42cm²

Page 61 Quick Test
1. Volume = 301.59cm³ (to 2 d.p.) and surface area = 251.33cm² (to 2 d.p.) OR 301.44cm³ and 251.2cm² if using π = 3.14
2. 24cm²

---

3. Circumference = 21.99cm (to 2 d.p.) and area = 38.48cm² (to 2 d.p.) OR 21.98cm and 38.47cm² if using π = 3.14

Page 63 Quick Test
1. $\frac{500\pi}{3}$ or 523.6cm³
2. 91.5cm²
3. $\frac{200}{3}$ or 66.7cm³
4. 108π or 339.3cm²

Pages 64–69 Review Questions

Page 64
1. 8 adult tickets = £308.80 and 4 child tickets = £51.04 [1]; £359.84 [1]
2. a) 311.961 [1]
   b) 0.311 961 [1]
3. −27 [1]
4. 24 combinations [1]
5. a) 9 [1]
   b) 35 [1]
   c) 9 OR 100 [1]
   d) 27 [1]
   e) 13 [1]
6. 64 [1]
7. Peter is correct [1]; $(2^3)^2 = 2^6 = 64$, $(2^2)^3 = 2^6 = 64$ [1]
8. $105 = 3 \times 5 \times 7$ [2]

Page 65
1. $k - g$ [1]
2. $12x - 5y$ [2] (1 mark for each correct term)
3. $\frac{36 + 27}{81}$ [1]; $\frac{63}{81} = \frac{7}{9}$ [1]
4. $6 + 10 = 5x - 2x$ [1]; $16 = 3x$ [1]; $x = \frac{16}{3}$ [1]
5. $b(5a - 3bc)$ [1]
6. $4x - 12 = 10$ [1]; $4x = 22$ [1]; $x = 5.5$ [1]
7. $x = -6$ [1]
8. a) $18x + 14$ [1]
   b) $18x + 14 = 56$ [1]; $x = \frac{7}{3} = 2\frac{1}{3}$cm [1]
9. a) $r^2 = \frac{V}{\pi h}$ [1]; $r = \sqrt{\frac{V}{\pi h}}$ [1]
   b) $r = \sqrt{\frac{50}{\pi \times 10}}$ [1]; $r = 1.26$ (to 3 significant figures) [1]

Page 66
1. $10^2 = k \times 5$ [1]; $100 = 5k$, $k = 20$ [1]
2. 1 part = £60 ÷ 12 = £5 [1]; Shares are (5 × £5) = £25, (7 × £5) = £35 [1]; Difference = £10 [1]
3. 6 hours = 360 minutes [1]; 360 : 4 = 90 : 1 [1]

1. a) Distance = Speed × Time = 1.5 × 1.5 [1]; 2.25m [1]
   b) $\frac{64}{8} \times 5 = 40$ miles [1]; zebra runs at 40mph, so the antelope is faster [1]
2. Mass = Density × Volume = 2700 × 4.5 [1]; = 12 150kg [1]
3. Pressure = $\frac{\text{Force}}{\text{Area}}$ [1]; $\frac{588}{0.0001}$ = 5 880 000Pa [1]

Page 67
1. $y + 2y + 3y = 180°$, $6y = 180°$, $y = 30°$ [1]; Largest angle = 90° [1]
2. $80° + 123° + 165° + 40° = 408°$ It is not quadrilateral, because the interior angles are greater than 360° in total [1]
3. Kite, rectangle, parallelogram, arrowhead [2] (1 mark for two or three correct)
4. Bearing = 180° + 054° = 234° [1]
5. 60° [1]
6. a) Sum = 6 × 180° [1]; 1080° [1]
   b) $\frac{1080°}{8} = 135°$ [1]
7. 3 × 6.5 = 19.5km [1]
8. a) $y + 5 + 3y - 16 + 2y + 5 = 180°$, $6y - 6 = 180°$ [1]
   b) $6y = 186°$, $y = 31°$ [1]
   c) $y + 5 = 36°$ [1]; $3y - 16 = 77°$ [1]; $2y + 5 = 67°$ [1]
9. Pauline is correct [1]; exterior angle is 180° − 158° = 22° [1]; number of sides = 360° ÷ 22 = 16.3̇6̇; it cannot be right because the number of sides must be a whole number [1]

Page 68
1. $6 \times \frac{4}{3} = 8$ [1]
2. $\frac{1}{16}$ [1]
3. $\frac{1}{8} \times 344 = 43$ [1]; 344 − 43 = 301 biscuits [1]
4. $\frac{(95 \times 6)}{5}$ [1]; £114 [1]
5. $\frac{(5.000)}{8} = 0.625$ [1]

1. $\frac{35}{100} \times £56 = £19.60$ [1]; £56 − £19.60 = £36.40 [1]
2. Richard is correct [1]; $\frac{30}{100} \times £40 = £12$, $\frac{40}{100} \times £30 = £12$ [1]
3. $\frac{85\,000}{215\,000} \times 100$ [1]; = 39.5% [1]
4. $\frac{15}{500} \times 100 = 3\%$ [1]

Page 69
1. a) 0.3 [1]
   b) 50 × 0.3 [1]; = 15 [1]
   c) No [1]; P(Georgia wins) = 0.6, so greater than 0.5 (0.5 would be fair). [1]
2. 28 + 10 + 35 = 73 [1]; 82 − 73 [1]; 9 [1]
3. a) Venn diagram with no crossover [1]; All labels correct [1]

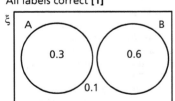

   b) 0 [1]
   c) 0.3 + 0.6 [1]; = 0.9 [1]

> Remember, mutually exclusive means P(A and B) = 0

4. $\frac{6}{10}$ **[1]**; $\frac{3}{5}$ **[1]**

Pages 70–75 Practice Questions

Page 70

1. a) i) 20, 23 **[1]**
   ii) +3 **[1]**

   b) i) −4, −8 **[1]**
   ii) −4 **[1]**

   c) i) $\frac{7}{9}$, $\frac{7}{27}$ **[1]**
   ii) ÷3 **[1]**

2. $24 - 4n$ **[2]** (1 mark if $-4n$ seen)

3. −2, 1, 4, 7, 10 **[2]** (1 mark for any three correct)

4. a) $3n + 11$ **[2]** (1 mark for each correct term)
   b) 311 **[1]**

5. a) 23 **[1]**; 30 **[1]**
   b) 3 **[1]**

6. a)

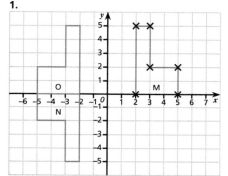 **[1]**; **[1]**

   b) $2n + 1$ **[2]** (1 mark for each correct term)
   c) 201 **[1]**

Page 71

1.

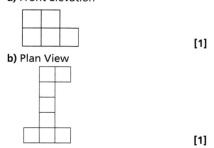

   a) Shape M plotted correctly **[1]**
   b) Shape N plotted correctly **[1]**
   c) Shape O plotted correctly **[1]**
   d) Reflection **[1]**; in the y-axis OR mirror line $x = 0$ **[1]**

2. a) Rectangle T is 9cm × 15cm **[1]**; Area = 135cm² **[1]**
   b) Area R = 15cm², Area T = 135cm² **[1]**; T is 9 times bigger. **[1]**

3. Draw a line and construct the perpendicular bisector of the line. **[1]**; Bisect the right angle. **[1]**

4. a) A circle **[1]**
   b) An arc of a circle **[1]**
   c) A circle **[1]**
   d) An arc of a circle **[1]**

5. a) Front Elevation

[1]

   b) Plan View

[1]

6. A, B and C **[1]**

7. a) 2 **[1]**
   b) 2 **[1]**

8.

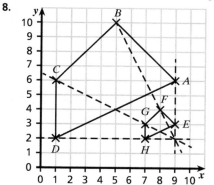

   a) Correct drawing of $ABCD$ **[1]**
   b) Correct drawing of $EFGH$ **[1]**
   c) Enlargement **[1]**; scale factor $\frac{1}{4}$ **[1]**; centre of enlargement (9, 2) **[1]**

9.

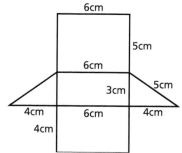

   a) Accurate drawing of net **[2]**
   b) 5 faces **[1]**

10. Sketch of 3D shape with matching front view **[1]**; side view **[1]**; and plan view **[1]**.

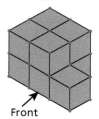

Front

Page 73

1. a)

x × 3 **[1]**   + 7 **[1]** y

   b)

x	−3	−2	−1	0	1	2	3
$y = 3x + 7$	−2	1	4	7	10	13	16

Fully correct **[2]** (1 mark if one incorrect value)

   c) Correctly plotted points **[1]**; straight line drawn **[1]**

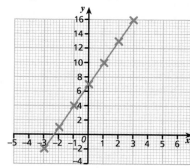

2. a) Sketch showing correct shaped curve **[1]**; correct x-intercepts **[1]**; and correct y-intercept. **[1]**

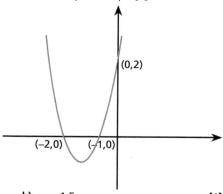

   b) $x = -1.5$ **[1]**

3. Fully correct graph with y-intercept at (0, −2) **[1]**; and a straight line crossing through points (−4, −18) and (4, 14) **[1]**

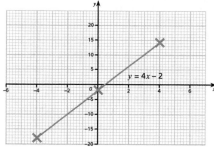

$y = 4x - 2$

4. Fully correct graph with y-intercept at (0, 3) **[1]**; and a straight line crossing through points (−2, −7) and (2, 13) **[1]**

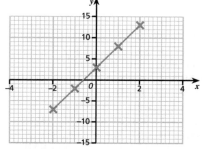

5. Gradient = −2 and y-intercept = (0, 5) **[1]**

Answers

6. Fully correct table **[1]**; and accurately plotted graph **[1]**

x	–3	–2	–1	0	1	2	3
y	34	17	6	1	2	9	22

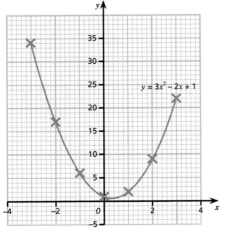

$y = 3x^2 - 2x + 1$

7. $\frac{-1-5}{3-(-3)} = \frac{-6}{6} = -1$ **[1]**; $5 = -1 \times (-3) + c$,

   $c = 2$ **[1]**; $y = -x + 2$ **[1]**

8. $m = -1$ **[1]**; $c = 5$ **[1]**; $y = 5 - x$

   OR $x + y = 5$ **[1]**

Page 74

1. a) 5^5 **[1]**
   b) 5^4 **[1]**
   c) $\frac{5^6}{5^3}$ **[1]**; $= 5^3$ **[1]**
2. $x^{2 \times 4}$ **[1]**; x^8 **[1]**
3. a) 7^{2+5-3} **[1]**; 7^4 **[1]**
   b) $7^{4-(-4)}$ **[1]**; 7^8 **[1]**
   c) $7^{3 \times -2}$ **[1]**; 7^{-6} **[1]**
4. Rebecca **[1]**; $2^2 \times 5^2 = 4 \times 25 = 100$ **[1]**

   > Because 2 and 5 are different numbers, the basic rules of indices do not apply.

5. 9^{-2} OR $x^{2 \times -2}$ **[1]**; $\frac{1}{81x^4}$ OR $\frac{1}{81}x^{-4}$ **[1]**
6. $x^{-1} + 1$ **[2]** (1 mark for each correct term)
7. $27r^6p^3$ **[2]**
8. a) 8×4 **[1]**; 32 **[1]**
   b) $\frac{27}{2}$ **[1]**; 13.5 **[1]**
   c) $\frac{1}{64}$ **[1]**
   d) 1 **[1]**

Page 75

1. a) Perimeter =
      $7 + (2 \times 1) + (2 \times 5) + 3 + (2 \times 2)$
      (or equivalent) **[1]**; 26cm **[1]**
   b) Area = $(7 \times 1) + (5 \times 3)$ **[1]**; 22cm² **[1]**
2. $6 \times 10 \times x = 300$ **[1]**; $x = 5$cm **[1]**
3. Area of square $= 36$cm² **[1]**; Area of circles $= 2 \times \pi \times 1.5^2 = 14.137...$ **[1]**;
   Shaded region $= 36 - 14.137...$ **[1]**;
   $= 21.9$cm² (to 3 significant figures) **[1]**
4. a) Volume of large cylinder =
      $\frac{3}{4} \times 6000\pi = 4500\pi$ **[1]**;
      $4500\pi = \pi \times 15^2 \times h$ **[1]**;
      $h = 20$cm **[1]**

b) Volume of small cylinder =
   $\frac{1}{4} \times 6000\pi = 1500\pi$ **[1]**;
   $1500\pi = \pi \times r^2 \times h = \pi \times r^3$ **[1]**;
   $r = 11.4$cm (to 3 significant figures) **[1]**
5. Volume of cone $= \frac{1}{3} \times \pi \times 3^2 \times 7 = 21\pi$ **[1]**;
   Volume of the hemisphere =
   $\frac{1}{2} \times \frac{4}{3} \times \pi \times 3^3 = 18\pi$ **[1]**; Volume of
   plastic needed $= 21\pi + 18\pi = 39\pi$ cm³ **[1]**

Pages 76–91 Revise Questions

Page 77 Quick Test
1. $y = -2x + 15$
2. 2

Page 79 Quick Test
1.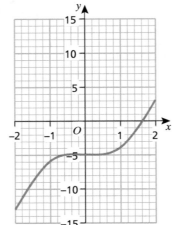

2. a) 60mph
   b) 30 minutes

Page 81 Quick Test
1.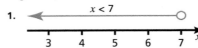

   $x < 7$

2. –5, –4, –3, –2
3. a) >
   b) <

Page 83 Quick Test
1. a) Angle ABC = Angle ADE
      (corresponding angles); Angle
      ACB = Angle AED (corresponding
      angles); Angle DAE is common to
      both triangles; so triangles are similar
      (three matching angles).
   b) $\frac{5}{10} = \frac{BC}{8}$ so $BC = 4$cm

Page 85 Quick Test
1. 13cm
2. $8^2 + 15^2 = 17^2$
3. $24^2 + 56^2 = C^2$, $C = 60.9$cm

Page 87 Quick Test
1. $\sin \theta = \frac{3.5}{8} = 0.4375$, $\theta = 25.9°$
2. $\cos 35° = \frac{x}{14}$, $x = 11$km

Page 89 Quick Test
1. a)
   b) 12° per person
   c) The pie chart, to show the proportion of pupils in the class who wear the different shoe sizes.

Page 91 Quick Test
1. a) 7.76
   b) 8
   c) 9
   d) 3

Pages 92–97 Review Questions

Page 92
1. LCM of 3 and 4 = 12 **[1]**; therefore, 29 will be common to both **[1]**
2. a)

Pattern Number	Perimeter (cm)
1	5
2	8
3	11
4	14
60	182 **[1]**
n	$3n + 2$ **[1]**

   b) $3n + 2 < 1500$ **[1]**; 499 pentagons **[1]**
3. –5, –2, 3 **[2]** (1 mark for one or two correct terms)
4. 66 **[1]**; 130 **[1]**

   > The difference is doubled each time.

Page 93–94
1. a) $X = (-5, 1)$ **[1]**; $Y = (-3, 5)$ **[1]**;
      $Z = (-1, 2)$ **[1]**
   b) $X = (1, -5)$ **[1]**;
      $Y = (5, -3)$ **[1]**; $Z = (2, -1)$ **[1]**
2. Lengths of rectangle D: $3 \times 3 = 9$cm
   and $5 \times 3 = 15$cm **[1]**; Area of rectangle
   C $= 3 \times 5 = 15$cm², area of rectangle
   D $= 9 \times 15 = 135$cm² **[1]**; Ratio $= 15 : 135$
   $= 1 : 9$ **[1]**
3. Volume of cuboid
   C $= 3 \times 4 \times 5 = 60$cm³ **[1]**;
   Volume of cuboid
   D $= 9 \times 12 \times 15 = 1620$cm³ **[1]**;
   Ratio $= 60 : 1620 = 1 : 27$ **[1]**
4. $A' = (3, 2)$ **[1]**; $C' = (6, 6)$ **[1]**;
   $B' = (5, 3)$ **[1]**; $D' = (4, 5)$ **[1]**
5. a) A vertical line **[1]**
   b) An arc of a circle **[1]**
   c) A horizontal straight line **[1]**
   d) An arc of a circle **[1]**

6. A square 4cm × 4cm **[1]**

7.

Not Drawn to Scale

3cm

7cm

D   8cm   E

a) Correct construction of triangle
   (see above) **[2]**
b) Angle FDE = 60° (+ or – 2°) **[1]**
c) Correct angle bisector of FED **[2]**

8. a) **[2]**

   b) **[2]**

   c) 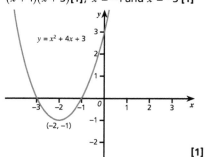 **[2]**

9.   Plan   Side

   a) Correct plan view **[2]**
   b) Correct side elevation **[2]**
10. a) CHOKE **[1]**
    b) Any appropriate word with a
       horizontal line of symmetry, e.g.
       BED, HIKE, BOX, BID **[1]**

Page 95
1. $m = \dfrac{5 - 8}{\frac{5}{6} - \frac{2}{3}} = -18$ **[1]**;

   $8 = -18 \times \left(\frac{2}{3}\right) + c, c = 20$ **[1]**;

   $y = -18x + 20$ **[1]**

2. $m = \dfrac{4}{2} = 2$ **[1]**;
   y-intercept = (0, 3)**[1]**;
   $y = 2x + 3$ **[1]**

3. $(x + 1)(x + 3)$**[1]**; $x = -1$ and $x = -3$ **[1]**

   $y = x^2 + 4x + 3$

   (–2, –1)

   [1]

4. $m = \dfrac{3}{4}$ **[1]**; $\left(0, \dfrac{1}{4}\right)$ **[1]**

5. a) $y = (x + 7)(x - 1)$ **[1]**; $x^2 + 6x - 7$ **[1]**;
      $a = 6, b = -7$ **[1]**
   b) –3 **[1]**

6. a)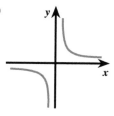

   [1]

   b)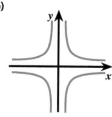

   [1]

7.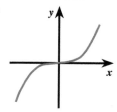

   [1]

Page 96
1. $\frac{1}{8}a^{-3}b^{15}$ **[1]**; $9a^{-4}b^6$ **[1]**; $\frac{9}{8}a^{-7}b^{21}$ **[1]**
2. True **[1]**; $x^{-6} = \dfrac{1}{x^6}$ **[1]**
3. a) 3^6 **[1]**
   b) 3^3 **[1]**
   c) 3^6 **[1]**
4. a) 5^{4+5-2} **[1]**; 5^7 **[1]**
   b) $5^{5-(-4)}$ **[1]**; 5^9 **[1]**
   c) $5^{3 \times 6}$ **[1]**; 5^{-18} **[1]**
5. Darcey **[1]**; $3^2 + 3^3 = 9 + 27 = 36$ **[1]**

   > The basic rules of indices do not
   > apply when adding terms.

6. 16^{-2} OR $x^{3 \times -2}$ **[1]**; $\dfrac{1}{256x^6}$ OR $\dfrac{1}{256}x^{-6}$ **[1]**
7. $x^2 + x^8$ **[2]** (1 mark for each correct term)

Page 97
1. a) $\frac{1}{2} \times 6 \times 8 \times 9$ **[1]**; 216cm³ **[1]**
   b) $\sqrt[3]{216}$ **[1]**; 6×12 **[1]**; = 72cm **[1]**
2. $\pi r^2 = 2\pi r$ **[1]**; $r = 2$ **[1]**
3. $\frac{1}{2}(2x + x) \times 3x \times 20 = 900$ **[1]**;
   $9x^2 = 90$ **[1]**; $x^2 = 10$ **[1]**; .
   $x = \sqrt{10}$ or 3.16cm **[1]**
4. $75 = 4 \times \pi \times r^2$ **[1]**;
   $r^2 = \dfrac{75}{4\pi}$ **[1]**; $r = 2.44$cm (to 3 significant
   figures) **[1]**
5. $\frac{1}{2} \times x \times 6 = 7.5$ **[1]**; $6x = 15$ **[1]**;
   $x = 2.5$ **[1]**
6. $5 \times 3.5 = 17.5m^2$ **[1]**; $0.5 \times 5 \times 1 = 2.5m^2$
   [1]; $17.5 + 2.5 = 20m^2$ **[1]**; 2 tins **[1]**

Pages 98–101 Practice Questions

Page 98
1. $m = 3$ **[1]**; $5 = 3 + c, c = 2$ **[1]**; $y = 3x + 2$ **[1]**

2. a) Esmai **[1]**
   b) 6mph **[2]** (1 mark for 2 miles in
      20 minutes)
   c) 15–20 minutes **[1]**; the part of
      Gemma's graph with the steepest
      gradient **[1]**
   d) 12.5 minutes **[1]**
   e) Esmai and Naval are level for first 5
      minutes **[1]**; Esmai then speeds up
      and overtakes Naval **[1]**; Esmai wins,
      Naval is second and Gemma is third. **[1]**
      (Accept any other valid points.)
3. Train accelerated from 0 mph to 30 mph
   over the first hour. It then travelled at a
   constant speed of 30 mph for 5 hours. It
   then accelerated again up to 50 mph in
   the next 3 hours. It then decelerated for
   the final 3 hours and came to rest. **[3]**
   (1 mark for one correct statement;
   2 marks for two correct statements)

Page 99
1. –1, 0, 1, 2, 3 **[1]**
2. $2x > 8$ **[1]**; $x > 4$ **[1]**
3. $4 \leqslant y \leqslant 12$ **[1]**; 4, 5, 6, 7, 8, 9, 10,
   11, 12 **[1]**
4. $-4 < x \leqslant 2$ **[2]** (1 mark for each side of
   inequality)

1. Angle ACB = Angle BDC = 90° **[1]**;
   Angle ABC = Angle DBC (the angle is
   common to both triangles) **[1]**; Angle
   BAC = Angle BCD (180° – Angle
   B – 90°), so the triangles are similar
   (three matching angles) **[1]**
2. a) 5cm **[1]**
   b) 20cm **[2]**

Page 100
1. $7.6^2 + 6.7^2 = y^2$ **[1]**; $57.76 + 44.89 = y^2$ **[1]**;
   $y = \sqrt{(102.65)} = 10.13$km **[1]**
2. $4^2 - 2^2 = f^2$ **[1]**; $16 - 4 = f^2$ **[1]**; $\sqrt{12} = f$,
   fence height = 3.46m **[1]**; No, because
   the fence height is 3.46m and Fang can
   only jump 3m. **[1]**
3. $13^2 - 5^2 = BD^2$ **[1]**; $169 - 25 = BD^2$,
   $BD = \sqrt{144}$ **[1]**; $BD = 12$cm **[1]**
4. $10^2 + 6^2 = b^2$ **[1]**; $100 + 36 = b^2$ **[1]**;
   $b = \sqrt{136} = 11.7$m (to 3 significant
   figures) **[1]**
5. $1.5^2 + 2^2 = 6.25$ **[1]**; $\sqrt{6.25} = 2.5$ **[1]**; The
   triangle is right-angled (Pythagoras'
   Theorem) **[1]**.
6. $3^2 + 3^2 = d^2$ **[1]**; $d = \sqrt{18} = 4.24$cm **[1]**
7. $\tan \theta = \dfrac{5}{3} = 1.6667$ **[1]**; $\theta = 59°$ **[1]**
8. a) $5^2 + 8^2 = CA^2$, $89 = CA^2$ **[1]**; $CA = \sqrt{89}$
      = 9.4km **[1]**
   b) $\sin CAB = \dfrac{8}{9.4} = 0.851$ **[1]**; $CAB = 58°$
      [1] OR $\tan CAB = \dfrac{8}{5} = 1.6$ **[1]**;
      $CAB = 58°$ **[1]**

   > Making a sketch will show that you
   > are dealing with a right-angled
   > triangle.

Answers

9. a) $\sin 32° = \dfrac{GH}{9}$ [1];

$GH = \sin 32° \times 9 = 4.77\text{cm}$ [1]

b) $\tan HGJ = \dfrac{6}{4.77}$ [1];

$\tan HGJ = 1.2579, \ 51.5°$ [1]

Page 101

1. a)

Number of Pieces of Fruit	Frequency
10	6
11	**21 [1]**
12	**13 [1]**
13	10
14	10

b) 60 [1]

c) 11 [1]

d) $6 \times 10 + 21 \times 11 + 13 \times 12 + 10 \times 13 + 10 \times 14$ [1]; $717 \div 60$ [1]; 11.95 pieces of fruit [1]

2. a) Drawn and labelled axes [1]; and accurately plotted points. [1]

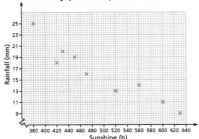

b) Negative correlation – as sunshine increases, rain decreases [1]

Pages 102–109 Revise Questions

Page 103 Quick Test

1. $1^2 \times 400 = 400$ OR $(0.9)^2 \times 400 = 324$

2. a) 240km
   b) 240000m

Page 105 Quick Test

1. $x = $ (approx.) -1.4 or 3.4
2. $x = 2, y = 1$

Page 107 Quick Test

1. Angle $XOY = 100°$
2. Circle of radius 4cm

4cm   Not drawn to scale

Page 109 Quick Test

1. $\begin{pmatrix} 2 \\ -6 \end{pmatrix}$

Pages 110–113 Review Questions

Page 110

1. a) 60mph [1]
   b) Constant speed [1]

2. a) i) A straight horizontal line [1]
      ii) 30 minutes [1]
   b) 4.30pm [1]
   c) i) $\dfrac{18}{0.5}$ [1]; 36km/h [1]
      ii) 6pm [1]

3. Gradient = 2 [1]; $y = 2x + c$, $6 = (2 \times 3) + c$ [1]; $y = 2x$ [1]

Page 111

1. $n = 3, 4, 5, 6, 7$ [1]
2. $3x > 21$ [1]; $x > 7$ [1]
3. $3 \leqslant y \leqslant 7$ [1]; 3, 4, 5, 6, 7 [1]
4. If t is number of televisions, $t > 6$ and $t \leqslant 20$ [1]; $6 < t \leqslant 20$ [1]
5. 13 [1]

1. 56° [1]; 64° [1]; 60° [1]
2. Shadow is $\dfrac{34}{8.5}$ times bigger = 4 times bigger [1]; height of tree = $5 \times 4 = 20$m [1]
3. Similar figures are identical in shape but can differ in size [1]; congruent figures are identical in shape and size. [1]
4. AAS [1]

Page 112

1. $10^2 + 5^2 = d^2$ [1]; $d = \sqrt{125}$, $d = 11.2$cm [1]
2. $x^2 + x^2 = 12^2$ [1]; $2x^2 = 144, x^2 = 72$ [1]; $x = \sqrt{72} = 8.49$cm [1]
3. a) Right-angled triangle or an isosceles triangle [1]
   b) $PR = 5$ units [1]
   c) $PQ = 5$ units [1]
   d) $5^2 + 5^2 = QR^2$ [1]; $QR^2 = 50$, $QR = \sqrt{50}$ [1]; $QR = 7.07$ units [1]
   e) Area = $\frac{1}{2}$ (base × height) [1]; $\frac{1}{2} \times 5 \times 5 = 12.5$ square units [1]
4. Sean was correct [1]; $9^2 = 81$, $40^2 = 1600$, $41^2 = 1681$ so $9^2 + 40^2 = 41^2$ [1] Pythagoras' Theorem works, so triangle is right-angled. [1]
5. $\tan \theta = \dfrac{\text{opp}}{\text{adj}}$, $\tan 63.15° = \dfrac{x}{80}$ [1]; $x = 80 \times \tan 63.15°$ [1]; $x = 158$m [1]
6. $\tan \theta = \dfrac{3}{5}$ [1]; $\tan \theta = 0.6, \theta = 30.964°$ [1]
7. $\sin 30° + \sin 60° = 0.5 + 0.8660 = 1.366$ [1]; $\cos 30° + \cos 60° = 0.8660 + 0.5 = 1.366$ [1]; Both answers are the same – Chevaun is incorrect [1]
8. a) $\sin 45° = \dfrac{x}{175}$ [1]; $x = 175 \times \sin 45° = 123.7$km [1]; $x = 124$km [1]
   b) 100km in 30 minutes, 50km in 15 minutes, 25km in 7.5 minutes [1]; 175km in 52.5 minutes [1]

Page 113

1. a) 90
   b) 1 book = $\dfrac{360°}{90} = 4°$ [1]; non-fiction = 80°, crime = 60°, children's = 200°, science fiction = 20° [1]; accurately drawn pie chart [1]

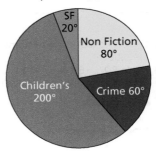

2. a) Biased, as she will only speak to people who use the library [1]
   b) A random [1]; selection of 100 people who live in Malmesbury [1]

3. a) Line of best fit drawn as per diagram below [1]; Accept 120 to 135 [1]

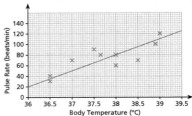

   b) The estimate is not reliable as it is outside the data range. [1]

Pages 114–117 Practice Questions

Page 114

1. $\dfrac{500 \times 8}{40}$ [1]; $= 100 \pm 25$ [1]

2. 4kg carrots £1.96 [1]; 1kg = 49p [1]

3. £657 = ($h \times 35$) − 218 [1]; $\dfrac{657 + 218}{35}$ [1]; = 25 hours [1]

4. a) $\sqrt{(6.2^2 - 3.6)} = 5.902541825$, $2.6 \times 0.15 = 0.39$ [1]; $5.902541825 \div 0.39 = 15.13472263$ [1]; 15.13 [1]
   b) 15.1 [1]

5. a) kilometres / km [1]
   b) grams / g [1]
   c) millilitres / ml [1]

6. 40km [1]

7. a) 9000 [1]
   b) 8800 [1]
   c) 8770 [1]

Answers

Page 115–116

1. $x^2 = 9$ **[1]**; $x = \pm 3$ **[1]**
2. **a)** Straight-line graph correct **[1]**; and curved graph correct **[1]**

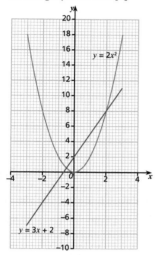

b) $x = -0.5$ **[1]**; and $x = 2$ **[1]**

> When graphs of simultaneous equations are plotted, the x-coordinates of the points of intersection give you your solutions.

3. $2x + x - 2 = 1$ **[1]**; $3x = 3$ **[1]**; $x = 1$ **[1]**; $y = -1$ **[1]**
4. **a)** $(x + 4)(x - 2)$ **[1]**
   b) $x = -4$ **[1]**; $x = 2$ **[1]**
5. $3a + 2p = 220$ and $6a + 2p = 340$ (or equivalent working) **[1]**; $3a = 120$ **[1]**; $a = 40$ pence **[1]**; $p = 50$ pence **[1]**
6. Add equations to eliminate y **[1]**; $3x = 12$, $x = 4$ **[1]**; substitute value for x to find y **[1]**; $y = 1$ **[1]**
7. Multiply first equation by 2 and second equation by 3 **[1]**; $y = 2$ **[1]**; substitute value for y to find x **[1]**; $x = 3$ **[1]**
8. **a)** Accept values of x from 0.5 to 0.9 **[1]**; and -2.5 to -2.9 **[1]**

b) Correct straight line from $(-3, -4)$ to $(3, 2)$ **[1]**

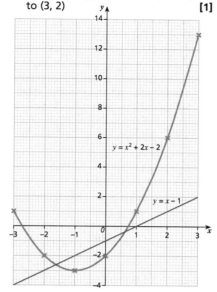

c) Accept values of x from 0.4 to 0.8 **[1]**; and -1.8 to -1.4 **[1]**
9. $2x = 8$ **[1]**; $x = 4$ **[1]**; $8 + y = 9$ OR $16 + y = 17$ **[1]**; $y = 1$ **[1]**
10. $x^2 + 3x - 4 = 0$ **[1]**; $(x - 1)(x + 4) = 0$ **[1]**; $x = 1$, $x = -4$ **[1]**
11. $a = 6$ **[1]**

Page 117

1. **a)** 40° **[1]**
   b) 60° **[1]**

1. **a)** Right-angled triangle **[2]**
   b) $(1, -2)$ **[1]**; $(5, -2)$ **[1]**; $(5, -4)$ **[1]**
   c) $(-6, 5)$ **[1]**; $(-2, 5)$ **[1]**; $(-2, 3)$ **[1]**

2. $\begin{pmatrix} 6 \\ -6 \end{pmatrix}$ **[2]**

Pages 118–121 Review Questions

Page 118

1. **a)** $805.975 \div 6.14 = 131.266\,286\,6$ **[1]**; 131.27 **[1]**
   b) 131 **[1]**
2. **a)** Per day £84 (adults) + £35.70 (child) = £119.70 **[1]**; Holiday costs $9 \times £119.70$ **[1]**; = £1077.30 **[1]**

> They book 12 days but only pay for 9 because of the special offer.

b) 5% of £1077.30 **[1]**; = £53.87 **[1]**
   c) 11.10am + 4 hours 20 minutes + 1 hour 34 minutes, flight arrives in Turkey at 5.04pm (17:04) in UK time **[1]**; Turkish arrival time = 7.04pm (19:04) **[1]**
   d) $3672 \div 8 = 459$ **[1]**; $459 \times 5 = 2295$ miles **[1]**

3. **a)** 55g (+ or – 10 grams) **[1]**
   b) 2.5m (+ or – 1 metre) **[1]**
   c) 350ml (+ or – 50 millilitres) **[1]**

Page 119–120

1. $\frac{1}{2} \times x \times (x - 2) = 1.5$ **[1]**; $x^2 - 2x = 3$ **[1]**; $x^2 - 2x - 3 = 0$ **[1]**; $(x - 3)(x + 1)$, $x = 3$ **[1]**

> Remember, x is a length in this question so x must be positive.

2. **a)**

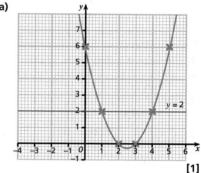

b) $x = 1$ **[1]**; $x = 4$ **[1]**
3. $(x + 9)(x - 1)$ **[1]**; $x = -9$ **[1]**; $x = 1$ **[1]**
4. $3a + 4d = 610$ and $5a + 2d = 550$ **[1]**; double equation 2 and subtract **[1]**; $a = 70$p **[1]**; $d = £1$ **[1]**
5. $x + y = 20$ **[1]**; $x - y = 4$ **[1]**; $x = 12$ **[1]**; $y = 8$ **[1]**
6. **a)** Correct straight line from $(-3, -10)$ to $(3, 14)$ **[1]**

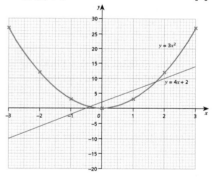

b) $x = 1.6$ to 1.8 **[1]**; $x = (-0.5)$ to (-0.3) **[1]**
7. $2x + x + 2 = 1$ **[1]**; $x = -\frac{1}{3}$ **[1]**; $y = \frac{5}{3}$ OR $1\frac{2}{3}$ **[1]**
8. $5x = 25$ **[1]**; $x = 5$ **[1]**; $10 - 2y = 6$ OR $15 + 2y = 19$ **[1]**; $y = 2$ **[1]**
9. $a = 2$ **[1]**

Page 121

1. **a)** arc **[1]**
   b) radius **[1]**
   c) circumference **[1]**
   d) diameter **[1]**
   e) chord **[1]**
   f) tangent **[1]**
   g) π **[1]**
   h) $A = \pi \times r \times r$ **[1]**
   i) $C = \pi \times$ diameter **[1]**

2. $8a + 6b$ **[1]**
3. Correctly translated shape **[1]**

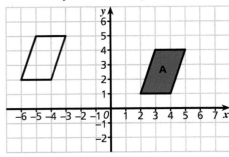

1. Trapezium below line C shaded **[1]**
2. $3x^2(x+2)$ **[2]** (1 mark for $3x^2$; 1 mark for correct brackets)
3. $3x + 9 - 5 = 2x - 4$ **[1]**; $3x + 4 = 2x - 4$ **[1]**; $x = -8$ **[1]**
4. $\frac{5}{7} \times \left(\frac{1}{5} - \frac{2}{5}\right) + \frac{18}{7}$ **[1]**; $\frac{17}{7}$ **[1]**
5. $-5x^2 + 10x - 2y$ **[2]** (1 mark for $-5x^2 + 10x$; 1 mark for $-2y$)
6. $4p^2y + 6py$ **[1]**
7. $x - 3 = -\frac{3}{5}$ **[1]**; $x = \frac{12}{5}$ **[1]**
8. $(x - 2)(x + 1)$ **[1]**
9. $30 = 60 - q^2$ **[1]**; $q = \sqrt{30} = 5.48$ **[1]**
10. a) $(x + 4)(x - 4)$ **[2]** (1 mark for each correct bracket)
    b) $x = 4$ **[1]**; $x = -4$ **[1]**
11. Ethan is correct **[1]**; $r^2 = \frac{25}{\pi}$,
    $r = \sqrt{\frac{25}{\pi}} = \frac{5}{\sqrt{\pi}}$ **[1]**

    You must square root both the numerator and denominator.

12. 6.677, 6.767, 6.77, 6.8 **[1]**
13. a) $45 = 5 \times 3 \times 3$ **[1]**; $= 5 \times 3^2$ **[1]**
    b) $105 = 3 \times 5 \times 7$ **[1]**
    c) 3×5 **[1]**; $= 15$ **[1]**
14. $\frac{31}{6} - \frac{7}{3}$ **[1]**; $\frac{31}{6} - \frac{14}{6}$ **[1]**; $\frac{17}{6}$ **[1]**
15. $P = 1.1 \times 1.1$ **[1]**; $= 1.21$, 21% increase **[1]**
16. Dave's Dongles: £16.20 for six months **[1]**; £18 for following six months, total £205.20 **[1]**; Ian's Internet: £14.62 for four months **[1]**; £17.20 for following eight months, total £196.08 **[1]**; Ian's Internet is cheaper **[1]**
17. a) 1408.44 **[1]**
    b) 1.40844 **[1]**
18. $1.5 \times 10^8 \div 3.5 \times 10^4$ **[1]**; 4285.7 (to 1 d.p.) $= 4.2857 \times 10^3$ **[1]**
19. Speed $= \dfrac{\text{Distance}}{\text{Time}}$ **[1]**
20. Exterior angle $= \dfrac{360°}{20} = 18°$ **[1]**; interior angle $= 180° - 18° = 162°$ **[1]**
21. $3n + 5$ **[2]** (1 mark for each correct term)
22. a) 2 **[1]**
    b) $(10 \times 1) + (21 \times 2) + (3 \times 16) + (4 \times 12) + (5 \times 6)$ **[1]**; $\frac{178}{65}$ **[1]**; 2.74 **[1]**
    c)

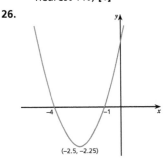

[2]
23. a) $F = kx$, $4 = 2k$ **[1]**; $F = 2x$ **[1]**
    b) 10 **[1]**
    c) $\frac{20}{2}$ **[1]**; 10 **[1]**
24. $x = 0$ **[1]**

25. a) $3 : 8$ **[1]**
    b) $\frac{20}{74} \times 100$ **[1]**; $= 27\%$ (to the nearest 1%) **[1]**
26.

(−2.5, −2.25) **[1]**
27. $3x - 4 = 2x - 1$ **[1]**; $x = 3$ **[1]**; $y = 5$ **[1]**
28. a) Angle $AOB = 180° - 50° = 130°$ (angles on a straight line add up to 180°) **[1]**
    Angle $x = (180° - 130°) \div 2 = 25°$ (isosceles triangle) **[1]**
    b) Angle $OBC = (180° - 50°) \div 2 = 65°$ (isosceles triangle) **[1]**
    Angle OBA = Angle $x = 25°$ (isosceles triangle) and Angle $ABC = 65° + 25° = 90°$ **[1]**
29. $25t^6$ **[2]**
30. $2 \times \pi \times 6 = 12\pi$ **[1]**; $12\pi \times \frac{115}{360}$ **[1]**; $12\pi \times \frac{115}{360} + 12$ **[1]**; 24.0 (to 3 significant figures) **[1]**
31. $\frac{6}{11} \times \frac{5}{11}$ **[1]**; $\frac{30}{121} \times 2$ **[1]**; $\frac{60}{121}$ **[1]**

    The bead is replaced each time.

32. a) $x = -2$ **[1]**; and $x = -1$ **[1]**
    b) The curve is symmetrical, so $x = -1.5$ **[1]**; $y = (-1.5)^2 + 3 \times (-1.5) + 2$ **[1]**; $y = -0.25$, (−1.5, −0.25) **[1]**

Glossary and Index

G

Geometric sequence   a sequence of numbers in which each term is the product of the previous term multiplied by a constant   43

Gradient   the measure of the steepness of a slope:

$$\text{gradient} = \frac{\text{vertical distance}}{\text{horizontal distance}}$$ 21, 52–53, 76–77

H

Hemisphere   a 3D shape that is half of a sphere, i.e. a dome with a circular base   63

Highest common factor (HCF)   the largest positive integer that will divide exactly into two or more numbers   12–13

Hypotenuse   the longest side of a right-angled triangle; opposite the right angle   84–85

I

Included angle   the angle formed by (between) two lines that meet   82

Independent   an event for which the outcome is not dependent on any other events   35

Index / indices (pl.)   a form of notation that uses a small digit to the top right of a number, to show the number of times by which the number is to be multiplied by itself   56–57

Inequality   a linear expression showing two quantities that are not equal; symbols used are $>, \geqslant, <, \leqslant$ 80–81

Input   the value put into a function   44, 52–53

Integer   any whole number, positive or negative, including zero   12

Intercept   the point where a line crosses the axes   52–55

Interior   inside   24

Intersection   the point at which two or more lines cross   104–105

Inverse (operation)   the opposite operation, e.g. subtraction is the opposite operation to addition and division is opposite to multiplication   12–17

Inverse proportion   as one quantity increases, the other quantity decreases   19

Irrational number   any real number that cannot be represented as a simple fraction / ratio of integers   27

Irregular   shapes in which some of the sides and angles are unequal   24

Isometric grid   a grid made up of equilateral triangles or dots, used for drawing 3D shapes   50–51

Isosceles   a triangle with two equal sides and two equal angles   22–23, 85, 107

K

Kite   quadrilateral in which two pairs of adjacent sides are equal   23

L

Linear equation   an equation that does not contain any variables over the power of 1, e.g. $x = 2y + 3$ 15, 52–53, 104–105

Linear graph   a graph of a linear function, represented by a straight line   52–53, 76–77

Linear sequence   a number sequence that increases by the same amount each time   44

Line graph   a graph where all the plotted points are joined by straight lines, often used to show continuous data   89

Locus / loci (pl.)   the path taken by a point that obeys certain rules   48–49

Lowest common multiple (LCM)   the lowest integer that is a multiple of two or more numbers   12

M

Magnitude   size   108

Mean   an average found by dividing the sum of all values by the number of values   90–91

Median   the middle item in an ordered sequence of items   90–91

Mode   the most frequently occurring value in a data set   90–91

Multiple   these appear in the 'times table' of the number   12

Multiplication   to work out the product of two or more values; the inverse of division; represented by ×   8–9

Multiplier   the number by which another number is multiplied; a decimal multiplier is used in percentage change calculations   30–31

Mutually exclusive   two or more outcomes that cannot happen at the same time   32–33

N

Negative correlation   describes a relationship between two variables, where when one variable increases the other decreases   91

Negative number   all numbers less than 0; shown using a minus sign (–)   10–11, 57

Net   a 2D composite shape that can be folded into a solid   50

nth term   the general term of a number sequence or an expression for it   42–45

Numerator   the top number of a fraction   26–27, 57

O

Obtuse   an angle between 90° and 180°   22

Opposite side   the side opposite an angle in a triangle   86–87

Output   the result of a function   44, 52–53

P

Parallel   lines that stay the same distance apart and never meet   22–23, 60, 76, 108–109

Parallelogram   a quadrilateral in which opposite sides are equal and parallel   23

Percentage   out of one hundred   20–21, 28–31, 102

Perimeter   the boundary or edge of a shape (and the length of that boundary)   58–59

Perpendicular   a line at 90° to another line   48–49, 60

Place value   the value of a digit in a number, based on its position within that number   10–11

Plan view   a 2D view looking down on a 3D shape   50–51

Pie chart   a circular chart used to illustrate statistical data, showing proportion   89

Polygon   a closed shape bounded by straight lines   24–25

Population   the entire pool from which a sample is drawn   90

Position-to-term rule   a rule that links the value of a term to its position in the sequence; can be used to work out any term in the sequence   42–43

Positive correlation   describes a relationship between two variables, where when one variable increases the other also increases   91

Positive number   any number greater than zero   10–11, 57

Power   see **Index**   12

Pressure   the ratio of force to area, i.e. $\text{pressure} = \dfrac{\text{force}}{\text{area}}$ 20

Primary data   data collected by you or on your behalf for an investigation   90

Prime factors   factors that are also prime numbers   13

Prime number   a number that has only two factors: itself and 1   12–13

Probability   a measure of how likely it is that an event or outcome will happen; can be expressed as a fraction, decimal or percentage   32–35

Proportion   describes the relationship between things or the parts of something, in terms of their comparative sizes or quantities   18–19

Pyramid   a 3D shape in which lines drawn from the vertices of the base meet at a point   62

Pythagoras' Theorem   a theorem that states that the square on the hypotenuse of a right-angled triangle is equal to the sum of the squares on the other two sides, i.e. $a^2 + b^2 = c^2$ 84–85

Pythagorean triple   a set of side lengths that commonly occur in right-angled triangles   84

Q

Quadratic expression / equation   an expression or equation that contains an unknown term with a power of 2, e.g. $y = 2x^2 + 3$ 16–17, 54–55, 104–105

Collins

GCSE 9-1
Maths
Foundation

Workbook

Linda Couchman and Rebecca Evans

Revision Tips

Rethink Revision

Have you ever taken part in a quiz and thought *'I know this!'* but, despite frantically racking your brain, you just couldn't come up with the answer?

It's very frustrating when this happens but, in a fun situation, it doesn't really matter. However, in your GCSE exams, it will be essential that you can recall the relevant information quickly when you need to.

Most students think that revision is about making sure you **know** stuff. Of course, this is important, but it is also about becoming confident that you can **retain** that *stuff* over time and **recall** it quickly when needed.

Revision That Really Works

Experts have discovered that there are two techniques that help with all of these things and consistently produce better results in exams compared to other revision techniques.

Applying these techniques to your GCSE revision will ensure you get better results in your exams and will have all the relevant knowledge at your fingertips when you start studying for further qualifications, like AS and A Levels, or begin work.

It really isn't rocket science either – you simply need to:

- **test yourself** on each topic as many times as possible
- **leave a gap** between the test sessions.

Three Essential Revision Tips

1. **Use Your Time Wisely**

   - Allow yourself plenty of time.
   - Try to start revising at least six months before your exams – it's more effective and less stressful.
   - Your revision time is precious so use it wisely – using the techniques described on this page will ensure you revise effectively and efficiently and get the best results.
   - Don't waste time re-reading the same information over and over again – it's time-consuming and not effective!

2. **Make a Plan**

   - Identify all the topics you need to revise (this Complete Revision & Practice book will help you).
   - Plan at least five sessions for each topic.
   - One hour should be ample time to test yourself on the key ideas for a topic.
   - Spread out the practice sessions for each topic – the optimum time to leave between each session is about one month but, if this isn't possible, just make the gaps as big as realistically possible.

3. **Test Yourself**

   - Methods for testing yourself include: quizzes, practice questions, flashcards, past papers, explaining a topic to someone else, etc.
   - This Complete Revision & Practice book provides seven practice opportunities per topic.
   - Don't worry if you get an answer wrong – provided you check what the correct answer is, you are more likely to get the same or similar questions right in future!

Visit our website to download your free flashcards, for more information about the benefits of these techniques, and for further guidance on how to plan ahead and make them work for you.

www.collins.co.uk/collinsGCSErevision

Contents

N Number   A Algebra   G Geometry and Measures

S Statistics   P Probability   R Ratio, Proportion and Rates of Change

1 Chocolate Easter eggs are packed 14 to a box. A shopkeeper wants 170 eggs.

How many boxes should he order?

Answer _____ [2]

2 Christine's father is 170cm tall. Christine is 28cm shorter than her father.

How tall is Christine?

Answer _____ [2]

3 Insert two pairs of brackets to make the following calculation correct:

$$8 + 5 \times 9 - 3 = 78$$ [1]

4 a) Write two hundred million in standard form.

Answer _____ [1]

b) Write 6.78×10^{-4} as an ordinary number.

Answer _____ [1]

5 Work out $(1.5 \times 10^4) + (3.5 \times 10^3)$.
Give your answer in standard form.

Answer _____ [3]

6 Work out the value of $\frac{(\sqrt{m})}{y}$ where $m = 8.1 \times 10^3$ and $y = 1 \times 10^{-2}$

Give your answer in standard form.

Answer _____ [3]

7 Work out $0.8645 \div 0.5$

Answer _____ [2]

Number 1, 2 & 3 (Cont.)

8 Find the value of ▲ if:

a) $-3 - ▲ = -10$

Answer _____ [1]

b) $-3 - ▲ = 1$

Answer _____ [1]

c) $-3 × ▲ = 27$

Answer _____ [1]

9 3, 7, 9, 12, 16, 20, 31
From this list choose:

a) Three prime numbers. Answer _____ [1]

b) Two numbers that are factors of 21. Answer _____ [1]

c) Three numbers that are multiples of 4. Answer _____ [1]

d) Two square numbers. Answer _____ [1]

e) The square root of 400. Answer _____ [1]

10 Write 76 as a product of prime factors.

Answer _____ [2]

11 Find the HCF of 684 and 468.

Answer _____ [3]

12 The lights on an aeroplane's wings flash every 12 seconds. The lights on a helicopter flash every 15 seconds. At a certain time both lights flash together.

How long will it be before this happens again?

Answer _____ [2]

Total Marks _____ / 30

Basic Algebra

1 Solve the equation $\dfrac{2x+4}{4} = 2$

Answer _____ [3]

2 Work out the value of the following expression when $x = -2$ and $y = 7$:

$4xy - x^2$

Answer _____ [2]

3 Expand and simplify $3x(x - y) + y(x + 5)$

Answer _____ [2]

4 Solve $4x + 7 = 6x - 5$

Answer _____ [2]

5 Simplify $4x - 2y + 8x$

Answer _____ [1]

6 Write $9xy - 3y^2 + 6x^2y$ in the form $ay(bx + cy + dx^2)$, where a, b, c and d are integers.

Answer _____ [2]

Total Marks _____ / 12

Factorisation and Formulae

1   Expand $(x + 4)(x - 2)$

Answer _____ [2]

2   Factorise $x^2 + 6x + 5$

Answer _____ [2]

3   The formula below links velocity, time and acceleration:

$v = u + at$

a)   Use the formula to find the value of v when $u = 15$, $a = 2.5$ and $t = 10$.

Answer _____ [1]

b)   Rearrange to make t the subject of the formula.

Answer _____ [2]

c)   Find the value of t, when $v = 25$, $a = 1.6$ and $u = 11$.

Answer _____ [1]

4   Factorise $x^2 - x - 2$

Answer _____ [2]

Total Marks _____ / 10

Ratio and Proportion

1 If $\frac{2}{7}$ of the pupils in a class are girls, what is the ratio of boys to girls?

Answer _____ [1]

2 **a)** A coach uses 11 litres of fuel to travel 161.7km. How far can it travel on 13 litres of fuel?

Answer _____ [2]

b) A large sack of dog biscuits feeds three dogs for 15 days.

For how many days would the same sized sack feed five dogs at the same rate?

Answer _____ [2]

3 £700 is divided between Sarah, John and James in the ratio 1 : 3 : 4.

How much more money than Sarah does John receive?

Answer _____ [3]

4 Simplify 15 millilitres : 3 litres

Answer _____ [1]

5 The formula $d = kt^2$ represents what happens when an apple falls from a tree.

d = distance (that the apple falls)
t = time
k = constant of proportionality

If $d = 20$ when $t = 2$, work out the constant of proportionality.

Answer _____ [2]

Total Marks _____ / 11

Variation and Compound Measures

1 Petra inherits £3000. She puts the money into a savings account that pays 2% compound interest each year.

    a) How much interest will Petra earn in the first year?

                        Answer _____ [2]

    b) How much interest will she have earned at the end of three years?

                        Answer _____ [3]

2 A greyhound runs 77.8 metres in eight seconds.

    Write down the greyhound's average speed in:

    a) Metres per second (to 3 decimal places).

                        Answer _____ [1]

    b) Metres per hour (to 2 decimal places).

                        Answer _____ [2]

3 A silver ring weighing 2g has a density of 10.49g/cm^3.

    Work out the volume of silver in the ring.
    Give your answer to an appropriate degree of accuracy.

                        Answer _____ [2]

Total Marks _____ / 10

Angles and Shapes 1 & 2

1   Work out the value of x.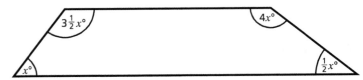

Answer _____ [2]

2   The interior angle of a regular polygon is 150°.

Work out how many sides the polygon has.

Answer _____ [2]

3   A helicopter leaves its base and flies 40km on a bearing of 050°. It then flies 30km on a bearing of 105°.

   a) Draw a scale diagram to show this information. How far is the helicopter from its base?

Answer _____ [2]

   b) On what bearing does the helicopter need to fly in order to return to its base?

Answer _____ [1]

Total Marks _____ / 7

Fractions

1 Write $\frac{45}{63}$ in its simplest form. 🖩

Answer _____ [1]

2 Neesha ate $\frac{2}{3}$ of her chocolate bar this morning and then ate $\frac{3}{5}$ of what was left in the afternoon. How much is left to eat tomorrow? 🖩

Answer _____ [2]

3 Which is larger, $\frac{7}{9}$ of 81 or $\frac{3}{5}$ of 110? You must show your working. 🖩

Answer _____ [2]

4 Express 14 minutes as a fraction of 2.5 hours. Give your answer in the simplest form. 🖩

Answer _____ [2]

5 Mr Tane jogs four and a half kilometres every afternoon.

How far will he run in total in the month of June?

Answer _____ [3]

6 Find the value of y if $y - 1\frac{1}{2} = \frac{3}{4}$ 🖩

Answer _____ [2]

Total Marks _____ / 12

Percentages 1 & 2

1 In five months, a population of rats increased in number by 20% and then by 35%.

If there were 150 rats originally, how many were there at the end of the five-month period?

Answer _____ [2]

2 Write down 180g as a percentage of 9kg.

Answer _____ [2]

3 In a small village school, 22% of the children caught chicken pox.

If 11 children caught chicken pox, how many children attended the school?

Answer _____ [2]

4 This year, Pratik grew 31 tomato plants. This is a 38% reduction on last year.

How many tomato plants did Pratik grow last year?

Answer _____ [2]

5 Temi paid tax on £14 000 at 24%. She paid the tax in 12 equal monthly instalments.

Work out how much tax she paid each month.

Answer _____ [2]

Total Marks _____ / 10

Probability 1 & 2

1 A spinner has five sides: red, blue, yellow, green and pink.

The table below shows the probability that the spinner will land on each colour.

Colour	Red	Blue	Yellow	Green	Pink
Probability	x	0.3	x	$3x$	0.2

a) Find the value of x.

Answer _____ [3]

b) Is the spinner fair? Give a reason for your answer.

_____ [2]

2 A bag contains 12 counters. Five of the counters are blue, three are yellow and the rest are red.

a) A counter is taken from the bag at random and then replaced.

Write down the probability that the counter is red.
Give your answer in its simplest form.

Answer _____ [2]

b) A counter is taken from the bag at random. It is then replaced and another counter is taken.

Show that the probability that one counter is blue and the other is yellow is $\frac{5}{24}$.

[2]

3 A veterinary practice surveyed its clients to find out what pets they owned.

95 clients took part. 75 clients owned a cat (C), 30 clients owned a rabbit (R) and 15 owned both.

a) Complete the Venn diagram to show this information. **[1]**

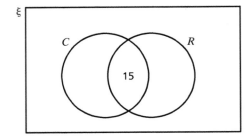

b) Write down the probability that a client owns neither a cat nor a rabbit.
Give your answer as a fraction in its simplest form.

Answer _____ **[2]**

4 A biased dice has five faces numbered 1 to 5.
The probability the dice lands on a 5 is 0.18
The dice is rolled twice and the score recorded.

a) Complete the probability tree diagram. 5′ means '**not** 5'. **[2]**

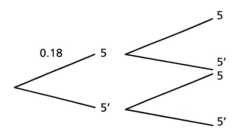

b) Calculate the probability the dice lands on a 5 on only one of the two rolls.

Answer _____ **[3]**

Total Marks _____ / 17

Number Patterns and Sequences 1

1 Here is a sequence of patterns made from matchsticks.

a) Draw the next pattern in the sequence. [1]

b) Complete the table below to show the number of matchsticks required for each pattern.

Pattern Number	1	2	3	4
No. of Matchsticks				

[2]

c) Write down the term-to-term rule for the sequence.

Answer _____ [1]

d) Oswald thinks this is an arithmetic sequence.

Is Oswald correct? Give a reason for your answer.

_____

_____ [2]

2 The following numbers form a geometric sequence:

3, 6, 12, 24, __, __

a) Write down the next two terms in the sequence.

Answer _____ [1]

b) The following numbers also form a geometric sequence:

5, 10, 20, _____ , 80, 160

Fill in the missing term. [1]

3 The nth term for a sequence of numbers is $3n - 2$.

Work out the first five terms of the sequence.

Answer _____ [3]

Total Marks _____ / 11

Number Patterns and Sequences 2

1 Here are the first three terms in a sequence of numbers: 8, 5, 2, __, __

    a) Write down the next two terms in the sequence.

                                  Answer _____   **[2]**

    b) Work out the expression for the nth term of the sequence.

                                  Answer _____   **[2]**

    c) Jennifer thinks that −15 is a number in this sequence.

        Is Jennifer correct? Explain your answer.

    _____   **[2]**

2 The patterns in the sequence below are constructed from circles and straight lines:

    a) Draw the next pattern in the sequence.   **[1]**

    b) Complete the table to show the number of circles and straight lines in the first five patterns of the sequence:

Pattern Number	1	2	3	4	5
Number of Circles					
Number of Straight Lines					

                                                       [3]

    c) Use your table to work out the nth term for the number of circles.

                                  Answer _____   **[2]**

    d) Use your table to work out the nth term for the number of straight lines.

                                  Answer _____   **[2]**

    e) Use your answers to parts **c)** and **d)** to calculate the number of circles and the number of straight lines in pattern number 50 of the sequence.

                              Circles: _____

                    Straight Lines: _____   **[3]**

Total Marks _____ / 17

Transformations

1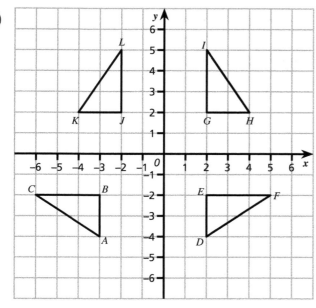

Describe the single transformation that maps:

a) Triangle ABC onto triangle DEF.

_____

_____ [2]

b) Triangle DEF onto triangle GHI.

_____

_____ [3]

c) Triangle DEF onto triangle JKL.

_____

_____ [2]

2 On the grid below plot the points: $A(2, 1)$, $B(4, 1)$ and $C(3, 5)$. Join the points together. Using construction lines, enlarge triangle ABC by scale factor 2, centre of enlargement $(0, 0)$ to form triangle DEF.

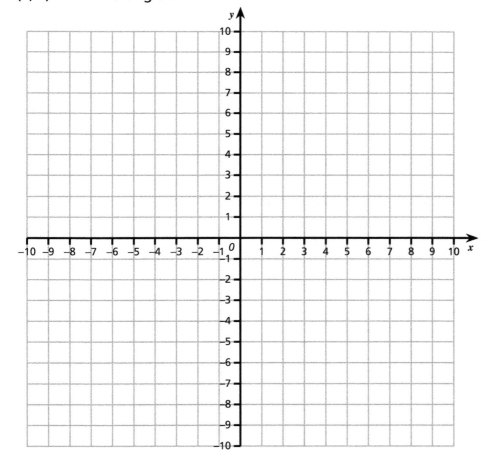

[3]

Total Marks _____ / 10

Constructions

1 Using a pair of compasses and a ruler, mark two points, C and D, that are 5cm apart.

Draw the locus of points that are equidistant from C and D.

[2]

2 Draw any triangle ABC.

Construct the bisectors of each angle using a pair of compasses and a ruler.

[3]

3 A pyramid has a rectangular base that is 3cm by 4cm and a height of 5cm.

Draw an accurate plan view of the pyramid.

[2]

Total Marks _____ / 7

Nets, Plans and Elevations

1 The diagram shows a cuboid made from 12 centimetre cubes.

On the isometric grid alongside it, draw a different cuboid made from 12 centimetre cubes.

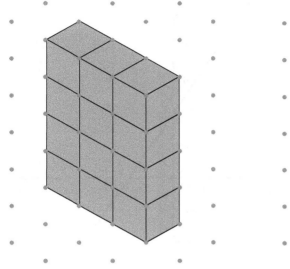 

[3]

2 The diagram shows a letter T made from five cubes.

On the grid alongside it, draw: **a)** the side elevation and **b)** the plan view.

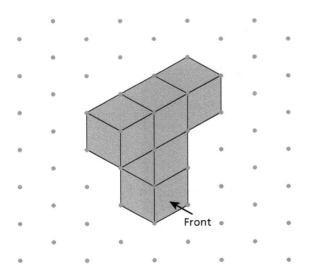

Front

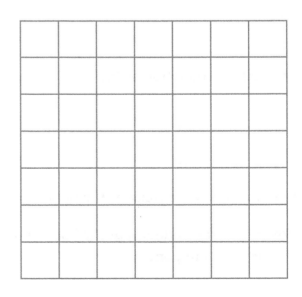

[4]

Total Marks _____ / 7

Linear Graphs

1 Work out the equation of the line shown.

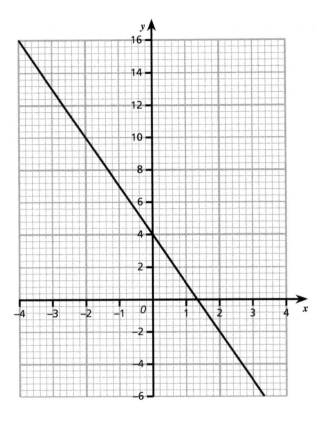

Answer _____ [3]

2 A line has the equation $5y + 2x = 7$

Write down the gradient of the line.

Answer _____ [2]

3 Work out the equation of the line that goes through points (1, 5) and (6, 15).

Answer _____ [3]

4 A graph crosses the y-axis at the point (0, 5) and the x-axis at the point (5, 0).

Write down the equation of the line in the form $ax + by + c = 0$, where a, b and c are integers.

Answer _____ [2]

Total Marks _____ / 10

Graphs of Quadratic Functions

1 A graph has the equation $y = 2x^2 - 7$

a) Complete the table below.

x	-2	-1	0	1	2
y					

[1]

b) Plot the graph of the equation on the axes below.

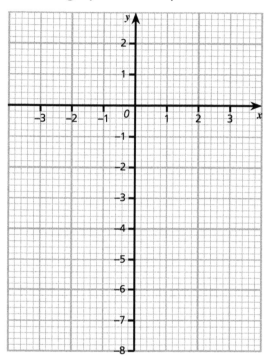

[2]

2 **a)** Sketch the graph of $y = x^2 + 5x + 4$

Clearly label all points where the graph crosses the axes.

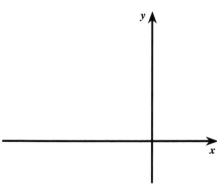

[3]

b) Write down the coordinates of the turning point.

Answer _____ [1]

Total Marks _____ / 7

Powers, Roots and Indices

1 Write down the following as a single power of 5.

a) $5^2 \times 5^8$

Answer _____ [1]

b) $5^6 \div 5^2$

Answer _____ [1]

c) $(5^2)^3$

Answer _____ [1]

d) $5^{-2} \times 5^6$

Answer _____ [1]

2 Simplify $(2x^2y)^3$

Answer _____ [2]

3 Clare thinks $5c^{-4}$ is $\dfrac{1}{5c^4}$

Martin thinks $5c^{-4}$ is $\dfrac{5}{c^4}$

Who is correct?
Show working to support your answer.

Answer _____ [2]

4 Solve $3^n = 81$

Answer _____ [1]

Total Marks _____ / 9

Area and Volume 1, 2 & 3

1 A rectangle has a length of 6cm and area of 24cm².

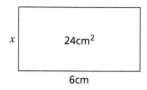

x 24cm²

6cm

a) Work out the width of the rectangle ($x$cm).

Answer _____ [2]

b) Calculate the perimeter of the rectangle.

Answer _____ [2]

2 A square has a side length of 6cm.

An equilateral triangle has the same perimeter as the square.

6cm

Work out the length of one side of the triangle.

Answer _____ [3]

3 The diagram below shows a hemisphere with a radius of 4cm.

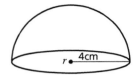

Calculate the volume of the hemisphere.
Leave your answer in terms of π.

[The volume V of a sphere with radius r is $V = \frac{4}{3}\pi r^3$]

Answer _____ [3]

4 The diagram below is the cross-section of a swimming pool.

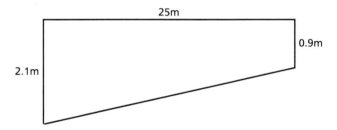

The swimming pool is 10m wide. The pool fills with water at a rate of 0.2m³ per second.

How many hours does it take to fill the pool completely?
Give your answer to 3 significant figures.

Answer _____ [4]

Total Marks _____ / 14

Uses of Graphs

1. x is directly proportional to y.

Sketch the graph of this relationship.

[2]

2. A line has the equation $2y = 3x + 5$

Work out the equation of the line that is parallel to it and goes through point (3, 6).

Answer _____ [4]

3. The formula $C = 3M + 2$ represents how the cost of a phone call is calculated by a telephone company, where C is the cost in pence and M is the number of minutes.

Write down the gradient of the line and use it to describe the rate of change.

[2]

Total Marks _____ / 8

Other Graphs

1 The graph below shows the journey of a car.

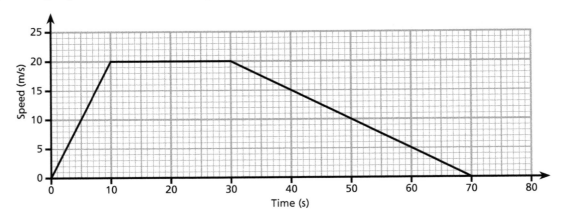

a) Describe the journey of the car.

_____

_____

_____ [3]

b) Calculate the distance covered by the car.

Answer _____ [3]

2 Sketch the graph of $y = x^3 - 1$ and label the y-intercept.

[2]

Total Marks _____ / 8

Inequalities

1. If $-6 \leqslant d \leqslant 2$ and $-5 \leqslant e \leqslant 5$, work out: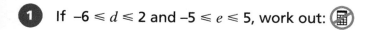

   a) The largest possible value of $d \times e$.

   Answer _____ [1]

   b) The smallest possible value of $d \times e$.

   Answer _____ [1]

2. a) Solve the inequality $7x + 6 \geqslant 41$

   Answer _____ [1]

   b) Write down all the integer values of x if $-2 < x \leqslant 2$.

   Answer _____ [1]

3. State whether each of the following statements is true or false:

   a) $4 > 4.01$ Answer _____ [1]

   b) $2.1 < 2.09$ Answer _____ [1]

   c) When $-1 < y < 4$, y has the values of 0, 1, 2, 3 Answer _____ [1]

4. Solve the inequality $6x - 2 < 4x + 12$

   Answer _____ [2]

5. Write down all the integer values of x that satisfy the following inequalities:

   a) $x > -1$ and $x < 3$

   Answer _____ [1]

   b) $x \leqslant 5$ and $x > 2$

   Answer _____ [1]

Total Marks _____ / 11

Congruence and Geometrical Problems

1

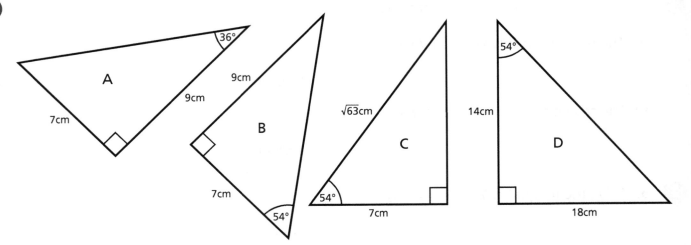

a) Which two triangles are congruent?
   Give a reason for your answer.

   Answer _____ [2]

b) Which triangles are similar to triangle A?

   Answer _____ [1]

2 A tree that is 4m high casts a shadow 9.5m long.

Work out the height of a lamp post that casts a shadow 38m long.

   Answer _____ [2]

3 A rectangle (A) has a length of 12cm and a width of 7cm. A similar rectangle (B) has a perimeter of 114cm.

By what scale factor would rectangle A need to be enlarged to produce rectangle B?

   Answer _____ [2]

Total Marks _____ / 7

Right-Angled Triangles 1

1   The two short sides of a right-angled triangle are 8cm and 9cm.

Work out the length of the longest side.

Answer _____ [3]

2   A triangle has sides of lengths 10cm, 24cm and 26cm.

Is it a right-angled triangle?
Show working to support your answer.

Answer _____ [3]

3   The diagonal of a square is 16cm in length.

Calculate the length of one side of the square.
Give your answer to 2 decimal places.

Answer _____ [3]

4   Use Pythagoras to calculate the length of a line joining the two points (–1, –2) and (3, 5).
You must show your working.

Answer _____ [3]

5   A yacht leaves harbour and sails 6.5km due north. It then sails 3.4km due west.

How far is the yacht from the harbour?

Answer _____ [3]

Total Marks _____ / 15

Right-Angled Triangles 2

1 A bee flies 25m away from its hive on a bearing of 052°. It then changes direction and flies due west.

How far does the bee need to fly in this direction before it is due north of its hive?

Answer _____ [2]

2 The string attached to a kite makes an angle of 41° with the ground.

If the shadow of the string on the ground is 23m long, how high is the kite in the sky?
Give your answer to the nearest metre.

Answer _____ [2]

3 A rectangle measures 8cm by 5cm.

Calculate the angle that the diagonal makes with the longest side.

Answer _____ [2]

4 A 12m ladder leans against the side of a house. The foot of the ladder is 4m from the base of the house wall.

What angle does the ladder make with the ground?
Give your answer to 1 decimal place.

Answer _____ [2]

Total Marks _____ / 8

Statistics 1

1 The data below shows the number of times that a group of students took their driving test before they passed.

Number of Driving Tests	Frequency
1	15
2	25
3	20
4	10
5	5

a) Draw a bar chart to represent this data. [3]

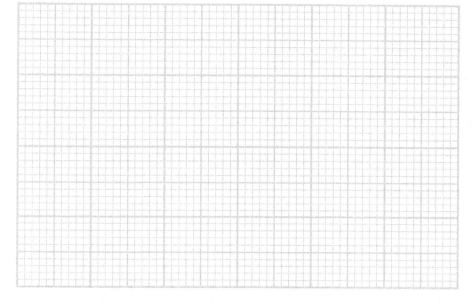

b) Draw a pie chart to represent this data.

c) Give one advantage of using a pie chart to represent this data and one advantage of using a bar chart.

_____

_____

_____

_____

[4]   _____ [2]

Total Marks _____ / 9

Statistics 2

1 The scatter diagram below shows total time spent studying and the marks in a mathematics test for 11 students.

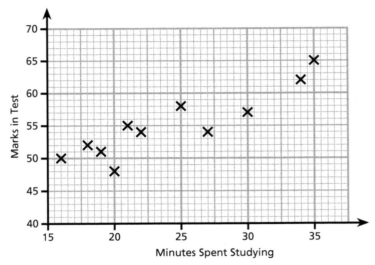

a) Another student took the test. They spent 15 minutes studying and scored 46 marks.

Add this student to the scatter diagram. [1]

b) Write down the type of correlation shown by the graph.

Answer _____ [1]

c) What might this correlation mean?

_____ [1]

d) Draw a line of best fit. [1]

e) Use your line of best fit to estimate the time spent studying by a student who scored a mark of 60 in the test.

Answer _____ [1]

2 Rebecca calculates the mean time taken for her class to run 100m.
She calculates a mean of 15.2 seconds for her 23 classmates, but realises she has accidentally used a time of 21.3 instead of 12.3

Correct the mean time taken.

Answer _____ [3]

Total Marks _____ / 8

Measures, Accuracy and Finance

1   Estimate the value of $(8.64 \times 0.864) \div (8.4 - 8)$ 🖩

                                       Answer _____   [2]

2   Members of the Crawshaw family enjoy camping holidays and often take their car to France by ferry. The total ferry charges for the two-way trip are: cars £46, plus £12.50 per adult and £8.70 per child. The campsite has a daily charge of €12.50 for cars, €10 per adult and €5 per child. The rate of exchange is €1 = £0.78

Calculate the total cost in pounds for the two parents and two children in the Crawshaw family to:

a)   Make a single ferry crossing, assuming a single trip is half the cost of a two-way trip.

                                       Answer _____   [2]

b)   Stay for three days at the French campsite.

                                       Answer _____   [2]

3

centimetres

litres   cubic metres

                    kilometres

millimetres

metres   millilitres

centilitres

Choose a word from those above to make each of these statements correct.

a)   The height of a room in a house is approximately three _____ .   [1]

b)   An average sized mug can hold about 350 _____ of liquid.   [1]

4   A train leaves Brighton station at 14:37. It passes through East Croydon station 52 minutes later. From East Croydon, it will take the train 19 minutes to get to London Victoria.

At what time will the train reach London Victoria?

                                       Answer _____   [2]

Total Marks _____ / 10

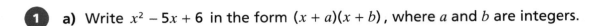

Quadratic and Simultaneous Equations

1 **a)** Write $x^2 - 5x + 6$ in the form $(x + a)(x + b)$, where a and b are integers.

Answer _____ [2]

b) Use your answer to part **a)** to solve the equation $x^2 - 5x + 6 = 0$

Answer _____ [2]

2 A square has side length $x + 3$ cm.
The value of the area of the square is the same as the value of the perimeter.

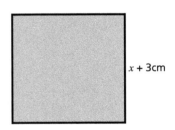
$x + 3$ cm

Work out the side length of the square.

Answer _____ [6]

3 Solve the simultaneous equations:

$x + y = 5$

$2x - y = 7$

Answer _____ [4]

Total Marks _____ / 14

Circles

1 Complete the following sentences:

   a) The distance all the way around the outside of a circle is called the _____. [1]

   b) The radius is _____ the diameter. [1]

   c) A straight line outside the circle, which touches the circle at one point, is called

      a _____. [1]

   d) A shape that is half a circle is called a _____. [1]

2 *ABCD* is a cyclic quadrilateral.

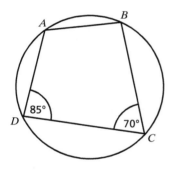

Calculate:

   a) Angle *ABC*.

                                    Answer _____ [2]

   b) Angle *DAB*.

                                    Answer _____ [2]

3 *O* is the centre of a circle. *OP* and *OQ* are radii.

   If angle *PQO* = 37°, calculate angle *POQ*.

                                    Answer _____ [3]

Total Marks _____ / 11

Vectors

1 Here are five vectors:

$\overrightarrow{KL}$ = 4p + 8q, $\overrightarrow{MN}$ = 8p + 16q, $\overrightarrow{OP}$ = –4p + 8q, $\overrightarrow{QR}$ = 12p – 24q

and $\overrightarrow{ST}$ = 12p + 24q

Which vectors are parallel?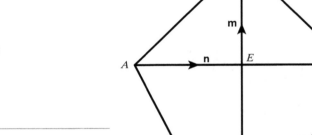

Answer _____ [3]

2 $ABCD$ is a kite. The diagonals BD and AC intersect at E.

$\overrightarrow{AE}$ = n, $\overrightarrow{DE}$ = 3m, $\overrightarrow{EB}$ = m

Work out the vector expressions for: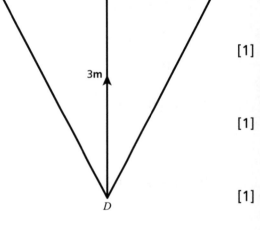

a) $\overrightarrow{DB}$

                 Answer _____ [1]

b) $\overrightarrow{CA}$

                 Answer _____ [1]

c) $\overrightarrow{DA}$

                 Answer _____ [1]

d) $\overrightarrow{AB}$

                 Answer _____ [1]

3 $ABCD$ is a quadrilateral where $\overrightarrow{AB}$ = **a**, $\overrightarrow{BC}$ = **b**, $\overrightarrow{CD}$ = **c** and $\overrightarrow{AD}$ = 2**b**

Name the type of quadrilateral.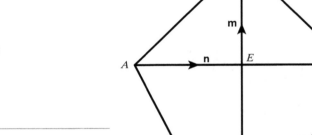

                                       Answer _____ [1]

Total Marks _____ / 8

Collins

GCSE (9–1)
Mathematics
Paper 1 (Non-Calculator)

F

Foundation Tier

Time: 1 hour 30 minutes

You may use:

- Geometrical instruments
- Tracing paper

Do not use:

- A calculator

Instructions

- Use **black** ink or black ball-point pen. You may use a HB pencil for graphs and diagrams.
- Answer **all** questions.
- Read each question carefully before you start to write your answer.
- Answer the questions in the spaces provided.
- Additional paper may be used if required.
- You must show all your working out with your answer clearly identified at the end of your solution. Marks may be given for a correct method even if the answer is incorrect.
- Diagrams are **not** accurately drawn, unless stated.

Information

- The total mark for this paper is 80.
- The marks for each question are shown in brackets **[ ]**.

Name: ....

Practice Exam Paper 1

1 (a) What is one million decreased by two?

Answer _____ [1]

(b) 3   8   12   15   27   60

From the numbers above, select:

(i) A cube number   _____ [1]

(ii) A prime number   _____ [1]

(iii) The lowest common multiple (LCM) of 12 and 15. _____ [1]

(c) Sandra says:

"If I double a prime number and then add three, I will always get a prime number for the answer."

Write down two numbers for which this statement is true and two numbers for which it is not true. Do not use the numbers 2 or 3.

True: _____ and _____ [1]

Not True: _____ and _____ [1]

2 Chris is making a run for his rabbits.
He needs two pieces of wood. One must be 1 m 55 cm long and the other must be 1 m 65 cm long.
The timber shop only sells wood in three-metre or four-metre lengths.

Work out:

(a) The total length of wood that Chris requires.

Answer _____ [1]

(b) The length of wood that he will have left over, if he buys the most suitable length of wood from the timber shop.

Answer _____ [1]

3   Below is a table of costs for posting a medium-sized parcel.

Weight (up to and including)	Price (2nd class)
1 kg	£5.20
2 kg	£8.00
5 kg	£13.75
10 kg	£20.25
20 kg	£28.55

(a) How much does it cost to send a parcel weighing 4700 g?

Answer _____   [1]

(b) Two parcels each weighing 5.7 kg are to be sent to the same address.

How much money would be saved by posting them together as one parcel?

Answer _____   [3]

(c) As part of a special promotion, the cost of posting a parcel that weighs more than 10 kg is reduced by 20%.

What is the new price?

Answer _____   [2]

Turn Over

4

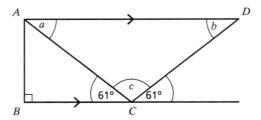

(a) (i) Work out the value of angle a.
You must give a reason for your answer.

_____ [2]

(ii) Work out the value of angle b.
You must give a reason for your answer.

_____ [2]

(iii) Work out the value of angle c.

Answer _____ [1]

(b) What type of triangle is triangle ACD?
You must give a reason for your answer.

_____ [1]

5   Write down whether each of the following statements is true or false:

(a) $2(x + 5) = 2x + 10$ is an identity. _____ [1]

(b) A function machine halves a number and then subtracts 11.

If the result is –6, the input number was 10. _____ [1]

(c) The line $y = 3x + 4$ crosses the y-axis at 4. _____ [1]

(d) If the perimeter of a square is 32 cm, then its area
is 1024 cm². _____ [1]

6   Max, Karen, Jayden and Naimah had a meal in a restaurant.

Max's meal cost £15.62, Karen's meal cost £12.47, Jayden's meal cost £19.01 and Naimah's meal cost £23.66.

Max paid for all the meals with one £50 note, two £20 notes and a £10 note.

(a) How much change did Max receive?

Answer _____ [2]

(b) If the friends decided to split the bill equally between the four of them, how much would they each have to pay?

Answer _____ [1]

Turn Over

7 Two counters are placed in a box.
One counter has the number 5 on one side and 6 on the other.
The other counter has the number 7 on one side and 8 on the other.

The two counters are taken out of the box and placed flat on a desk.
The two numbers facing upwards are added together.

(a) What is the probability that the total will be 13?

Answer _____ **[1]**

(b) What is the probability that the total will be less than 13?

Answer _____ **[1]**

(c) This is carried out 200 times.

Approximately how many times would you expect the total to be 14?

Answer _____ **[1]**

8   **(a)** Simplify $5m + 6g + 4g - 8m$

Answer _____   **[1]**

(b) Simplify $6 + 4(e - 5)$

Answer _____   **[1]**

(c) Factorise $15a - 20y$

Answer _____   **[1]**

(d) Simplify $d^2 \times d^2 \times d^2$

Answer _____   **[1]**

Turn Over

9   (a) Use a ruler and protractor to accurately draw an angle of 56°.   [1]

(b) Bisect the angle you have drawn.
    You must show all your construction lines.   [2]

10 **(a)** Estimate the answer to $\frac{(51.2 \times 109.6)}{(4.3 + 15.9)}$

Answer _____ **[2]**

(b) If $x = 3.2 \times 10^4$ and $y = 2.3 \times 10^5$, work out the value of $x + y$.
Give your answer in standard form.

Answer _____ **[2]**

(c) Write 0.000 681 2 correct to 3 significant figures.

Answer _____ **[1]**

(d) Work out $5 + 4 \times 3 - 14 \div 2$

Answer _____ **[1]**

Turn Over

11   (a) A house was bought for £450 000.
Since it was bought, house prices have risen by 5%.

What is the new value of the house?

Answer _____ [3]

(b) In a test, Steven scored 14 out of 20.
In a different test, Peter scored 18 out of 25.

Who achieved a better result?
You must show your working.

Answer _____ [3]

12 A children's zoo has 18 rabbits in an enclosure.
It has enough food to last the rabbits in the enclosure for 20 days.
Another 18 rabbits are added to the enclosure.

How long will the same amount of food last the rabbits in the enclosure now?

Answer _____ **[2]**

Turn Over

13

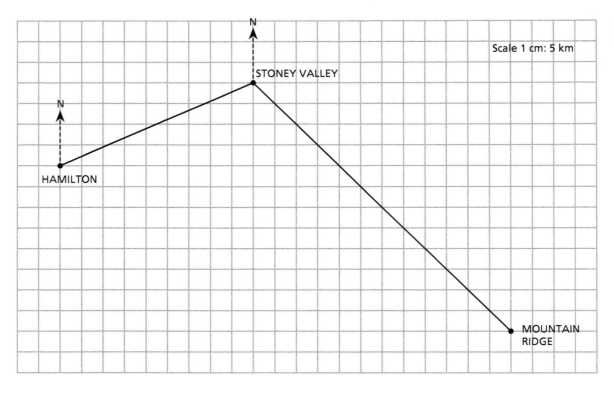

The scale drawing shows three towns in Canada.

(a) What is the actual distance in kilometres between Hamilton and Mountain Ridge?

Answer _____ **[1]**

(b) What is the bearing of Stoney Valley from Hamilton?

Answer _____ **[1]**

(c) Jamie leaves Stoney Valley at 11.47am.
He cycles to Mountain Ridge at a speed of 15 km/h.

Will Jamie arrive at Mountain Ridge before 3 pm?
You must explain your answer clearly.

_____ **[1]**

14 **(a)** Complete the table of values for $x^2 - 2x - 3$.

x	−2	−1	0	1	2	3	4
y	5		−3			0	

[2]

(b) Draw the graph of $y = x^2 - 2x - 3$ using values of x from −2 to 4.   [1]

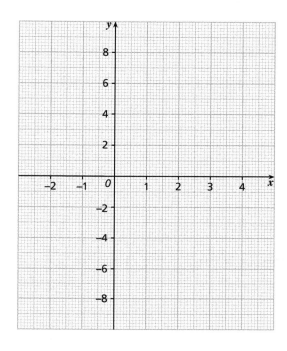

(c) Using your graph, find the values of x for which $x^2 - 2x - 3 = 0$.

Answer _____ [2]

(d) Write down the equation of the line of symmetry for $y = x^2 - 2x - 3$

Answer _____ [1]

Turn Over

Practice Exam Paper 1

15   Here are the ingredients for making 18 oaty biscuits.

110 g butter
80 g sugar
130 g oats
4 dessert spoons of golden syrup

(a) How much sugar would be needed to make nine oaty biscuits?

Answer _____ [1]

(b) Simon has 194 g of oats.

Is this enough to make 27 oaty biscuits?
You must show your working.

Answer _____ [3]

(c) If 4 kg of sugar cost £4.50, what is the cost of the sugar used in the recipe for 18 oaty biscuits?

Answer _____ [2]

(d) Melissa makes 45 oaty biscuits.
Overnight, $\frac{4}{9}$ of the biscuits are eaten by mice.

How many biscuits are left?

Answer _____ [2]

16   Barry said:

"The lengths, in centimetres, of the sides of a right-angled triangle can be represented by: $x + 1$, $3x + 4$ and $2x + 2$."

(a) Write down and simplify an expression for the perimeter (P) of the triangle.

Answer _____   **[2]**

(b) If the perimeter of the triangle is 49 cm, work out the lengths of each of the three sides of the triangle.

Answer _____   **[3]**

(c) Jeremy said that Barry had made a mistake, because it would not be possible to draw this triangle.

Who is correct?
You must give a reason for your answer.

_____

_____   **[2]**

Turn Over

17

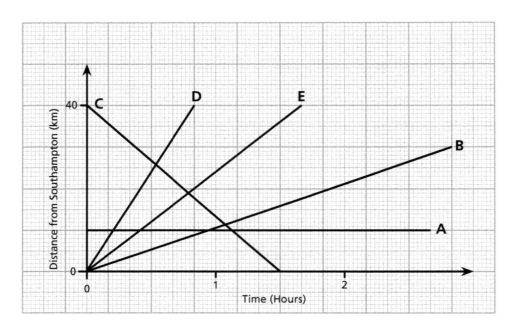

The lines on the distance–time graph represent certain events.

Write down the letter of the line that corresponds with each of the following events.

(a) A wind turbine in the Solent, 10 km off shore from Southampton.

Answer _____ **[1]**

(b) A car ferry travelling from the Isle of Wight to Southampton.

Answer _____ **[1]**

(c) A person swimming from Southampton to the Isle of Wight.

Answer _____ **[1]**

(d) A hovercraft leaving Southampton.

Answer _____ **[1]**

(e) A car ferry leaving Southampton.

Answer _____ **[1]**

End of Test

Collins

GCSE (9–1)
Mathematics
Paper 2 (Calculator)

F

Foundation Tier

Time: 1 hour 30 minutes

You may use:

- A scientific calculator
- Geometrical instruments
- Tracing paper

Instructions

- Use **black** ink or black ball-point pen. You may use a HB pencil for graphs and diagrams.
- Answer **all** questions.
- Read each question carefully before you start to write your answer.
- Answer the questions in the spaces provided.
- Additional paper may be used if required.
- Where appropriate, you should show your working out. Marks may be given for a correct method even if the answer is incorrect.
- Diagrams are **not** accurately drawn, unless stated.

Information

- The total mark for this paper is 80.
- The marks for each question are shown in brackets **[ ]**.
- Use the π button on your calculator or take π to be 3.142 unless the question says otherwise.

Name: ....

Practice Exam Paper 2

1 A survey was carried out to collect data about how often people visited the theatre.
It was conducted by asking people who were leaving a theatre to answer a few questions.
A section of the questionnaire is shown below.

(i) How old are you?

  20 to 30   30 to 40   40 to 50   50 to 60   Over 60

(ii) How many times do you visit the theatre?

  Not often   Sometimes   Many times

(a) Explain why the data collected will be biased.

_____

_____   [1]

(b) Write an improved version of each question.

(i) _____

_____

_____

_____   [1]

(ii) _____

_____

_____

_____   [1]

2   A train leaves Smithrington Station at 10.43 am. It travels 98 km to Bingham Station and the journey takes 1.75 hours.

Calculate:

(a) The train's arrival time at Bingham Station.

Answer _____   **[2]**

(b) The average speed of the train for the journey.

Answer _____   **[2]**

3   In Yishkon, Canada, the temperature outside a house is −15 °C.
Inside the house, the temperature is 18 °C.

(a) How much higher is the temperature inside the house than outside?

Answer _____   **[2]**

(b) The formula to convert degrees Celsius (C) to degrees Fahrenheit (F) is:
$F = \frac{9}{5} \times C + 32$

Use the formula to calculate the temperature inside the house in degrees Fahrenheit.

Answer _____   **[2]**

Turn Over

4   The total weight of the ingredients used to make a chocolate cake is 480 grams.
     The cake is made from flour, sugar, eggs and chocolate in the ratio 7 : 4 : 2 : 2

     (a) Calculate the weight of each ingredient.

         Flour   _____

         Sugar   _____

         Eggs   _____

         Chocolate   _____
                                                                                          [5]

     (b) A cake with ingredients weighing a total of 720 grams takes one hour to bake.

         Work out how long it will take for the 480 gram chocolate cake to bake.

                                         Answer _____   [1]

     (c) $\frac{1}{5}$ of the chocolate cake is eaten in the morning.
         $\frac{3}{10}$ of the remainder is eaten in the afternoon.

         What fraction of the cake is left?

                                         Answer _____   [3]

5   A patio is in the shape of an L.
        It is constructed from 1 m² paving stones.

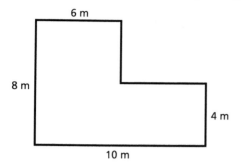

6 m

8 m

4 m

10 m

(a) Calculate the perimeter of the patio.

Answer _____ [1]

(b) Calculate the area of the patio.

Answer _____ [1]

(c) All the paving stones are rearranged to form a square patio.

Work out the length of one side of the square patio.

Answer _____ [1]

(d) Each paving stone costs £2.58.

What was the total cost of the paving stones used to create this patio?

Answer _____ [1]

Turn Over

6   Mrs Harris has bought some kitchen floor tiles.
Each tile is in the shape of a regular hexagon.

(a) In the space below, show how Mrs Harris could lay the tiles so that there are
no gaps between them. You must draw at least four tiles.

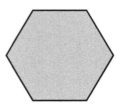

[1]

(b) Calculate the size of an interior angle of one tile.

Answer _____   [2]

(c) Box A contains 12 hexagonal tiles and costs £55.08.
Box B contains 15 hexagonal tiles and costs £68.55.

Which box of hexagonal tiles is the best buy?
You must justify your answer.

Answer _____   [3]

7

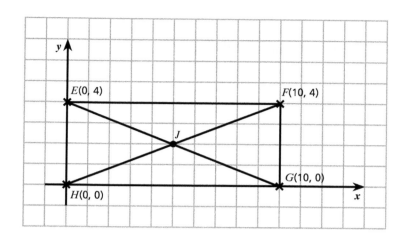

(a) The coordinates of J are: _____ **[1]**

(b) The coordinates of the midpoint of line GH are: _____ **[1]**

(c) As a fraction in its simplest form, the gradient of the line HF is:

Answer _____ **[2]**

(d) The area of triangle HJG is:

Answer _____ **[2]**

Turn Over

8   The mean weight of five men is 87 kg.
The weights of four of the men are: 82 kg, 84 kg, 85 kg and 91 kg.

Calculate the weight of the fifth man.

Answer _____ **[3]**

9   **(a)** In each of the calculations below, ▲ stands for one of the following signs:
+, −, ×, or ÷

Work out which sign should replace ▲ for the calculation to be correct.

(i) 17 ▲ 1.4 = 15.6 _____ **[1]**

(ii) 60 ▲ 1.5 = 40 _____ **[1]**

(iii) 2.8 + 4.7 ▲ 3.1 = 17.37 _____ **[1]**

(b) In each of the statements below, ▲ stands for a number.

Work out which number should replace ▲ for the statement to be correct.

(i) 824.637 to two decimal places is 824.6▲ _____ **[1]**

(ii) 824.637 to three significant figures is 82▲ _____ **[1]**

10 An 8.2 kg turkey costs £24.60.

(a) What is the cost per kilogram?

Answer _____ **[1]**

(b) 1 kg is about 2.2 pounds in weight.

What is the approximate weight of the turkey in pounds?

Answer _____ **[1]**

(c) The instructions state that the turkey must be cooked for 30 minutes per pound, plus an extra 30 minutes.

Calculate how long, to the nearest hour, the turkey must be cooked for.

Answer _____ **[3]**

Turn Over

11 Sean said, "When $x = 4$, then the value of $3x^2$ is 144."
James said, "When $x = 4$, then the value of $3x^2$ is 48."

Who is correct?
You must show how you got to your answer.

Answer _____ [2]

12 On the isometric grid below, draw a cube with a volume of 27 cm³.

[3]

13 **(a)** Insert one of the symbols $<$ or $>$ to make each statement true.

   (i) 3.3 _____ 3.2   [1]

   (ii) −3.3 _____ −3.2   [1]

(b) Write down all the possible integer values for y if:
$-2 \leqslant y < 4$

                                          Answer _____   [1]

(c) Solve the inequality:
$4x - 5 < 31$

                                          Answer _____   [1]

14 A bumblebee leaves its nest and flies 30 m due north.
It then flies 45 m due west to a buddleia bush.

(a) Calculate the shortest distance from the buddleia bush back to the nest.
Give your answer to the nearest metre.

                                          Answer _____   [4]

(b) Calculate the bearing of the nest from the buddleia bush.
Give your answer accurate to 1 decimal place.

                                          Answer _____   [4]

Turn Over

15 A park has a circular pond with a radius of 10 metres.
Hyacinth bulbs are planted every 40 cm around the circumference of the pond.
Use $\pi = 3.142$

(a) How many bulbs are planted?
Give your answer to the nearest whole number.

Answer _____ **[3]**

(b) The depth of the water in the pond is 30 cm throughout.

Calculate how many litres of water there are in the pond.
$1000 \text{ cm}^3 = 1$ litre

Answer _____ **[3]**

16

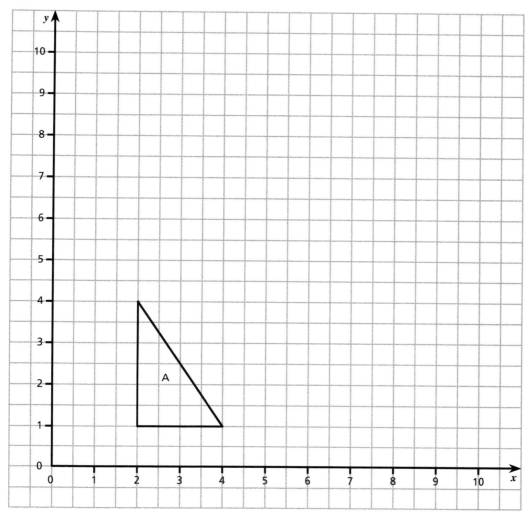

Enlarge triangle A by scale factor 2, centre of enlargement (1, 1).

[3]

Turn Over

17 State whether each of the following statements is true or false for the simultaneous equations below:

$3x + 2y = 16$

$2x + 3y = 19$

(a) $5x + 5y = 35$

Answer _____ **[1]**

(b) $x - y = -3$

Answer _____ **[1]**

(c) $x > y$

Answer _____ **[1]**

(d) $x = 2$

Answer _____ **[1]**

(e) $y = 6$

Answer _____ **[1]**

End of Test

Collins

GCSE (9–1)
Mathematics
Paper 3 (Calculator)

F

Foundation Tier

Time: 1 hour 30 minutes

You may use:

- A scientific calculator
- Geometrical instruments
- Tracing paper

Instructions

- Use **black** ink or black ball-point pen. You may use a HB pencil for graphs and diagrams.
- Answer **all** questions.
- Read each question carefully before you start to write your answer.
- Answer the questions in the spaces provided.
- Additional paper may be used if required.
- Where appropriate, you should show your working out. Marks may be given for a correct method even if the answer is incorrect.
- Diagrams are **not** accurately drawn, unless stated.

Information

- The total mark for this paper is 80.
- The marks for each question are shown in brackets **[ ]**.
- Use the π button on your calculator or take π to be 3.142 unless the question says otherwise.

Name: ....

Practice Exam Paper 3

1   Write these numbers in order, smallest first.

   0.04   40% $\frac{1}{4}$

   Answer _____   [2]

2   What is 600 : 12 000 as a ratio in its simplest form?
    Circle the correct answer.

   60 : 1200   6 : 12   1 : 20   6 : 20   [1]

3   Divide £240 in the ratio 1 : 5

   Answer _____   [2]

4   Calculate 15% of 60.

   Answer _____   [2]

5 Insert one of the symbols $<$, $>$ or $=$ to make each statement true.

(a) -4 _____ -6 [1]

(b) 3^0 _____ 3 [1]

(c) 9% _____ 0.09 [1]

6 Expand and simplify $3(x + 2) + 2(x + 3)$

Answer _____ [2]

7 A tin contains four different types of biscuit.
A biscuit is taken from the tin at random.
Some of the probabilities of taking each type of biscuit are shown below.

Biscuit	Digestive	Rich Tea	Cookie	Shortbread
Probability	0.3	0.2		0.1

(a) Complete the table. [1]

(b) What is the probability that a digestive or a shortbread is taken from the tin?

Answer _____ [1]

(c) The tin contains 50 biscuits.

Work out how many shortbread biscuits there are in the tin.

Answer _____ [2]

Turn Over

8   (a) Draw the graph of $3x + y = 2$ for values of x from -2 to 3.

x	-2	-1	0	1	2	3
y	8		2			

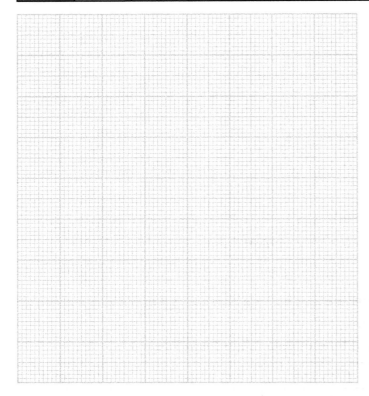

[3]

(b) Rearrange the equation $3x + y = 2$ to make y the subject.

Answer _____ [1]

(c) Write down the gradient of the line.

Answer _____ [1]

(d) Write down the coordinates of the y-intercept of the line.

Answer _____ [1]

9 Lize invests £9000 in an account for three years.
The account pays 3% compound interest per annum.

At the end of the three-year period, Lize decides to buy a new car using the money in the account. The car costs £10 000.

How much extra money does Lize need to buy her new car?
Give your answer to the nearest pound.
You must show all of your working.

Answer _____ [4]

10 Solve the following equations:

(a) $4y = 20$

Answer _____ [1]

(b) $50 - p = 20$

Answer _____ [1]

(c) $3x - 3 = 9$

Answer _____ [2]

(d) $16 = \frac{2x}{5} + 6$

Answer _____ [3]

Turn Over

11 A function is represented by the following function machine.

Input ——— $\div 2$ ——— $+9$ ——→ Output

(a) The first output is 31.

Work out the value of the first input.

Answer _____ [2]

(b) A number is put into the machine. The output is the same number.

Work out the value of the number.

Answer _____ [2]

12 The diagram shows a cylindrical soup can with a diameter of 8 cm.

(a) Calculate the total area of the two circular faces of the can.
Leave your answer in terms of π.

Answer _____ **[3]**

(b) The volume of the can is 192π cm³.
Work out the height of the can.

Answer _____ **[2]**

(c) The curved surface area of the can is covered by a paper label.

Work out the area of the label.
Give your answer to 1 decimal place.

Answer _____ **[3]**

Turn Over

13

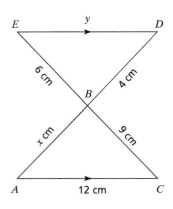

(a) Explain why triangles BED and ABC are similar.

_____

_____

_____ **[1]**

(b) Work out the value of x.

Answer _____ **[2]**

(c) Work out the value of y.

Answer _____ **[2]**

14   **(a)** On the axes below sketch the graph of $y = x^3$

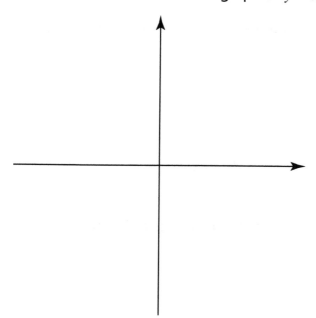

[2]

(b) On the axes below sketch the graph of $y = \dfrac{1}{x}$

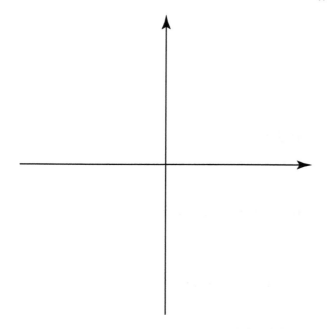

[2]

Turn Over

15 Dan, Neil, Chris and Dave are playing a table tennis tournament.

Dan scores four more points than Neil. Neil scores three points fewer than Chris.
Dave scores twice as many as Neil.
The total number of points scored is 97.

Work out how many points each player scored.

_____ **[4]**

16 Millie collected data about the height and shoe size of the members of her class.
The data is shown in the diagram below.

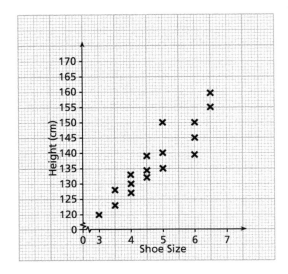

(a) Describe the relationship between height and shoe size.

_____ **[1]**

(b) Use the diagram to predict the height of a pupil with shoe size 5.5.

Answer _____ **[1]**

(c) Use the diagram to predict the height of a pupil with shoe size 7.

Answer _____ **[1]**

(d) Explain which of these predictions is more reliable.

_____

_____ **[1]**

17 Find an expression for the nth term of the following sequence:

3   7   11   15   19   ...

Answer _____ **[2]**

18

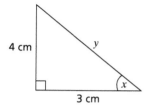

(a) Calculate the length of side y.

Answer _____ **[3]**

(b) Work out the size of angle x.

Answer _____ **[3]**

Turn Over

19   A restaurant offers eight flavours of ice cream, six different toppings and nine
     different sauces.

     You can order the following:
     • Ice cream with topping
     • Ice cream with sauce
     • Ice cream with sauce and topping.

     Work out how many different possible orders there are.

                                              Answer _____   **[4]**

20   Solve the equation $x^2 - 9x + 8 = 0$

                                              Answer _____   **[2]**

21   Five bags of sand and four bags of gravel weigh 340 kg.
     Three bags of sand and five bags of gravel weigh 321 kg.

     Ben buys six bags of sand and eight bags of gravel.
     His van has a safe carrying load of 500 kg.

     Ben's friend Sam thinks it is not safe to travel with all the sand and gravel.

     Is Sam correct?
     You must show how you got your answer.

                                              Answer _____   **[4]**

End of Test

Answers

Workbook Answers

You are encouraged to show all your working out, as you may be awarded marks for method even if your final answer is wrong. Full marks can be awarded where a correct answer is given without working but, if a question asks for working, you must show it to gain full marks. If you use a correct method that is not shown in the answers below, you would still gain full credit for it.

Page 148 – Number 1, 2 & 3

1. $170 \div 14 = 12$, with remainder [1]; 13 boxes [1]
2. $170 - 28$ [1]; 142cm [1]
3. $(8 + 5) \times (9 - 3) = 78$ [1]
4. a) 2×10^8 [1]
   b) 0.000678 [1]
5. $1.5 \times 10^4 = 15\,000$ [1]; $3.5 \times 10^3 = 3500$ [1]; $18\,500 = 1.85 \times 10^4$ [1]
6. $\sqrt{m} = \sqrt{8100} = 90$ [1]; $y = 0.01$ [1]; $\frac{\sqrt{m}}{y} = \frac{90}{0.01} = 9000 = 9 \times 10^3$ [1]
7. 1.729 [2]
8. a) $\blacktriangle = 7$ [1]
   b) $\blacktriangle = -4$ [1]
   c) $\blacktriangle = -9$ [1]
9. a) 3, 7, 31 [1]
   b) 3, 7 [1]
   c) 12, 16, 20 [1]
   d) 9, 16 [1]
   e) 20 [1]
10. $2 \times 2 \times 19$ OR $2^2 \times 19$ [2]
11. $684 = 2^2 \times 3^2 \times 19$ [1]; $468 = 2^2 \times 3^2 \times 13$ [1]; HCF $= 2^2 \times 3^2 = 36$ [1]
12. LCM of 12 and 15 is 60 [1]; 1 minute [1]

Page 150 – Basic Algebra

1. $2x + 4 = 8$ [1]; $2x = 4$ [1]; $x = 2$ [1]
2. $-56 - (-2^2)$ [1]; -60 [1]
3. $3x^2 - 3xy + xy + 5y$ [1]; $3x^2 - 2xy + 5y$ [1]
4. $2x = 12$ [1]; $x = 6$ [1]
5. $12x - 2y$ [1]
6. $a = 3, b = 3, c = -1, d = 2, 3y(3x - y + 2x^2)$ [2] (1 mark for 2–3 correct terms)

Page 151 – Factorisation and Formulae

1. $x^2 + 4x - 2x - 8$ [1]; $x^2 + 2x - 8$ [1]
2. $(x + 1)(x + 5)$ [2] (1 mark for each correct bracket)
3. a) $v = 15 + (2.5 \times 10) = 40$ [1]
   b) $v - u = at$ [1]; $t = \frac{v - u}{a}$ [1]
   c) $t = \frac{25 - 11}{1.6} = 8.75$ [1]
4. $(x - 2)(x + 1)$ [2] (1 mark for each correct bracket)

Page 152 – Ratio and Proportion

1. $5 : 2$ [1]
2. a) $161.7 \div 11 = 14.7$km [1]; $14.7 \times 13 = 191.1$km [1]
   b) Food would last $(15 \times 3) = 45$ days for 1 dog [1]; $45 \div 5 = 9$ days [1]
3. One part is £700 $\div$ 8 = £87.50 [1]; John receives £87.50 $\times$ 3 = £262.50 [1]; £262.50 − £87.50 = £175 more than Sarah [1]
4. $15 : 3000 = 1 : 200$ [1]
5. $20 = k \times 2 \times 2$ [1]; $k = 5$ [1]

Page 153 – Variation and Compound Measures

1. a) $\frac{£3000}{100} \times 2\%$ [1]; = £60 [1]
   b) £3000 $\times \left(1 + \frac{2}{100}\right)^3$ [1]; = £3183.62 [1]; £3183.62 − £3000 = £183.62 interest [1]
2. a) Speed = $77.8 \div 8 = 9.725$m/s [1]
   b) Speed = $9.725 \times 60 \times 60$ [1]; = $35\,010$m/h [1]

   Speed = Distance ÷ Time

3. Volume = $2 \div 10.49$ [1]; = 0.191cm³ (to 3 decimal places) OR 0.19cm³ (to 2 decimal places) [1]

   Volume = Mass ÷ Density

Page 154 – Angles and Shapes 1 & 2

1. $9x = 360°$ [1]; $x = 40°$ [1]
2. Exterior angle $(= 180° - 150°) = 30°$ [1]; number of sides = $360 \div 30 = 12$ [1]
3. a) Correct scale drawing (see sketch) [1]; distance = 62km (+/− 2km) [1]

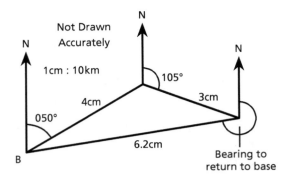

b) Bearing 253° (+/– 2°) **[1]**

Page 155 – Fractions

1. $\frac{5}{7}$ **[1]**

2. $\frac{1}{3}$ left for the afternoon **[1]**; $\frac{2}{15}$ left for tomorrow **[1]**

3. $\frac{7}{9}$ of 81 = 63 **[1]**; $\frac{3}{5}$ of 110 = 66, so $\frac{3}{5}$ of 110 is larger **[1]**

4. 2.5 hours = 150 minutes, $\frac{14}{150}$ **[1]**; $\frac{7}{75}$ **[1]**

5. 30 days in June **[1]**; 4.5 × 30 **[1]**; = 135 km **[1]**

6. $y = \frac{3}{4} + \frac{3}{2}$ **[1]**; $y = \frac{9}{4}$ OR $2\frac{1}{4}$ **[1]**

Page 156 – Percentages 1 & 2

1. 20% increase = 180 **[1]**; 35% increase on 180 = 243 rats **[1]**

2. 9kg = 9000g **[1]**; $\frac{180}{9000} \times 100 = 2\%$ **[1]**

3. $\frac{22}{100} \times c = 11$ **[1]**; $c = \frac{11}{22} \times 100 = 50$ children **[1]**

4. $31 \times \frac{100}{62}$ **[1]**; 50 plants **[1]**

5. $\frac{£14\,000}{100} \times 24 = £3360$ **[1]**; $\frac{£3360}{12} = £280$ **[1]**

Page 157 – Probability 1 & 2

1. **a)** $5x + 0.5 = 1$ **[1]**; $5x = 0.5$ **[1]**; $x = 0.1$ **[1]**

   b) No **[1]**; not all outcomes are equally likely **[1]**

2. **a)** $\frac{4}{12}$ **[1]**; $\frac{1}{3}$ **[1]**

   b) $\frac{5}{12} \times \frac{3}{12}$ **[1]**; $\frac{15}{144} = \frac{5}{48}$,

   $\frac{5}{48} + \frac{5}{48} = \frac{10}{48} = \frac{5}{24}$ **[1]**

> Remember, a blue counter could be taken, followed by a yellow OR a yellow, followed by a blue.

3. **a)** 60, 15, 5 correct on diagram (see below) **[1]**

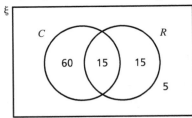

   b) $\frac{5}{95}$ **[1]**; $= \frac{1}{19}$ **[1]**

4. **a)** 0.82 seen **[1]**; completely correct tree **[1]**

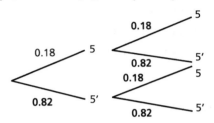

   b) 0.18 × 0.82 = 0.1476 **[1]**; 0.1476 × 2 **[1]**; = 0.2952 **[1]**

Page 159 – Number Patterns and Sequences 1

1. **a)** Correctly drawn fourth pattern **[1]**

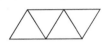

   b) Fully correct table **[2]** (1 mark for 3 correct values)

Pattern Number	1	2	3	4
No. of Matchsticks	3	5	7	9

   c) Add 2 **[1]**

   d) He is correct **[1]**; it goes up by the same amount each time **[1]**

2. **a)** 48, 96 **[1]**

   b) 40 **[1]**

3. 1, 4, 7, 10, 13 **[3]** (2 marks for any three terms correct, 1 mark for attempting to substitute a value between 1 and 5 for n into $3n - 2$)

Page 160 – Number Patterns and Sequences 2

1. **a)** –1 **[1]**; –4 **[1]**

   b) $11 - 3n$ **[2]** (1 mark if $-3n$ is seen)

   c) n is not an integer (whole number) when $11 - 3n = -15$ **[1]**; No **[1]** (second mark will only be awarded if a correct explanation is given)

2. **a)** Correct drawing of fourth pattern **[1]**

   b) Fully correct table **[3]** (1 mark for one column correct; 2 marks for one row correct)

Pattern Number	1	2	3	4	5
Number of Circles	4	6	8	10	12
Number of Straight Lines	4	7	10	13	16

c) $2n + 2$ **[2]** (1 mark for each correct term)
d) $3n + 1$ **[2]** (1 mark for each correct term)
e) $2 \times 50 + 2$ and $3 \times 50 + 1$ **[1]**; circles: 102 **[1]**; straight lines: 151 **[1]**

Page 161 – Transformations

1. a) Reflection **[1]**; in line $x = -\frac{1}{2}$ **[1]**

   b) Rotation **[1]**; anticlockwise 90° **[1]**; centre of rotation (0, 0) **[1]**

   c) Reflection **[1]**; in line $y = x$ **[1]**

2. One mark for each correct vertex of triangle DEF (all construction lines must be seen) **[3]**

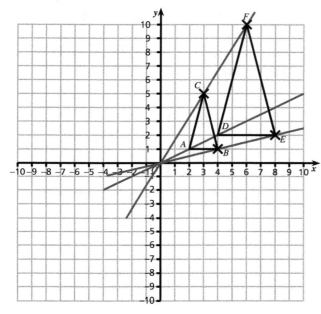

Page 162 – Constructions

1. Correct construction of the perpendicular bisector of CD **[2]**

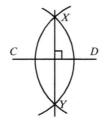

Not Drawn to Scale

2. Correct construction of the bisectors of the three angles **[3]**

3. Accurate rectangle 3cm by 4cm **[1]**; diagonals of rectangle drawn **[1]**

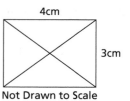

Not Drawn to Scale

Page 163 – Nets, Plans and Elevations

1. A correctly drawn cuboid measuring either: 2cm × 2cm × 3cm OR 6cm × 1cm × 2cm, OR 12cm × 1cm × 1cm **[3]** (1 mark for each correct side length)

2. a) Side elevation drawn as a rectangle of height 3cm and width 1cm **[2]** (1 mark for each correct side length)

   b) Plan view drawn as a rectangle 3cm by 1cm **[2]** (1 mark for each correct side length)

Page 164 – Linear Graphs

1. $m = \frac{-12}{4} = -3$ **[1]**; $c = 4$ **[1]**; $y = -3x + 4$ **[1]**

2. $y = \frac{-2x + 7}{5}$ **[1]**; $= -\frac{2}{5}$ **[1]**

3. $m = \frac{15 - 5}{6 - 1} = 2$ **[1]**; $5 = 2 \times 1 + c$, $c = 3$ **[1]**;
   $y = 2x + 3$ **[1]**

4. $x + y = 5$ **[1]**; $x + y - 5 = 0$ **[1]**

Page 165 – Graphs of Quadratic Functions

1. a)

x	−2	−1	0	1	2
y	1	−5	−7	−5	1

[1]

   b) Points plotted accurately **[1]**; joined with a smooth curve **[1]**

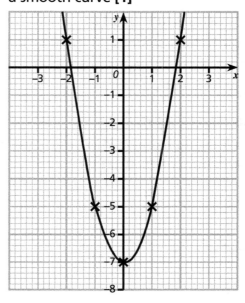

2. a) Correct shape graph **[1]**; crossing x-axis at (–1, 0) and (–4, 0) **[1]**; crossing y-axis at (0, 4) **[1]**

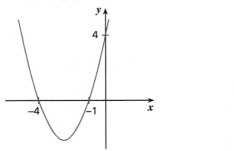

> Remember to factorise and solve the expression when it is equal to zero (= 0).

b) (–2.5, –2.25)   **[1]**

Page 166 – Powers, Roots and Indices

1. a) 5^{10} **[1]**
  b) 5^4 **[1]**
  c) 5^6 **[1]**
  d) 5^4 **[1]**
2. $8x^6y^3$ **[2]** (1 mark for each correct term)
3. Martin **[1]**; $5c^{-4}$ is $5 \times \dfrac{1}{c^4} = \dfrac{5}{c^4}$ **[1]**
4. $3^4 = 81$, so $n = 4$ **[1]**

Page 167–168 – Area and Volume 1, 2 & 3

1. a) $\dfrac{24}{6}$ **[1]**; 4cm **[1]**
  b) $2 \times 6 + 2 \times 4$ **[1]**; = 20cm **[1]**
2. $6 \times 4 = 24$ **[1]**; $\dfrac{24}{3}$ **[1]**; 8cm **[1]**
3. $\dfrac{4}{3} \times \pi \times (4)^3$ **[1]**; $\dfrac{256\pi}{3} \div 2$ **[1]**; $\dfrac{128\pi}{3}$ **[1]**
4. Area of cross-section $= \dfrac{1}{2} \times (2.1 + 0.9) \times 25 = 37.5$, volume $= 37.5 \times 10 = 375$ **[1]**;
$375 \div 0.2 = 1875$ seconds **[1]**; $1875 \div 3600$ **[1]**;
$= 0.521$ hours (to 3 significant figures) **[1]**

> 3600 seconds = 1 hour

Page 169 – Uses of Graphs

1. Straight line graph drawn **[1]**; correct direction of line and through (0, 0) **[1]**

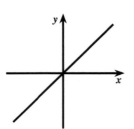

2. $y = \dfrac{3}{2}x + \dfrac{5}{2}$, attempt to make y the subject **[1]**;
$m = \dfrac{3}{2}$ **[1]**; $6 = \dfrac{3}{2} \times 3 + c$, $c = \dfrac{3}{2}$ **[1]**;
$y = \dfrac{3}{2}x + \dfrac{3}{2}$ OR $2y = 3x + 3$ **[1]**

3. Gradient = 3 **[1]**; the cost increases by 3p per minute **[1]**

Page 170 – Other Graphs

1. a) Accelerates for the first 10 seconds, from stationary to 20m/s **[1]**; drives at a constant speed for 20 seconds **[1]**; decelerates for the next 40 seconds to 0m/s **[1]**
  b) $(\frac{1}{2} \times 10 \times 20) + (20 \times 20) + (\frac{1}{2} \times 40 \times 20)$ **[1]**; $100 + 400 + 400$ **[1]**; = 900m **[1]**

> Break down the area below the graph into two triangles and a rectangle.

2. Correct y-intercept (0, –1) **[1]**; correct shape of curve **[1]**

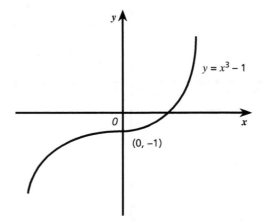

Page 171 – Inequalities

1. a) 30 (–6 × –5)   **[1]**
  b) –30 (–6 × 5)   **[1]**
2. a) $x \geqslant 5$ **[1]**
  b) 2, 1, 0, –1   **[1]**
3. a) False   **[1]**
  b) False   **[1]**
  c) True   **[1]**
4. $2x < 14$ **[1]**; $x < 7$ **[1]**
5. a) 0, 1, 2   **[1]**
  b) 3, 4, 5   **[1]**

Page 172 – Congruence and Geometrical Problems

1. a) A and B **[1]**; AAS OR SAS **[1]**
  b) B and D   **[1]**

2. $\frac{38}{9.5} = \frac{\text{height of lamp post}}{4}$ **[1]**; lamp post = 16m **[1]**

3. Perimeter of A = 38cm **[1]**; perimeter of B = 114cm, so scale factor = 3 **[1]**

Page 173 – Right-Angled Triangles 1

1. $x^2 = 8^2 + 9^2$ **[1]**; $x = \sqrt{145}$ **[1]**; $x = 12.04$cm **[1]**
2. $26^2 = 676$, $24^2 = 576$, $10^2 = 100$ **[1]**; $24^2 + 10^2 = 26^2$ **[1]**; so yes, it is a right-angled triangle **[1]**
3. $a^2 + a^2 = 16^2$ **[1]**; $2a^2 = 256$ **[1]**; $a = 11.31$cm **[1]**
4. $x^2 = 4^2 + 7^2$ **[1]**; $x = \sqrt{65}$ **[1]**; $x = 8.06$ units **[1]**
5. $d^2 = 6.5^2 + 3.4^2$ **[1]**; $d = \sqrt{53.81}$ **[1]**; $d = 7.34$km **[1]**

Page 174 – Right-Angled Triangles 2

1. $\sin 52° = \frac{x}{25}$ **[1]**; $x = 19.7$m **[1]**
2. $\tan 41° = \frac{x}{23}$ **[1]**; $x = 19.99 = 20$m to the nearest metre **[1]**
3. $\tan\theta = \frac{5}{8} = 0.625$ **[1]**; $\theta = 32°$ **[1]**
4. $\cos\theta = \frac{4}{12} = 0.33333$ **[1]**; $\theta = 70.5°$ **[1]**

Page 175 – Statistics 1

1. **a)** Bar chart with five bars drawn not touching **[1]**; correct heights **[1]**; correctly labelled axes **[1]**

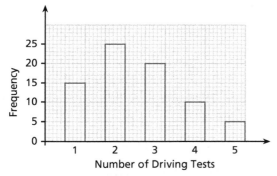

b) $\frac{360}{75} = 4.8$ **[1]**; sectors: 72°, 120°, 96°, 48°, 24° **[1]**; completely correct diagram **[2]** (1 mark for three correct sections)

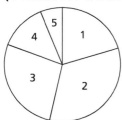

Each person is worth 4.8 degrees, so: Size of Sector = Frequency × 4.8

c) Pie charts can be used to compare proportions **[1]**; bar charts show exact frequency **[1]**

Page 176 – Statistics 2

1. **a)** Point plotted at (15, 46)　　　　　　**[1]**
   b) Positive　　　　　　　　　　　　　**[1]**
   c) Increase in time studying leads to increase in mark　　　　　　　　　**[1]**
   d) Line drawn (see diagram below)　　**[1]**
   e) 28–32 minutes　　　　　　　　　　**[1]**

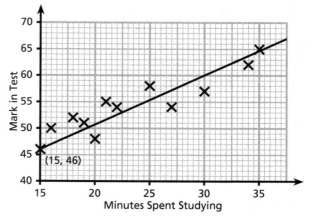

2. $15.2 × 23 = 349.6$ **[1]**; $349.6 − 21.3 + 12.3 = 340.6$ **[1]**; mean $= 340.6 ÷ 23 = 14.8$ **[1]**

Page 177 – Measures, Accuracy and Finance

1. $(10 × 1) ÷ (0.5)$ **[1]**; $= 20$ **[1]** OR $(9 × 1) ÷ (0.5)$ **[1]**; $= 18$ **[1]**
2. **a)** £23 + (2 × £6.25) + (2 × £4.35) **[1]**; = £44.20 **[1]**

   Read the question carefully. The prices given were for a two-way trip and the question asks for costs for a single trip.

   b) (3 × 12.5) + 60 + 30 = 127.5 euros **[1]**; 127.5 euros = £99.45 **[1]**
3. **a)** metres　　　　　　　　　　　　　**[1]**
   b) millilitres　　　　　　　　　　　　**[1]**
4. 14.37 + 52 minutes + 19 minutes **[1]**; 15:48 **[1]**

Page 178 – Quadratic and Simultaneous Equations

1. **a)** $(x − 3)(x − 2)$ **[2]** (1 mark for each correct bracket)
   b) $x = 3$ **[1]**; $x = 2$ **[1]**
2. $P = 4(x + 3)$ **[1]**; $A = (x + 3)(x + 3)$ **[1]**; $4x + 12 = x^2 + 6x + 9$ **[1]**; $x^2 + 2x − 3 = 0$ **[1]**; $(x + 3)(x − 1) = 0$ **[1]**; $x = 1$, length = 4cm **[1]**
3. $3x = 12$, attempt to add the equations **[1]**; $x = 4$ **[1]**; $4 + y = 5$, attempt to substitute in to find y **[1]**; $y = 1$ **[1]**

Page 179 – Circles

1. a) circumference [1]
   b) half [1]
   c) tangent [1]
   d) semi-circle [1]
2. a) Angle ABC = 180° – 85° [1]; 95° [1]
   b) Angle DAB = 180° – 70° [1]; 110° [1]
3. Angle OPQ = Angle PQO [1]; Angle POQ = 180° – 74° [1]; 106° [1]

Page 180 – Vectors

1. $\overrightarrow{KL}$ = 4p + 8q [1]; $\overrightarrow{MN}$ = 8p + 16q [1]; $\overrightarrow{ST}$ = 12p + 24q [1]
2. a) 4m [1]
   b) –2n [1]
   c) 3m – n [1]
   d) n + m [1]
3. Trapezium [1]

Page 181 – Practice Exam Paper 1 (Non-Calculator)

1. a) 999 998 [1]
   b) i) 8 OR 27 [1]
      ii) 3 [1]
      iii) 60 [1]
   c) True: any two correct answers, e.g. 5 and 7 [1]; Not True: any two correct answers, e.g. 11 and 23 [1]
2. a) 3m 20cm OR 3.2m [1]
   b) 4m – 3m 20cm = 80cm OR 0.8m [1]
3. a) £13.75 [1]
   b) 2 × £20.25 = £40.50 [1]; 2 × 5.7kg = 11.4kg, which costs £28.55 [1]; saving = £40.50 – £28.55 = £11.95 [1]
   c) 20% of £28.55 = £5.71 [1]; new price = £28.55 – £5.71 = £22.84 [1]
4. a) i) a = 61° [1]; alternate angle [1]
      ii) b = 61° [1]; alternate angle [1]
      iii) c = 58° [1]
   b) Isosceles triangle, two angles are equal [1]
5. a) True [1]

   An identity is an equation that is true for all values of x.

   b) True [1]

   $(-6 + 11) \times 2 = 10$

   c) True [1]
   d) False [1]

Side Length of Square = Perimeter ÷ 4

6. a) Total = £70.76 [1]; change = £100 – £70.76 = £29.24 [1]
   b) £70.76 ÷ 4 = £17.69 [1]
7. a) $\frac{2}{4} = \frac{1}{2}$ [1]
   b) $\frac{1}{4}$ [1]
   c) $\frac{1}{4}$ × 200 = 50 times [1]
8. a) $10g - 3m$ [1]
   b) $4e - 14$ [1]
   c) $5(3a - 4y)$ [1]
   d) d^6 [1]
9. a) Accurately drawn angle of 56° (+/– 2°) [1]
   b) Construction lines showing two sets of arcs [1]; a straight line accurately drawn through the angle and intersecting arcs to give two equal angles of 28° [1]

10. a) $\frac{50 \times 100}{4 + 16} = \frac{5000}{20}$ [1]; = 250 [1]
    b) 32 000 + 230 000 = 262 000 [1]; 2.62×10^5 [1]
    c) 0.000 681 [1]
    d) 5 + 12 – 7 = 10 [1]

    Remember to use BIDMAS.

11. a) 10% of £450 000 = £45 000 [1]; 5% = £22 500 [1]; new price = £450 000 + £22 500 = £472 500 [1]
    b) Steven: $\frac{14}{20}$ × 100 = 70% [1]; Peter: $\frac{18}{25}$ × 100 = 72% [1]; Peter achieved a better result [1]
12. 20 ÷ 2 [1]; = 10 days [1]

    Twice as many rabbits, means food lasts half as long.

13. a) 63km (+/– 3km) [1]
    b) 066° (+/– 3°) [1]
    c) Yes, his journey takes $\frac{48}{15}$ = 3 hours 12 minutes, so he arrives at 2.59pm. [1]
14. a) Table with all values correct [2] (1 mark for three correct values)

x	–2	–1	0	1	2	3	4
y	5	0	–3	–4	–3	0	5

b) Accurately plotted graph **[1]**

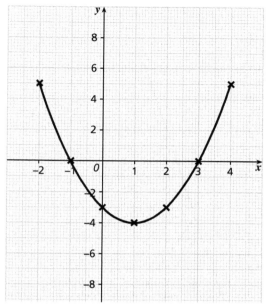

c) $x = -1$ **[1]**; $x = 3$ **[1]**

> Look at the points where the graph crosses the x-axis.

d) $x = 1$ **[1]**

15. a) 40 grams **[1]**
    b) 27 biscuits require $(130 \div 2) \times 3$ **[1]**; $= 195$g of oats **[1]**; no, there are not enough oats (1g short) **[1]**
    c) 4000g is 450p **[1]**; 80 grams is $450 \div 50 = 9$p **[1]**
    d) $\frac{4}{9} \times 45 = 20$ **[1]**; $45 - 20 = 25$ left **[1]**

16. a) $P = x + 1 + 3x + 4 + 2x + 2$ **[1]**; $6x + 7$ **[1]**
    b) $6x + 7 = 49$ **[1]**; $6x = 42$, $x = 7$cm **[1]**; lengths are 8cm, 25cm, and 16cm **[1]**
    c) Jeremy is correct **[1]**; $8^2 + 16^2 < 25^2$, so it is not a right-angled triangle OR $8 + 16 < 25$, so it is impossible to draw this triangle **[1]**

17. a) A **[1]**
    b) C **[1]**
    c) B **[1]**
    d) D **[1]**
    e) E **[1]**

Page 197 – Practice Exam Paper 2 (Calculator)

1. a) The data is biased because only people who had already visited a theatre were surveyed. **[1]**

b) i) Age ranges should not overlap (as it is continuous data), e.g. $20 \leqslant a < 30$, $30 \leqslant a < 40$, etc. **[1]**
   ii) The question must be given a time frame, e.g. How many times do you visit the theatre in a year? **[1]**

2. a) Journey time: 1 hr 45 min **[1]**; arrival time: 12.28 pm **[1]**
   b) $S = \frac{D}{T} = \frac{98}{1.75}$ **[1]**; $= 56$km/h **[1]**

3. a) $18 - (-15)$ **[1]**; $= 33°C$ **[1]**
   b) $F = \frac{9}{5} \times 18 + 32$ **[1]**; $= 64.4°F$ **[1]**

4. a) 480g = 15 parts, 1 part = $480 \div 15 = 32$g **[1]**; flour = 224g **[1]**; sugar = 128g **[1]**; eggs = 64g **[1]**; chocolate = 64g **[1]**
   b) $\frac{480}{720} \times 60 = 40$ mins **[1]**

> Convert 1 hour to 60 minutes first.

   c) $\frac{3}{10} \times \frac{4}{5} = \frac{6}{25}$ **[1]**; $\frac{1}{5} + \frac{6}{25} = \frac{5}{25} + \frac{6}{25} = \frac{11}{25}$ **[1]**; $\frac{14}{25}$ is left **[1]**

> Read the question carefully. $\frac{3}{10}$ of the remainder (not the original amount) is eaten in the afternoon.

5. a) 36m **[1]**
   b) $(8 \times 6) + (4 \times 4) = 64$m² **[1]** (there are alternative ways of breaking down the shape to find its area)
   c) Length of one side of square: $\sqrt{64m^2} = 8$m **[1]**
   d) $64 \times £2.58 = £165.12$ **[1]**

6. a) At least four tiles correctly drawn **[1]**

   b) $4 \times 180° = 720°$ **[1]**; $720° \div 6 = 120°$ **[1]** OR Exterior angle = $360° \div 6 = 60°$ **[1]**; interior angle = $180° - 60° = 120°$ **[1]**
   c) Box A: one tile costs £4.59 **[1]**; Box B: one tile costs £4.57 **[1]**; Box B is the best buy **[1]**

7. a) (5, 2) **[1]**
   b) (5, 0) **[1]**
   c) $\frac{4}{10}$ **[1]**; $\frac{2}{5}$ **[1]**
   d) $\frac{1}{2} \times (10 \times 2)$ **[1]**; $= 10$ square units **[1]**

8. $\frac{(82 + 84 + 85 + 91 + x)}{5} = 87$ **[1]**;

$(82 + 84 + 85 + 91 + x) = 435$ **[1]**;

$x = 435 - 342 = 93$kg **[1]**

9. a) i) −   **[1]**

   ii) ÷   **[1]**

   iii) ×   **[1]**

  b) i) 4   **[1]**

   ii) 5   **[1]**

10. a) $24.60 \div 8.2 = £3$ **[1]**

  b) $8.2 \times 2.2 = 18.04$ pounds   **[1]**

  c) $18.04 \times 30 = 541.2$ minutes **[1]**; total time
$= 541.2 + 30 = 571.2$ minutes **[1]**;
$571.2 \div 60 = 9.52$ hours, 10 hours (to the nearest hour) **[1]**

11. $3 \times 4^2 = 3 \times 16 = 48$ **[1]**; James is correct **[1]**

12. Correct drawing showing a cube measuring 3cm **[1]**; by 3cm **[1]**; by 3cm **[1]**

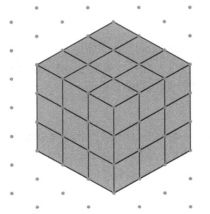

13. a) i) $>$ **[1]**

   ii) $<$ **[1]**

  b) $-2, -1, 0, 1, 2, 3$ **[1]**

  c) $4x < 36$, $x < 9$ **[1]**

14. a) $45^2 + 30^2 = x^2$ **[1]**; $x^2 = 2025 + 900 = 2925$ **[1]**; $x = \sqrt{2925} = 54.08$m **[1]**; $x = 54$m (to the nearest metre) **[1]**

  b) $\tan \theta = \frac{30}{45} = 0.6667$ **[1]**; $\tan^{-1} 0.6667$, $\theta = 33.69°$ **[1]**; bearing $= 90° + 33.7°$ **[1]**; $= 123.7°$ **[1]**

15. a) $C = \pi \times D = 3.142 \times 2000 = 6284$cm **[1]**; number of hyacinth bulbs is $6284 \div 40$ **[1]**; $= 157$ **[1]**

  b) Volume of cylinder $= \pi r^2 h$ **[1]**; volume $= 3.142 \times 1000 \times 1000 \times 30 = 94\,260\,000$cm³ **[1]**; $= 94\,260$ litres **[1]**

16. Correct enlargement with vertices at (3, 1) **[1]**; (7, 1) **[1]**; and (3, 7) **[1]**

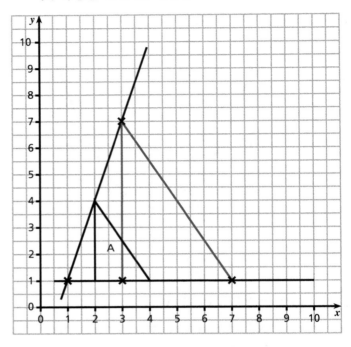

17. a) True   **[1]**

  b) True   **[1]**

  c) False   **[1]**

  d) True   **[1]**

  e) False   **[1]**

Page 211 – Exam Practice Paper 3 (Calculator)

1. $0.04, \frac{1}{4}, 40\%$ **[2]** (1 mark if order is incorrect but an attempt was made to change $\frac{1}{4}$ and 40% into decimals)

2. $1 : 20$ **[1]**

3. $£40 : £200$ **[2]** (1 mark for each correct amount)

4. $\frac{60}{100} \times 15$ **[1]**; $= £9$ **[1]**

5. a) $-4 > -6$ **[1]**

  b) $3^0 < 3$ **[1]**

  c) $9\% = 0.09$ **[1]**

6. $3x + 6 + 2x + 6$ **[1]**; $5x + 12$ **[1]**

7. a)

Biscuit	Digestive	Rich Tea	Cookie	Shortbread
Probability	0.3	0.2	0.4 **[1]**	0.1

  b) $0.3 + 0.1 = 0.4$ **[1]**

  c) 50×0.1 **[1]**; $= 5$ **[1]**

8. a) Correct table **[1]**

x	−2	−1	0	1	2	3
y	8	5	2	−1	−4	−7

Remember − × − = +

All points plotted accurately **[1]**; straight line connecting all points **[1]**

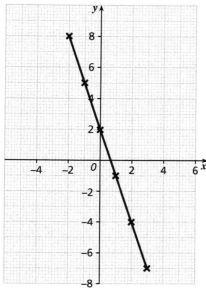

b) $y = 2 - 3x$ OR $y = -3x + 2$ **[1]**
c) −3 **[1]**
d) (0, 2) **[1]**

9. Money in account: £9000 × 1.03³ **[1]**; = £9834.54 **[1]**; extra money needed: £10 000 − £9834.54 **[1]**; = £165.46 **[1]**

10. a) $y = 5$ **[1]**
b) $p = 30$ **[1]**
c) $3x = 12$ **[1]**; $x = 4$ **[1]**
d) $10 = \dfrac{2x}{5}$ **[1]**; $50 = 2x$ **[1]**; $x = 25$ **[1]**

11. a) $(31 - 9) \times 2$ **[1]**; 44 **[1]**
b) $\dfrac{x}{2} + 9 = x$ **[1]**; $x = 18$ **[1]**

12. a) $\pi \times 4^2 = 16\pi\,\text{cm}$ **[1]**; $16\pi\,\text{cm} \times 2$ **[1]**; $= 32\pi\,\text{cm}$ **[1]**
b) $\dfrac{192\pi}{16\pi}$ **[1]**; = 12cm **[1]**
c) Circumference = $2 \times 4 \times \pi = 8\pi$ **[1]**; $8\pi \times 12$ **[1]**; = 301.6 cm² **[1]**

13. a) The angles in triangles BED and ABC are the same **[1]**
b) $\dfrac{9}{6} = \dfrac{x}{4}$ **[1]**; $x = 6$cm **[1]**
c) $\dfrac{6}{9} = \dfrac{y}{12}$ **[1]**; $y = 8$cm **[1]**

14. a) Correct shape of graph **[1]**; in correct quadrants **[1]**

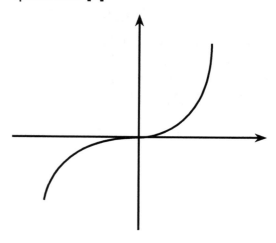

b) Correct shape of graph **[1]**; in correct quadrants **[1]**

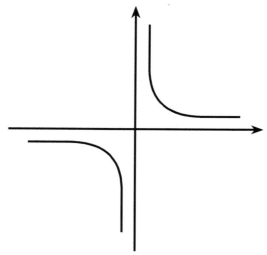

15. Neil = x , Dan = $x + 4$, Chris = $x + 3$, Dave = $2x$ (or equivalent) **[1]**; $x + x + 4 + x + 3 + 2x = 97$ **[1]**; $x = 18$ **[1]**; Neil = 18, Dan = 22, Chris = 21, Dave = 36 **[1]**

16. a) Positive correlation OR as height increases, shoe size increases **[1]**
b) Any answer in the range 140–145 **[1]**
c) Any answer in the range 155–165 **[1]**
d) The prediction for shoe size 5.5 is more reliable as it is within the data range (or equivalent statement) **[1]**

17. $4n - 1$ **[2]** (1 mark for each correct term)
18. a) $y^2 = 16 + 9 = 25$ **[1]**; $y = \sqrt{25}$ **[1]**; $y = 5$cm **[1]**
    b) $\tan x = \frac{4}{3}$ OR $1.\dot{3}$ **[1]**; $\tan^{-1} 1.\dot{3}$ **[1]**;
       $= 53.1°$ (to 1 decimal place) **[1]**
19. $8 \times 6 = 48$ and $8 \times 9 = 72$ **[1]**;
    $8 \times 9 \times 6 = 432$ **[1]**; $48 + 72 + 432$ **[1]**; $= 552$ **[1]**
20. $(x - 8)(x - 1)$ **[1]**; $x = 8$ and $x = 1$ **[1]**

21. $5s + 4g = 340$kg and $3s + 5g = 321$kg **[1]**;
    $g = 45$kg and $s = 32$kg **[1]**; $6s + 8g = 552$ **[1]**;
    Sam is correct as the total load is greater than 500kg **[1]**

Set up two equations from the information given. Then multiply the equations to eliminate the g terms.

ACKNOWLEDGEMENTS

The authors and publisher are grateful to the copyright holders for permission to use quoted materials and images.

All images are © Shutterstock.com

Every effort has been made to trace copyright holders and obtain their permission for the use of copyright material. The authors and publisher will gladly receive information enabling them to rectify any error or omission in subsequent editions. All facts are correct at time of going to press.

Published by Collins
An imprint of HarperCollins*Publishers* Ltd
1 London Bridge Street
London SE1 9GF

HarperCollins*Publishers*
Macken House, 39/40 Mayor Street Upper, Dublin 1, D01 C9W8, Ireland

© HarperCollins*Publishers* Limited 2021

ISBN 9780008112547

First published 2015

This edition published 2021

10 9

British Library Cataloguing in Publication Data.

A CIP record of this book is available from the British Library.

Commissioning Editors: Rebecca Skinner and Emily Linnett
Project Leader: Richard Toms
Project Management: Rebecca Skinner
Authors: Linda Couchman and Rebecca Evans
Cover Design: Sarah Duxbury and Kevin Robbins
Inside Concept Design: Sarah Duxbury and Paul Oates
Text Design and Layout: Jouve India Private Limited
Production: Niccolò de Bianchi
Printed and bound in the UK using 100% Renewable Electricity at CPI Group (UK) Ltd

MIX
Paper | Supporting responsible forestry
FSC™ C007454

This book is produced from independently certified FSC™ paper to ensure responsible forest management.
For more information visit: www.harpercollins.co.uk/green